Two Fingers on the Jugular

Two Fingers on the Jugular

A Motorcycle Journey across Russia

by

Lawrence Bransby

Copyright and Acknowledgements

Copyright Lawrence Bransby 2018

Facebook, Website

Lawrence Bransby has asserted his right to be identified as the Author of this work in accordance with the Copyright, Designs and Patents Act 1988.

All rights reserved. No part of this publication may be reproduced or transmitted in any form or by any means, electronic or mechanical, including photocopy, recording, or any information storage and retrieval system, without permission in writing from the copyright owner.

Cover design by Clive Thompson (cliveleet@gmail.co.za)

ISBN 9781793240989

Every effort has been made to seek permission to use copyright material reproduced in this book. The publisher apologises for those cases where permission might not have been sought and, if notified, will formally seek permission at the earliest opportunity. All quotes inserted after chapter headings, unless otherwise attributed, have been taken from "Second Hand Time" by Svetlana Alexievich, published by Fitzcarraldo Editions, London. Permission for the use of these quotes has been formally requested.

"The idea was to go. The point of motorcycling was to leave."

From *The Greasy Hand Preachers* - a film by Arthur de Kersauson & Clement Beauvais

"Russia is an enormous lunatic asylum. There is a heavy padlock on the door, but there are no walls."

Tatyana Tolstaya

FOREWORD

My wife died lied last week and now loneliness creeps through the corridors of my life and peoples the rooms of our home with memories of her presence...

The phone next to my bed rang at a time most normal people are asleep and immediately I knew that the time had come. Hospital nurses don't usually bother to call in the cold, blue hours of the morning and speak with gentle, restrained voices for any other reason: *I think you should come now...*

No details needed to be given; the meaning that hid in the silence between her words was clear.

Mechanically, I pulled on my clothes, pushed my bike out of the garage then rode to the hospital through silent, rain-washed streets. I left my bike in a lifeless car park puddled with water and made my way through the echoing, neon-lit corridors that I'd followed so many times before over the years, to sit at my wife's bedside watching as slowly, month by month, she had wasted away.

We all knew she was dying, had known for years and had had time to prepare. But somehow, I found, the reality is very different from the expectation; difficult to grasp, to put into a mental box.

What does one think of, riding a motorbike through dark streets towards an inevitable parting? Or while walking along echoing, bone-white corridors to the bedside of your dying wife? Nothing profound, really; small, inconsequential things, if I remember rightly: *It's finally happening...*

I found myself standing outside the bubble of my thoughts, outside my body, and observing myself acting the husband walking to the bedside of his dying wife.

And how am I going to live my life now?

And then she was there, gauntly thin, trapped between the whiteness of sheets. My wife...

I held her wasted hands; spoke to her those loving things one always wishes one had said more often during better times. She responded just once, momentarily, briefly, barely conscious.

Did she hear me? Was she aware of my presence? Probably not.

What does one say at a time like this? *We made it...* I found myself telling her, holding her thin fingers. *We made it...*

43 years... Against the odds, we had made it. Stayed true. Honoured our vows.

I sat down next to her bed. The ward was silent, mute, the nurses going about their nursey business with calm efficiency, as they do; all the old, sick, mumbling women now asleep, even the senile ones who enliven the daylight ward with their desperate, inarticulate cries.

I focused on my wife. Her breathing was so slow I found myself watching and waiting for the next breath to come and wondering: *Has she gone yet?* And then the next slow breath would come...

And the next...

And the next...

... spaced further apart... and then further... and then, at some time in the early hours, it didn't come.

I waited a long time.

Her breast was still.

Finally I called the nurse - *I think she's gone.*

She stood next to the bed and watched with me a while, then she turned to me and nodded. She was young and sweet and kind. She told me she would get the on-call doctor and she left me. I waited with the now still person who had been my wife, waiting for someone to tell me what to do.

Eventually the doctor came and did the required tests. Then he too nodded and told me, *Yes, she's gone...* Both he and the nurse were gentle with me.

And then I walked out of the hospital, alone, got on my bike and rode home alone to climb into my cold bed.

No one can prepare you for the loneliness of an empty house, the silence of its walls.

And sometimes, I find, in the early-morning hours, I long for the arms, not of my wife, but, strangely, of my mother, as she holds a little boy close to the warmth of her soft breast and I howl my anguish into the night.

The empty years stretch ahead like a threat and I'm afraid.

And still, now, perhaps it's a photograph that snags the corner of my eye, or the smell of clothes she used to wear, bedclothes she slept in, familiar objects that inhabit our home and are indelibly connected to her, call up that pressure behind the eyes, the tickle in the throat that releases all to easily the benison of tears.

And, so, I find I'm having to learn all over again how to live this strange thing called *life;* coming to terms with the absurdity of cooking a meal for one, of shopping for one, watching television alone, having no one to share things with.

The immediate I can fill easily with activity; it's the 30-ish years (we're a long-lived family – my Dad is 93) that lie ahead that fill me sometimes with a sense of despair.

So I occupy myself with hectic activity, keeping at bay the fiends that lurk in images of old men in shirtsleeves watching passers-by from lonely balconies, imagining what might have been; of lonely men slurping micro-waved soup with Jerry Springer while they stare at the telephone wondering whether one of their children might remember to phone.

Message to self: Enough of the self-pity, mate. Man up and get on with it - there's a whole world out there to explore.

But I believe these things needed to be said. I need to lay my wife to rest with the dignity of some sympathetic mention. Those of you who have followed my travels over the years will have got to know her: How she accepted without hysteria my statement that I was going to ride across Africa when we emigrated to the UK from South Africa in 1997; and then, a few days later, she accepted with similar *sang froid* my informing her that I was going to take our son with me – even though he was still at school at the time; her stoic acceptance of the many times I left her alone at home while I swanned off on another motorcycle adventure. I honour her for that, for understanding my need to throw a leg over my bike and head off into the far away without playing the guilt card.

So, life goes on. My faith and the deep knowledge that Glynis and I will meet again one day and talk over the good times together (and laugh at the bad) make the empty days easier to bear. And I am blessed with two supportive children who have become my dearest friends, and three delightful, irrepressible grandchildren who continue to keep me young. And, to be honest, there are certain benefits to being a widower: I can eat a whole rib-eye steak and no longer have to share; I can bring my bikes into the conservatory because it's cold and wet in the garage and I could hear them complain; I can weld the frame of my new desk in the lounge before the carpets are laid, play my music very loud, bring my gym into the dining room (after I've made space by getting rid of the dining room table).

But another journey was calling...

The Premise

A long journey by bike was needed to fill my wife-less void. And Russia was calling again. The lure of Vladivostok had been tugging with increasing insistence in the back of my mind for years, all through my wife's illness and long decline. The name itself speaks of far-off, remote places - *Vlad-i-vos-tok* - that unmistakeable Russian twist of the tongue and lip-curl around the syllables, the harsh glottal stop at the end that brings to mind vast distances and Siberian wastes and a hardy, dogged people who now, unlike in the past, *choose* to inhabit one of the harshest and most sparsely-populated stretches of land on this earth.

This would be my seventh journey into the Land of Putin; but other than a week-long visit to Omsk in Siberia where I was hosted by teachers at a Russian English-language school, all have all been within touching distance of the West, like a hesitant swimmer afraid to venture too far out to sea in case unfriendly currents drag him away from the security of the known.

The first two journeys I did alone - Kaliningrad (which can hardly be called Russia, bordered as it is by Poland and Lithuania and, just a short distance across the Bearing Sea, Denmark) and which still clings with a grim determination onto its German roots despite every effort by the Soviets at Russianisation; the second to Murmansk, that defiant northern warm-water port that, with the suicidal assistance of the Royal and Merchant Navies, fought off determined German attacks despite the near obliteration of their city by the Luftwaffe. But Murmansk is just a short spitting distance from northern Norway, resting one shoulder against the West, as it were. The third trip, a great leap deeper into the taiga to Archangel and then back to Murmansk, I undertook with my son, Gareth, with whom I had crossed Africa on two old XT500s when he was just seventeen. After our Russian trip we continued to travel together each year - Morocco and Central Asia, four further journeys that made me value him increasingly as a travel companion.

But this Russian journey I would undertake alone. I had left my faithful little DR350 in Osh, Kyrgyzstan, after our last journey into Central Asia and the plan was to fly to Osh and pick her up from where she had been languishing for the past eighteen months while my wife wasted away. I would then ride her across Kyrgyzstan, Kazakhstan and into Russia, turn right at Omsk and ride to Vladivostok then turn back, following a different route wherever possible, to the furthest western border of Russia before making my way home.

That was the plan, anyway.

I dug out my map of Russia, opened it up on the lounge floor and muttered, "Oh, shit!"

What I saw scared me more than a little.

Humour me here - get a map of Russia and lay it out. Find Murmansk and Archangel - up high on the extreme left of the map, rubbing shoulders in a companionable way with Norway and Finland, almost friends despite the terrible conflicts of the past. Now cast your eye across the 11 time zones of Russia to where it reaches out a finger to Alaska. And it brings to mind that my last venture into Russia - Archangel (which at the time had seemed rather adventurous) - is just a child's hop-skip-and-jump away from Western Europe. The *vastness* of Russia... the mind-numbing *emptiness* of it; a land so huge that the mind balks at it; everyday experience gives one nothing with which to compare and one's brain shies away from its conception. The largest country in the world - 6.6 million square miles in area, bigger than the entire surface area of Pluto, nearly twice the size of the United States, *seventy* times bigger than the United Kingdom. Outer Mongolia, the place that has become synonymous with extreme isolation, is cosmopolitan by comparison. To those hardy people living in the Russian far east, mainland Russia is part of another *world*, so detached as to be of little consequence to their everyday lives.

To be honest, I was more than a little fearful about the journey. The DR350 was old and, in a land ocean of this size, just a minnow; I would be alone both physically - without my son - and emotionally, the loneliness of knowing that, at home, increasingly far away as I rode eastwards across the curve of the globe, there would no longer be the warm, living presence of my wife and friend who would have been there to greet me when I returned home, the house still peopled by her life-smell, the excited bark of dog-welcome, the indifferently-comforting, musky-warm presence of her cats.

And then there was the barrier of an unknown language (a smattering of Russian and sign language can get one only so far.)

But it got worse. Looking at the map I realised that Vladivostok is very far from the eastern edge of Russia. Within spitting distance from Rocket Man's North Korea, granted, but if I wanted to travel across the *whole* country (as I did), I would need to push a little further. I tracked the road north and then followed it east until it reached the coast at Magadan. Just - what? another 5000ks or so. And back again, of course. Just another 10,000ks to prove a point.

Gareth came to visit and I shared with him my proposed route. He too mentioned that, if I wanted to do the job properly, I would need to reach Magadan. So that was it, then - Magadan.

Later, researching the Vladivostok - Magadan route on the Internet, I realised with a sinking heart that, as the track turns east from Yakutsk, the 2025ks to Magadan, the Kolyma Highway, is also the notorious Road of Bones. In my naivety, I had thought that the Road of Bones headed north of my intended route, ending somewhere in a mosquito-infested swamp above the Arctic Circle. I had even thought it might be an interesting diversion to leave my bike with a friendly Russian and hitch a ride on a truck up the Road of Bones and back. Just for the hell of it. Because I'm too much of a coward to do it on my own.

Now, suddenly, I found myself faced with attempting what is generally regarded as one of the most remote, dangerous and challenging roads in the world. *Twice.* Alone.

And I was even more afraid.

Of course, I didn't *have* to do it. I could stop at Vladivostok and then turn around and head back to the Russian Caucasus and still feel that I'd achieved something very few have done. But I felt I must attempt it. If I didn't, I would always know, deep down, that I'd left the job half done, that I hadn't the balls to do it properly. I just wished Gareth were coming with me. He has the strength of character and an empathy with things mechanical that breed confidence. I asked him if he'd take three months off work and join me but he just laughed. I know if he could, he'd do it like a shot. In fact, he said, "There's an abandoned Summer Road somewhere around there..." and started looking at the map.

I pulled it away from him. "That would be another *Gareth* road," I told him. And *Gareth* roads are notorious...

*****

I've always tried to do two things when I write about my motorcycle adventures: First, I like to be honest about my feelings and reflections and, second, I try not to big up the danger of any part of the trip. It's good to have a little humility. But, to be brutally honest, the Road of Bones scared the hell out of me; and what I read and watched on the Internet did nothing to dispel that fear. In fact, it compounded it.

Here's a taste from Wikivoyage:

Independent travel in Kolyma is serious adventure, with the very real possibility of death. The area is essentially lawless, undeveloped, barely populated, and unbelievably remote. Just getting to either terminus at Magadan or Yakutsk is an adventure in itself - travelling along the road makes this look like buying a bus ticket in comparison. Every year dozens of people die in the region from drowning, freezing, car accidents, starvation, tick-borne encephalitis, alcohol poisoning, fires, crime, wild animals, or they just disappear. While travellers in the region are rewarded with nature, adventure, and so on, there is none of the safety net that accompanies nearly every other area that people travel, such as health care, consular support, English speakers, law enforcement, telecoms, etc.

The Kolyma Highway is one of the most dangerous roads in the world. The biggest risk by far is death by car accident due to unsafe driving, bad roads, unmaintained vehicles, or a combination of all three. A local proverb advises "the slower you go, the faster you'll get there". In particular, large trucks can throw up enormous clouds of dust in dry weather, which can easily hide an oncoming vehicle. Maps are generally out of date by a decade or more. Many towns listed on the maps will be either abandoned or completely vanished. Only a few towns have a single hotel, though in the more remote towns almost anyone you speak to will be extremely helpful.

Many towns lack police, but not people with financial problems, so either camp out of town or don't look rich. Drunken people are more common in winter, and can occasionally be bothersome. Bears and other wildlife enjoy a fearsome reputation...

This is probably somewhat extreme, but it did little to calm my troubled breast.

I showed it to my daughter and she suggested that I delay this trip for another five years or so because she'd rather I didn't die quite so soon.

I attempted to get as much information about the route as I could. Evidently, it's safer to ride it in mid winter because, in the extreme cold, it turns into an ice road and the rivers are easy to cross. It becomes impassable during the thaw and then, from mid June to the end of September it is passable - unless it rains. Then it turns into a swamp. So they say. And the rivers are impossible to cross because of high water.

And it's crossing rivers that bring me out in a cold sweat. Crossing them *alone* does not bear thinking about.

I was confused. On the Internet there seemed to be a parallel universe: On the one hand I was faced with videos and descriptions of the Road of Bones that made me realise that it would be impossible to attempt alone and then I read about trucks "throwing up enormous clouds of dust". If trucks cross from Yakutsk to Magadan then, surely, so can I. And trucks couldn't negotiate the sodden, deep-mud tracks, the rotten-timbered bridges that are shown with such masochistic glee by travellers on Youtube.

Furthermore, fuel would be a problem because villages in this remote region are far apart. This from someone who has ridden it:

"The Kolyma Highway can be ridden in four days, but there is very little fuel. Fill up whenever you can: Yakutsk - Khandyga - (418 km); Khandyga - Ust-Nera - (561 km); Ust-Nera - Yagodnoe - (495 km); Yagodnoe - Magadan - (522 km)."

I managed to make contact with a Russian biker in Magadan and asked him: *"Can I ride the Road of Bones and, if so, when is the best time to attempt it?"*

He replied: *"Hi. If you not be try to ride on Road of Bones (old Summer Road). Best time for visit Magadan is second half of June to mid of August."*

A faint glimmer of understanding began to lighten the darkness in my brain. I asked him to clarify and he replied: *"New road is working federal road its condition is good. Old road near Tomtor, I not recommend travel alone on this road."*

And at last I understood: trucks and dust: *new road*; swamp and rotten bridges, *Old Summer Road*, the Youtube road, the road Gareth wants to ride.

I was relieved. Yes, I could do it (but then, perhaps, as always happens, I might meet a group of intrepid bikers along the way who plan to attempt the Old Summer Road, the *real* Road of Bones, and I could ask if I could join them).

On Gareth's next visit, he told me he would love to ship his bike to Yakutsk and ride the Old Summer Road with me. And I'd so love him to be able to do it. But time and cost make this a non-starter, sadly. What an adventure it would be!

I had a vague idea where I wanted to go but hadn't yet tied it down so, one morning, I laid out my maps and roughed out a route and totalled up the distances. My heart sank: 33,000ks. That's from Osh, Kyrgyzstan, across Kazakhstan to Omsk in Siberia, turn right to Magadan in the Russian far east, back to Moscow, then south-west to the Caucasus and then home to the UK via Ukraine...

Bummer. 360ks per day, *every day* for three months, with no breathing space for breakdowns. I'd done my usual and bitten off more than I could chew, especially without Gareth around to help look after the bike.

I contacted Sasha, the Russian biker whom Gareth and I had met on the side of the road on our way to Archangel and who had invited us to join him and the Black Bears on their annual club jolly to the White Sea coast. We've kept in contact over the years and I hoped to meet up with him again. But I also wanted him as a contact during the journey, someone whom I could get hold of if I were in trouble, ask if he would put the word out on Russian social media in case there were any bikers nearby who might offer assistance. He replied:

"So, are you going to cross Russia alone or with Gareth? Yes, of course I try to help to you if you will need it during your grand trip. I'll try to find some local and send him for help, or translate the conversation or whatever you will be needed as help. I'm living in Moscow at the moment.

So if you will be able to meet me and my family we will be very pleased to! You can stay in my house as long as you want."

I told him about the 33,000ks and reflected on the hugeness of Russia. His reply, from the point of view of the Kolyma Highway, was rather concerning:

"Yep. Russia is sooooo huge. All our problems are because of the size also. To get that 33k your bike have to be in very very good condition, keeping in mind that awful roads on the east part of the country. Needless to say that places are dangerous to go alone. I don't want to scare you, but we had a number of tragedies there. Poor and angry aborigines can be dangerous. I would recommend you do not stay overnight with suspicious people, and do not camp on well-viewed areas."

I had heard stories about "aborigines" in the far east killing travellers for their money; somewhere else, I read: *"Certain very isolated villages suffer from the unpredictable side effects of chronic alcoholism... where locals are frequently drunk and armed with knives",* and I could not forget a photograph taped to the plastics of a bike belonging to one of the Russian bikers we had met. When Gareth asked who it was, he told us that this biker had ridden to Vladivostok fulfilling a life-long dream, but one night, on his way back, drinking with some locals in a remote village, he refused a drink. One of the locals took umbrage, left the room and came back a short time later with a shot-gun which he used to blow the biker's head off. Evidently the police knew who the culprit was but, being corrupt (as most Russian police are, we were told), they wouldn't prosecute. Bikers throughout Russia were taping the photograph of the murdered man on their bikes in an attempt to force the police to arrest the culprit.

Now, having experienced this propensity of Russians to invite one to their table and ply one with vodka regardless of the time of day or night, I was concerned. Not being a heavy drinker, I did not want to spend my three months in Russia getting drunk, fending off men overcome by alcohol-induced bonhomie or constantly looking over my shoulder to check whether some yokel was aiming a shotgun at my head. I decided on a cunning plan and asked Sasha whether he could translate:

Dear Sir, Please do not be offended. I have a serious medical condition and cannot drink much alcohol. If I drink too much I will become very ill and might die. Hope you will understand. Thank you.

I planned to have this on a laminated card in my wallet and, after a few drinks, show it to my drunken buddies with a regretful look on my face.

A short while later, Sasha replied with a Russian message that, when translated, said: *"I don't want to drink with you, buddy."*

Not quite what I was looking for; I didn't think showing a drunk Russian man that message would be altogether wise.

Shasa sent me another, entirely different message, in Russian, then a third that, translated, said: *"I can take two shots but really don't want more".*

I replied: *"You've confused me now. Which Russian should I use? I can't give some big Russian biker a note that says 'Piss off, Ivan, I don't want to drink with bloody Russians' - he'll want to kill me."*

Finally, Sasha recommended one that he assured me would be fine and I printed it out and tucked it in my wallet.

*****

For a three-month stay in Russia, you need a business visa; for a business visa, you need a letter of invitation. I paid £150 for some spurious piece of paper generated from who knows where - some dingy room in Moscow, probably, right next door to the Kremlin Bureau of Cyber Disinformation, but that, I hoped, would tick the box labelled: *Letter of Invitation* - supposedly from a Russian company with whom I do business and that will fulfil the requirements of the Russian Consulate. Surely they must know that these are mostly fake - like the made-up hotel bookings that are another requirement for the issuing of a visa. I can remember a suspicious Russian border official on a previous trip pointing to a hotel that had been booked in a city about a thousand kilometres south of where we were heading and me mumbling something about us going there first. He gave me a sideways look and stamped my passport.

But all this was probably moot after the attempted murder of ex-Russian double agent Sergei Skripal and his daughter Yulia in Salisbury using the Soviet-made, weapons-grade nerve agent Novichok. Reprisals were announced and Russian counter-reprisals soon followed, despite evidence as plain as bloody footprints leading straight to the door of the Kremlin.

Similar to the case of Alexander Litvinenko, former officer of the FSB who defected to the UK and received political asylum, murdered by a lethal dose of Polonium 210 shortly after he openly accused Putin of ordering the assassination of Anna Politkovskaya. Later investigation revealed distinct polonium trails left by assassins Andrey Lugovoy and Dmitry Kovtun in three attempts to administer the radioactive poison, the last of which succeeded.

Would the Russians even allow me in?

Sasha's response to the Skripal murder: *"It is all about unwritten law for ex-KGB workers: You only can get in the organization. Going to get out? - you're dead man. They basically don't care what you guys think about all of this. They just follow by the barbaric paradigm of loyalty and betrayal."*

I decided to peel the Union Jacks off my petrol tank and claim to be South African when asked by vodka-soaked, rightwing louts where I'm from. And I wouldn't be telling a lie - I *am* from South Africa.

What about the bike?

Normal people attempting a journey of this magnitude would spend long months preparing it. With the DR stuck in Kyrgyzstan, I didn't have that opportunity. The best I could do was to contact the guys at MuzToo and ask them to check it out. After a few weeks, I got this email:

Hi Lawrence
I rigged up an XT battery on the back of your bike, stuck some fuel in and Kolyer took it for a test ride. All seems to be good. Oil and air filter in good condition. Runs well. Brake pads good etc... The speedo cable is missing so you may want to bring one of those. The two panniers here but only two inner tubes in them (1 front 1 rear).

Right, bike prepared, then...

Two days before I catch my flight to Osh, I see this on a social media post above a photograph of an active Russian nuclear submarine, looking efficient but peaceful: *"Goodbye America... Oooooh..."*

A Russian biker, whose father was *"Commander of communications atomic cruiser, proud and love"* (translated) mentions that his main entertainment when a boy was to *"walk on a military base in far taiga"*.

Reading between the lines, the child's teacher had treated him unjustly and he responded by threatening to get his dad to *"press the button and school dead"*.

Needless to say, *"Dad called to school"*. I'm sure he had some explaining to do.

"What about the submarine?" another Russian asks.

"She drowned..." (smiley face).

Alexi comments in Russian: *"Same bullshit. Let it remain at the level of exercise."*

Tongue in cheek, I respond: *"Please don't fire missiles at America until I get back to the UK. I'll let you know when it's safe,"* to which Alexi snaps back:

"Too late. UK will be the first. Fucking bitch Theresa set you up."

Oh, dear. It seems feelings in Russia might be a little tenser than I hoped. My decision to cover the British flag on my tank with the bright and cheerful South African one is, I think, a wise one.

(Of course his name is not Alexi - I made that up. I don't want him to wake up one morning with weapons-grade polonium smeared on his doorknob.)

I respond with: *"Hope you don't punch me in the face if we meet up on our travels. Bikers are buddies - right?"*

He sends me a smiley-face emoji so I think all will be well...

Chapter One

Sky is beautiful anywhere

"A Communist is someone who's read Marx, an anti-communist is someone who's understood him" - Russian joke.

I manage to lose my passport even before I board my flight from Manchester airport. After a few minutes of panicky searching, I become aware of a uniformed man with a frowney face holding up a passport that I assume is mine, looking about for the cretin who left it in the X-Ray scanner tray when he removed his belt, wallet, shoes and other stuff that might be used to blow up the aircraft. I retrieve it, cursing myself for the idiot that I am and wondering, not for the first time, whether the spectre of dementia is beginning to stalk the portals of my mind.

Another man wearing a uniform takes exception to the plastic five-litre petrol container that I have attempted to smuggle into my cabin bag. He confiscates it, of course.

My mini-electric tyre pump also perplexes him and he calls his supervisor. A man with important-looking spaghetti on his epaulettes examines the pump from all angles then asks, "Do you have the connection for this?" - holding the plug end for me to see.

"No, it's on the bike," I tell him, sad to see my pump go the way of the fuel container but he says,

"No, it's fine," and hands it back to me. I assume he thinks that if I have the actuating mechanism on my person then I might just blow up the plane. (My little joke - get it? "Blow up the plane -" No? It's a *pump?* Oh, forget it.)

He digs deeper into my bag and comes up with my container of spares - wheel bearings, brake pads, jumper leads etc - examines each carefully and deems them acceptable. Then he finds my set of Allen keys; he holds them up with two fingers as if they offend him. "You can't take these on the plane, sir," he informs me sternly.

"Why not?"

"They're tools," he says, logically.

What do you think I'm going to do with them - start dismantling the plane from the inside as soon as we leave the ground? I want to ask him, but don't. They arrest people who make sarcastic comments in airports.

Eventually I am allowed to board and, somewhat lighter now, we take off for Dusseldorf and Moscow. And as the evening dies to night, I look out of the window onto a thick layer of cumulus cloud so soft and thick you could lie on it. The whole sky has turned a muted pink, bruised on the edges with purple, the moon hanging bright in the sky just a day or two from full.

I turn to the old man who sits alongside me, bald and jerking with what I assume to be cerebral palsy, his face and nose bruised from a fall, and ask, "Are you Russian?"

"Yes," he says.

"Eta ochin kraisiva," I say, practicing my Russian and pointing to the sunset outside the window. He smiles and nods.

His wife, a comfortable, homely woman with frizzed hair whom I have watched during the flight holding her husband's jerking hands so he can drink what is left of his tea after the spillage, turns to me and says in heavily-accented English, "Yes, beautiful. But it is not Russia. It is sky. And sky is beautiful anywhere."

And with that reminder of the universality of beautiful things, the borderlessness of the elements, all the tensions behind the attempted murder of the Schipols and the tit-for-tat merry-go-round that followed fall away and I am welcomed into Russia.

As soon as the wheels touch down on the tarmac, the passengers, in true Soviet style, applaud vigorously - the pilot for getting us safely to our destination without killing us all and the plane, too, I assume, for reaching Moscow with all its bits still attached.

*****

Then on, across the Kazakh steppe to Kyrgyzstan. Osh meets me off the plane with a slap in the face; heavy rain is being blown sideways by a fierce wind.

My taxi driver speaks to me non-stop in Russian whilst dodging potholes, leaning out the window to spit, and sipping from a gaily-painted hip flask. He addresses me as if I am a fluent Russian speaker, oblivious of my incomprehension, but I know enough to recognise the usual questions asked of every traveller to remote areas: *Where are you from?* "Ah! Manchester United!" (Open window, spit, close window, wash mouth out with vodka.) *Where are you going? How old are you? How many children do you have?*

When he asks me about my wife, not knowing the Russian for: "She is dead -" I mime, attempting to maintain some form of delicacy in the action but, I believe, merely conveying to the man (open window, spit, close window) that she is still sleeping in Manchester. He doesn't understand so I give up.

(Spit, drink vodka.)

We pass a petrol station and he looks with a reproachful glance at a sign that advertises fuel at the equivalent of 40p a litre. He shakes his head, spits, and says bitterly, *"Benzin, ochin daragea."*

I don't tell him we are paying over £1.30 a litre in the UK.

We make our way through rain-wet streets to a hostel. It is early morning and I have had no sleep. I collapse onto a bed in a dark room but after an hour I have to get up; I can't sleep; I need to get to my bike, to see what condition it's in after two years, to know that it will, at least, start.

I need to know...

I take another taxi and we make our way into the outskirts of town. The rain has stopped. Over the gravel and through the large metal gates, enter the premises of MuzToo. Kolyer is there, the skinny Russian mechanic who is, as always, crouched over the entrails of a bike with his bony knees pressed against his chest. He greets me with an embarrassed smile and keeps on working.

Afraid of what I might see, I make my way over the long-grassed courtyard and peer into the rough, open-fronted, corrugated-iron-roofed shed that shelters about thirty tired-looking adventure bikes in various stages of disrepair. And there, pushed far back between a clutter of other bikes and furred with two years' of dust and bird-droppings and rat-shit, are the two bikes.

They look bad. Gareth's DR, engine open and covered with a cloth, leans against mine as if for company.

(For those of you who haven't read *A Pass Too Far*, we had abandoned Gareth's bike near the end of Matt's Pass in Tajikistan two years before with a seized engine; then, when the track ended against a cliff face and a deep river, we abandoned my bike too and walked out. We rescued my bike two days later and rode back to Osh two-up, abandoning Gareth's DR in the mountains. How it came to be back in the land of the living, leaning against my bike in the shed, I have briefly recounted in a postscript to this book.)

I look at my bike in the dim light, see my soft panniers strapped to the frame with tie-downs and looking as if they've just been rescued from the dump, my instrument cluster strapped in place with zip-ties after having been ripped off in a crash in soft sand, pannier rack roughly welded where I'd re-positioned it using pieces of scrap metal found in a grassy corner of the courtyard, various straps and cords hanging in the dirt.

I move Gareth's bike out of the way, careful to leave the piece of cloth over the open crank-case, and manoeuvre my bike over the concrete drain and out into the sunlight.

Standing in the long grass, exposed to the light, it doesn't look any better; in fact, it looks worse and I am afraid.

I set to work: fit the new battery first - I need to hear the engine. Turn the key and the green light shows dimly through the covering of dust. The engine fires on the second attempt and putters to itself like a sewing machine badly in need of a service. At least it runs. Re-fit pannier racks, mount GPS holder, remove wheels and replace bearings, pump up tyres. The spare parts I have brought for my rear brake callipers are the wrong size so I remove the pad mounting bolts, beat them straight with a hammer and re-fit them with the worn sides turned away. It's loose and wobbly but the brakes work. The indicators are dead and I have no speedo cable or horn but can cope with that.

I stand back and look at it - rough, dirty, travel-stained, old... What on earth was I thinking? Am I going to set off across Russia on *this?*

But, hey, it's got two wheels and an engine that runs so I suppose it's ready to go.

And then my daughter decides to have her baby early while on holiday in Spain.

I'm a grandfather again...

Chapter Two

Horses in the mountains

Old Russian joke: "Where do I sign up for the Communist Party?"
"At the psychiatrist's"

I wake late after a restless night worrying about the many miles ahead of me on an old bike, my daughter and my grandson who is critically ill in intensive care.

It being Ramadan, there is no breakfast on offer at the hostel so I drink coffee in the now hot Kyrg sunshine, my possessions scattered about on the ground, and wonder where and how I can fit them on the bike. Even though I've pared everything to the bone, there still seems too much stuff.

The normal planning and preparation time, perhaps a brief shakedown trip to see that everything is as it ought to be, the physical presence of the bike to trial pack your stuff, have been denied me. After a two-year break, I'm riding blind.

But by ten everything is ship-shape. She fires up willingly and I set off to brave the congested streets of Osh, looking for the main road north to Bishkek. I manage ten kilometres before a policeman wielding a fluorescent baton waves me down. The speed camera mounted on a tripod next to his patrol car looks ominous. He speaks no English but it is clear that I have been caught speeding - the proof is on the camera screen, which he points to with an authoritative finger: 67 in a 50 zone. He presents me with a clipboard onto which an official-looking document is clamped, his finger directing my eye to what I assume says: *The fine for exceeding the speed limit by 10-20kph is 500 Som* - about $5.00. I take out my wallet and hand over a S500 note, which he takes and shoves into his back pocket.

My suspicions are raised. His action is a little too hasty. I tap the clipboard and mime that I want my receipt. He balks and fills the space with talk. I tap the clipboard again, more insistently, tell him in English that if I pay a fine I want a receipt; anything else is a bribe and I don't do bribes. He becomes unctuous, dropping his voice and moving closer - obvious signs to the experienced traveller. By now he has the S500 note hidden in the palm of his hand; he cups it loosely level with his belt - that gesture that is universally recognised as signalling the beginning of a covert exchange of money for favours. He makes whispered: "Oi, this is a bribe transaction taking place here - *capeesh?"* noises while glancing nervously at his fellow officer.

I shake my head and prod the form on the clipboard a third time - I want my receipt. Unexpectedly, he thrusts the note back into my hand and says curtly, "Goodbye -" waving me away as one would an annoying fly.

The outskirts of Osh fall away; the clutter and dirt softens and is given a certain grandeur by the high, snow-capped Alau and Alaykuu Mountains that follow me for the next sixty kilometres. Shortly after the small town of Uzgen the road turns ninety degrees to the right and, with the mountains now behind me, I face north for the first time towards Kazakhstan and, eventually, Russia. At last I am on my way and, suddenly, there come upon me feelings of elation and loneliness that are almost visceral in their intensity.

And then on over the rolling hills of northern Kyrgyzstan, through small villages and towns, each with its own resident traffic cop under the shade of a tree, pointing a radar gun down the road.

The land dries and turns brown, the earth and rocks showing through. It is hot. I stop and drink sweet, black coffee, the engine smelling distressed in the still air. On the road, trucks bellow past and small children wave.

I am making slow progress but I assure myself there is no rush; the tens of thousands of kilometres ahead will still be there when I reach them but as always with me, the compulsion is to push on, getting the distance under my wheels.

Then on past the Moldo Too mountains, their pastel strata in soft shades of pink and brown and burnt umber and pale yellow, the blue-green waters of the Toktogel Reservoir following me down steep-sided clefts in the rock. From out of the dust-flecked air comes the rank smell of goats grazing, leaving the sweetness of foliage crushed by their hooves; and horses, sleek and nimble, carrying still within their genes the wildness and abandon that ran through the blood of their ancestors who roamed this place long before roads scoured its steep flanks. Later I come upon ice-blue lakes that reflect the dark peaks of mountains in their still waters, so beautiful that I catch my breath and say aloud, "Oh! Oh!"

Then on into the setting sun, the air cooling and the mountains muted in shadow; in the steep valleys it turns dark and cold, smelling of dust and ancient rocks and road-tar holding still within itself the heat of the day.

By evening I chance upon a quaint guesthouse with cold beer and Simon, an Australian cyclist, to keep me company - beard and hair untrimmed and unkempt, face wind-whipped and leathery from fourteen months on the road - and I know that all is well with the world.

*****

The road skirts the northern end of Toktogul Reservoir and immediately begins to climb. A clear river, almost aquamarine with snowmelt, tumbles alongside and, on the edge, itinerant bee-keepers display their pale yellow wares, rough wooden hives making crooked lines in the long grass, the air filled with their heavy, sweet perfume. The bee boxes are brightly coloured but predominantly blue, as if a job lot of that colour has been made available on the cheap throughout Kyrgyzstan. Tucked behind in the long grass amongst a clutter of stuff is always a gypsy-like caravan on wheels, a rustic home-from-home alongside his busy little workers.

I am slowed by herds of horses, fat as butter and sleek-skinned, making their way up the pass to the high pastures, skittish newborn foals keeping close to their mothers. Before and behind the herd, some with as many as fifty horses together, ride the herders, mounted and waving red flags. And always, ranging alongside as if surveying their charges, are large, hairy dogs who pay no attention to me other than giving me a slanty-eyed glance as I pass.

I continue to climb, the pass itself rising for well over 100ks until I reach the snow line and stop to close the vents in my jacket and don the jumper I stuffed into my bag as an afterthought, assuming I would be struggling in the heat for most of the way. At first it is old ice, grey and embedded with gravel, blocks left behind from the previous year's snowfall, metres high; then the new snow, white and crisp, and I try to hold within myself what's left of my body-warmth as I shiver for hours across the rock-strewn, high Alpine plateau, one mountain being replaced by another and yet another as I peer ahead, mentally pleading for the inevitable descent.

A harsh, cold wind knocks me about, the sky heavily overcast and threatening rain. Over the final pass, snow starts to fall, crisp and white against the dark sky, but at last the road begins to descend, the air warms and I can feel my fingers again. Yurts appear like smooth, white mushrooms on the mountainsides and, with them, more horses and flocks of dark-haired sheep.

A long, downhill slalom of about thirty kilometres takes me to the plains that signal the beginning of the Kazakh steppe. I so miss Gareth, knowing how he loved the challenge of these tight switchbacks, would speed up and rush ahead then slow and watch for me to catch up further down the track. I look ahead, hoping to see him but he's not there. I'm riding alone and again a deep wrench of loneliness comes upon me, my daughter and her newborn child dangerously ill and hospitalised in a foreign country too and I wonder whether I should be there with her.

All I can do is pray.

The wind, still blowing, snatches up dust and sand that turn the atmosphere milky and erase the entire Alatau Mountain Range behind me so that, unless you knew otherwise, the snow-capped peaks I have just ridden across throughout the day might not be there at all.

Needing to change money, I stop at the first town I come to after descending the mountains and am taken in hand by a young lad who informs me that he is a primary school teacher of English and needs to practice. He leads me to a dark shop selling clothing and bolts of brightly-coloured cloth and introduces me to a man who could be a caricature of a middle-eastern Jew. I could have been inside a Dickens novel and almost expect him to rub his fingers together and mutter slyly about interest. I show him my US dollars and a calculator appears in his hand, as if by magic. I don't know the exchange rate but trust him and accept the rather large figure - 57,000 comes to mind - that he offers me.

I nod and he counts out the notes.

Outside in the heat, bone-thin women, begging, block the pavement, and the desperation in their eyes stays with me for a long time.

I pass into Kazakhstan with brief formality and keep my wheels pointing north towards a town called Shu, 160ks away. At first the road is in good condition but it soon deteriorates - as is to be expected in Kazakhstan; battered and beaten-up, it seems unsure whether it ought to remain a tar road or revert to its preferred state of dirt. But it isn't a bike-breaker and I appreciate the age-lines on its face that give it character and make the ride more interesting.

On either side of me the steppe disappears to the horizon in gentle, rolling curves, the grass a deep green at this time of the year and tugged about by the wind. The sky is still dark and roiling with heat-thunder but every so often a shaft of sunlight breaks through and pools the grass and the flowers with bright colours, making silhouettes of the rooks that twist and wheel with their wings bent against the wind. Occasionally a line of wooden telephone poles, strapped to concrete posts sunk into the soil and leaning as if tired, step their way in straight lines towards the horizon.

A rail line joins us and we cross the steppe together, meeting up at a junction town whose name I don't catch (if it had one). Wind-swept and desolate, rusting carcasses of vehicles, abandoned factories and buildings seem to define it. Yellow-painted, above-ground gas pipes snake about the road verge, lifting themselves in dusty rectangles over every road and house entrance. There is no fuel and I am running low. But I see what looks like a place that might serve coffee and stop. An unfinished porch has been crudely constructed from abandoned railway sleepers. Inside, a middle-aged woman wearing a cardigan and slippers flashes her gold teeth at me and we agree that she will bring me coffee.

I sit at a table covered with a plastic sheet decorated with bright red poppies and she carefully arranges a sheet of newspaper in front of me as a place mat. Glass mug, bottle of coffee and sugar, hot water in an enamelled metal teapot decorated with flowers. The coffee - black of course - is sweet and strong. The inside walls, constructed from clapboard and bits of flattened tins, are painted pink and on the walls hang bright baskets of plastic flowers. A Kazakh truck driver joins me at my table and shares his biscuits with me. He assures me there is no fuel available here but can be obtained at Shu, sixty kilometres further on.

Outside, the wind continues to blow dust into the air and the dark clouds darken further with the lateness of the day.

Time to move on...

I ride slowly to conserve fuel, the little DR puttering along happily in a relaxed frame of mind.

Finally Shu appears, a rambling railway junction town, and I fuel up. A young man who speaks some English leads me to the hotel.

There is no news from my daughter...

Chapter Three

Dried fish in the wind

'Putin the democrat' is our shortest joke.

It's a long, cold road that runs for about 2000ks from Kyrgyzstan in the south to the Russian border close to Omsk in Siberia. The road - I have considered calling it a "track" but I'll stick to "road" for now - is almost straight with the occasional twisty bit thrown in, I assume, for elegant variation. It runs close-ish to the border with Mongolia and crosses, with little exception, pure steppe, that vast expanse of undulating grassland that used to be the haunt of wild horses, Siberian ibex and marauding Khans. It hasn't changed much. One comes across the occasional herd of sheep. I saw a dog. A wide, reed-banked river meanders its way across the flat land, deep and slow flowing and smelling of mud and the rotting bodies of barbel and bream in the shallows.

After a long time a small line of hills shrugs itself out of the sand, their strangeness giving some perspective to this endless plain. The soil is dry and sandy but manages to sustain a scattering of hardy grasses and spiked shrubs that click and rattle in the wind - but always the sand shows through as if the land is struggling to resist the slow encroachment of the desert. I pause briefly to pay my respects at the place where a biker died on this road, his memorial constructed from the remains of his bike and helmet, a poignant reminder that death exists close to life here amidst the sand and the murmuring grasses of the steppe.

Even now, in late spring, there is a chill to the air, a pale sun in a pale sky providing little warmth. I have difficulty conceiving of this desolation in mid winter; the Kazakhs who live here must be a hardy breed, able to cope with privations of which we in the cosseted West can have little conception.

Occasionally a nondescript, breezeblock structure appears on the roadside and holds out the promise of warm tea or coffee, perhaps a scrambled egg or two for weary travellers or the hardy drivers of trucks who wrestle their lumbering beasts along this battered road. Then rail lines appear with their dipping wires; abandoned water towers rise from the steppe and signal a rail junction with its straggle of houses and workshops that remind one of hastily-erected frontier towns, dry, dusty and impermanent.

So little of this land, despite its vastness, is cultivated; probably the meagre rainfall cannot sustain it, as the Russians discovered when they launched the Virgin Lands Project, their ill-fated attempt at intensive cotton cultivation in Kazakhstan. It could, perhaps, sustain a sparse level of pastoral enterprise but I came across only one herd of sheep in 400ks.

The road itself has been constructed in the manner of Russian roads throughout the taiga - probably easier because no trees need to be felled in these barren steppes. There just aren't any. The road itself is built on a low causeway, raised about four feet above the ground. The soil for this is simply dug from either side, leaving deep trenches that fill with water in the rainy season and are quickly populated by reeds; these create an impression of fertility by lining the road with green and hosting large flocks of blackbirds which rise and scatter like flung stones at my passing. On top of this soil causeway a thin layer of aggregate and tar are laid and this serves as the road - that is until the heavy trucks squash and squish and masticate it into high, undulating ridges and the surface breaks through and the potholes breed and multiply like mushrooms.

I come across one lonely work team with a tractor patching a few potholes but considering that there are 5,963,872,514 of the buggers on that road (I counted), they really are pissing into the wind. I do appreciate, though, the occasional sign along the way that warns me that humps and bumps can be expected (I thank the Kazakh government for this - without the warning, I would never have known); like half way up a steep pass with a thousand twisty bits, you come across a random sign that tells drivers to be careful of curves in the road - and you think to yourself, "Why?"

While I sip sweet, black coffee at a truck-stop café, a Kazakh woman of a certain age, ample girth and a winsome smile, asks her daughter (who has a little English) to tell me that she would like me to take her back to England. I tell her that she can ride on the back of my bike. She laughs and says nooo she's too fat. I vehemently disagree and make a slim-girl, Coca-Cola-bottle shape with my hands and give her ample curves an admiring glance. I swear she blushes and then she gives me a hug.

Later, for hours I ride alongside the bird's-egg blue Lake Balkhash, 16,400 sq km in size and sharing its vast basin with China. Old men crouch on the roadside in the sun, watching over crude wooden structures upon which dried fish twist and flutter in the wind like large, winter-grey leaves. I pull over to speak to a man with wrinkled, leathery skin who sits on a rock next to his ancient, blue-painted Izh two-stroke motorcycle and sidecar. As I approach, he stands and offers me his seat; it is a gesture that could have graced a lady's afternoon tea. I make myself comfortable on his smooth rock and look at the dried fish hanging from a piece of wire that he has rigged from his motorcycle to a wooden pole propped up with rocks. Leaning against the sidecar wheel is a rough, hand-painted sign held in place with string.

He stoops into the sidecar, lifts a blanket that he has used to keep the flies off, and selects a dried fish for me to eat. I accept it in the African way, with two hands expressing gratitude, dig out a leathery piece of flesh with my fingers and eat it. It is very salty and the taste reminds me of the earthy interior of smoke-filled Lesotho huts. The fish's head, tail and fins are still attached, the empty eye sockets making a convenient hole through which to pass a piece of wire.

Trucks bellow past on their way to and from the large industrial town of Balkhash several miles away, from whose copper foundries a sickly yellow pollution darkens the sky. (Later, when I pass through the town, people in the street can be seen wearing cloth masks over their mouths and noses.)

I sit and he stands and I dutifully pick flakes of dry flesh off the bones of my leathery fish and attempt, out of politeness, to eat. He walks over and admires my bike; I stand and admire his - both bikes have character, the patina of long, hard lives etched into their frames and skin. He is proud of his catch, lifting the blanket and showing me his fish, some of them two feet long, the flesh slashed into cubes on the bones before being smoked to the consistency of old saddles.

Wanting to honour me more as his roadside guest, he detaches a clutch of dried fish - about six in total - attached by a piece of wire through their eye sockets and presents them to me with a smile. I remonstrate; it is too much. I won't eat them, anyway, and this is his livelihood. He presses them into my hands. As a compromise, I select one and gesture that I will be happy with that but only the whole clutch as a gift is acceptable to him. Despite my protestations, he hangs the wire loop of fish over my handlebars. I try to offer him money but he refuses: it is a gift. I push a note into his pocket - "For coffee -" I tell him, to make the proffered money more acceptable like, *Have a drink on me, mate...* but it won't do. He removes the note and thrusts it back into my pocket. I give up gracefully. To protest further would be to disrespect his gift.

I offer him water - it's all I have - and he drinks. I drink too, without wiping the spout. (You only share spit with those with whom you closely bond, so I'm told.) Not to be outdone, he fills my water bottle from a container stored in the sidecar then says something to me. I manage to understand that he wants to see some UK money. Fortunately I have a 50p coin in my wallet left over after my flight and I give him this, showing him the bass-relief of the queen. He is happy with his gift and I, as so often before, am touched by the generosity of complete strangers.

And, no, I didn't eat the fish.

*****

I spend the night in the apartment of a Texan I chanced upon and who offered me a bed for the night. Over breakfast I ask him the inevitable question one wants to ask any reasonably adult American (is that an oxymoron?): *What do you think of Donald Trump?* (I don't say: *That loud-mouthed, pussy-grabbing, bad-hair excuse for a man you inexplicably elected for your president...* and I try to keep my face and voice neutral.)

"He's getting the job done," he answers, almost warily, as if making an indecent suggestion. "But he should be more careful about what he says," he adds as an afterthought.

Yeah, right! I want to say, but I don't.

He warms to his topic: Obama was the worst president in the history of America; he encouraged terrorism, wanted to bring America down to a level with the rest of the world, he openly encouraged the murder of policemen (I assume he meant white policemen), he was two-faced and Obama-Care was a disaster.

Well, that puts me in my place, doesn't it? (I decide not to ask him about guns.)

"What about his lies?" I venture, keeping my voice gentle in case he decides to punch me in the face.

"All politicians lie," he explains.

"And that makes it *right?*" I ask.

"It was a choice between lying Hillary and Trump who also lies," he explains, clearly annoyed. "But he's making America great again -"

I'm sure I've heard that somewhere before, I think to myself.

*****

Memorial and graveyard just off the road: "To the victims of oppression who have gained eternal rest in Kazakh soil."

I think they mean the bloody Russians...

Some random thoughts (one gets to thinking a great deal on the long, empty road, alone):

- The only real advantage a man has over a woman is that men have been designed to pee standing up.
- Why don't they take all the white South African farmers (the ANC doesn't like them very much and would appreciate it if they left) and give them farms here? Like in the Karoo, they would make this semi-desert bloom.
- I'm glad it's not raining. (Not a wise thought because now, for sure, dark clouds will begin to form.)
- America, we need you now - don't you care about your sons and daughters?
- If small holes in the road were repaired quickly, they wouldn't become big holes.

The distinctive smell of new rain on warm tar is not a happy one for the long-distance motorcycle traveller. It usually presages a day of misery.

I tuck my chin into my neck in a futile attempt to slow the insidious ingress of water under my clothes and onto my skin, and press on over a rain-slick road towards the town of Petropavlovsk and the border with

Russia. The sky is low and dark and miserable, the colour of "old pots and pans" as one poet aptly described it, the wind gusting hard in my face, the land flat and uninteresting.

Signs direct me straight north to the border at Petropavlovsk but my GPS suggests, in a helpful sort of way, that I might consider taking a more interesting road east that will enable me to cross into Russia just south of Omsk. If I keep on the boring, straight road I will be guaranteed a warm bed for the night; the alternative road, small and wiggly, shows just two villages before the border. The rain makes me favour the direct route; the *me* in me leans towards the latter.

I write this in the warmth of a cosy eating establishment cum petrol station 140ks before the turning where I need to make a decision. There is one positive about riding through the cold and rain on a bike: the random coffee stops are, by comparison, all the more of a blessing. A homely woman (all middle-aged women seem "homely" in Kazakhstan, for some reason) brings me strong coffee and a warm pasty thing that, together, wipe away the cold unpleasantness of the morning road. She smiles and says, "*Thank you!*" in an English accent, mimicking me, obviously enjoying the foreign sounds on her tongue.

Back on my bike, heading north: the rain has stopped (briefly), my coffee drunk, pasty eaten and, whilst my wife might be dead, my grandson is alive. Life goes on; the gyre continues to turn. All is good with the world - well, maybe not Trump's. (I'm sorry, my dear American friends, but anyone with hair like that deserves to be mocked.)

Then, just for spite, the rain beats down again like a bully and I ride on with my chin tucked into my neck. Which road to take? Straight on and a warm bed... small, interesting road with uncertain expectations; easy but boring... more difficult but interesting... I'm wet and cold and my body craves comfort...

As the road begins to fork, the decision is made and I lean into the slip road to the right. To hell with comfort, I'm a traveller, not a tourist. Immediately the traffic disappears and I have the road to myself: narrow and lumpy, it makes its meandering way through rain-wet grassland, empty of people or buildings. The sky is dark with cloud and a blustery wind slaps me about but I am filled with a sense of adventure. The easy way, the straight path, is for wimps, I tell myself, for men who lack a certain something deep down where these things matter. Yes, the small road... the road not taken... Ah, Robert Frost, you have captured so the elusive spirit of travel:

> Two roads diverged in a wood, and I-
>
> I took the one less travelled by,
>
> And that has made all the difference.

The rain intensifies; the afternoon darkens into evening and I need to find somewhere dry to lay my head. Then, at last, I see a sign that buoys my spirit: a bed - 25ks. Cold and wet and stiff from a long day's ride, trying to keep the water out of my clothes, I rejoice aloud into my helmet.

I come across a village of cow dung and the skeletons of trucks. Fences with missing slats lean into long grass and thin dogs and chickens scratch about in vacant lots, looking for food. I stop in the mud outside a small shop and ask the two young ladies behind the counter about accommodation. They look perplexed, shrug and shake their heads. *No hotels here, mate.*

I mime my all too obvious distress and rest my head on my hands in sleeping posture. They are sympathetic and both pick up their phones. After a few calls, one looks up and smiles at me - yes, she seems to imply, someone will take me in for the night. She tries to give me directions but I don't understand and I'm just not prepared to head off into a strange village on the off chance that I might stumble upon the right house. Eventually the lady indicates that she will take me there if I put her on the back of my bike. With difficulty, she climbs on and, with her sweet arms tight around my waist, we head along muddy side streets until I see a woman and a small boy standing in front of a gate, looking expectant. I deliver my young lady back to the shop and return.

My hostess, whose name is Tamara, opens the gate and I squeeze my bike through. In front of me is a shed-like structure made of chipboard, flattened tin and tarpaper. She ushers me inside. The roof is corrugated asbestos without a ceiling and has the appearance of an old cowshed. There is a bed in one corner, a small table and an old gas stove with the oven door hanging off its hinges. A flowered bed sheet hung over baling twine separates the room from the shed junk that occupies the other half. The floor is made of rough concrete and large, broken flags. Outside, a tethered dog yelps, a flock of geese hiss at me and, in the back garden, two cows low mournfully, as they do.

Tamara, a short, portly lady in her sixties, I would assume, bustles about me in motherly fashion, most concerned about my well being. In tow is a thin waif of a boy, about ten years old, who tugs at my sleeve and goes *Vroom vroom!* He likes my bike.

When I drag off my rain-soaked boots, she presents me with a pair of brightly-flowered women's slippers to wear inside. She insists I remove my wet clothes and hang them on strings tied across the strangely warm room. She opens a door and shows me my own personal banya: wood fire heating a large pot of water that steams comfortably under its lid, an enamel bowl filled with rocks and a bucket of cold water smelling faintly of benzene. With the waif accompanying me, I strip off and wash in water almost too hot to bear, sloshed over my body with a plastic dipper.

Fresh and sweet smelling, I unpack, wheel the bike onto the verge and, with the waif's help, change the oil. Afterwards, because his eyes beg me to, I give him a ride up and down the street. "*Vroom vroom!*" he goes, clinging to the handlebars. Later, he takes me for a walk along the muddy streets between roughly-constructed but neat little houses, each with vegetable garden and loose chickens out back. When we return, Tamara presents me with an old beanie and a tattered jacket to keep me warm. They belonged to her husband, she tells me.

The little boy disappears and I don't see him again.

When it is dark, while I sit at the oil-cloth-covered table, writing, Tamara cuts up tomatoes and a cucumber, the Central Asian staple, and heats a pot of soup on the gas stove. Later, while we eat, she idly spoons jam from a bowl then, with it still in her mouth, sips tea from a large cup. (Saves on the cost of sugar, I suppose.) On the walls are a picture of the Madonna and child and sepia daguerreotype photographs of a young Tamara, her stiffly-posed husband and a small child.

We communicate with difficulty but without tension. She, too, has lost her partner, a husband of many years and, like me, she lives alone. Perhaps it is this that creates a bond between us that I can feel. I have been welcomed into her home like a friend and, later, with the exertion of the day hanging heavily on my eyelids, she offers me tea and we two sit at the table - me with my zip-less borrowed jacket and my woman's slippers, she in dressing gown and with her hair down - and drink black tea and eat thick hunks of bread with toxic-looking red jam spread with a spoon and we talk using sign language and the few words we have in common like old companions at peace with each other's company.

That night, I sleep well on an old couch with ornate, scrolled back rest until I wake in the wee hours hearing the wind howl about the building and rattle loose sheets of tin nailed to the walls and the lonely sound of rain on the roof. Outside, chickens make that throaty sound that all fowls make when the morning is near. And, despite the warm care of my bed and this woman, I am afraid. In the wet, throughout the previous day, the DR had hesitated and missed and every time its little heartbeat showed signs of distress I became filled with a sense of dread. The distance that stretches ahead of me is frightening.

Strangely, as one naturally does when travelling alone with a machine as one's only companion, I have come to love this little bike with a deep affection, am conscious of it outside leaning against its side stand looking tired and forlorn. Then, too, already I am tired and not sure that my ageing body will cope with what I am proposing to put it through on this trip. Once across Russia on a reliable, modern bike - OK; one and a half times across on an old trail bike might be asking too much of both of us. If I weren't alone, I think I would be fine. Traversing the vast, threatening remoteness of the Russian far east by myself terrifies me.

So, I lie awake, hoping the rain will stop, hearing the wind make mournful sounds in the night outside, my aloneness in this vast and seemingly empty world very real in the centre of my chest.

Chapter Four

No foreigners allowed

"I'm sick of hearing how bad life was under socialism. I'm proud of the Soviet era! It wasn't 'the good life' but it was regular life. We had love and friendship... dresses and shoes... The young can adapt while the old die in silence behind closed doors."

It can sometimes be more difficult getting out of a country than getting in...

I wake to the noise of farm animals preparing to greet the day. My dear hostess cooks me breakfast of fried eggs, onions and some of those disgusting, pale sausages made of cows' lips and lungs and stuff you don't bear reflecting upon.

I load my bike under a blustery sky, dark with incipient rain and set off along the muddy track to the tar road. My little waif is nowhere to be seen.

From then on the day turns feral. A Siberian gale batters me across the rutted, pot-holed road through a sodden, empty landscape all morning and into the afternoon while rain pokes needles through my skin.

Finally, in the mid afternoon, signs appear indicating the imminent approach of the border; ahead, smudged by pouring rain, are buildings and a gate. I am tired, wet, cold - but, never fear: just 100ks north is Omsk, the welcoming faces of my friends Rimma and Sasha, a warm shower, a warming shot of vodka...

But like flies to wanton boys are we to the gods - they torment us for their sport; fate or karma was about to poke me in the eye as payback for my smugness. I approach the large, metal gate. A uniformed man steps out of his cubicle into the rain, crosses his arms over his chest and shakes his head. There is no mistaking the gesture: the border is closed.

I remonstrate. He shakes his head, but points me towards the main building. I speak earnestly to a man who seems to be in charge; he, too, shakes his head. I plead with a nice Russian lady over the telephone who speaks good English. But all are adamant: this particular border crossing is for the exclusive use of Kazakh and Russian citizens; no foreigners allowed; no exceptions made.

"You must go back to the border at Petropavlovsk," the Russian lady tells me - the border that I was just 100ks away from yesterday when I stupidly decided to be the big adventurer and take the small road and ride 300ks east through atrocious, arctic weather. The 300ks I now have to ride again, west, into the wind, through the rain and the cold, to that turning off the main road and then another 100ks north to Petropavlovsk (the border I had sneered at, a border for wimps in air-conditioned, luxury cars, cars with heaters) and then 300ks east again, in Russia, to my friends' apartment in Omsk that is now just a hop and a skip away from where I now stand. I can almost *smell* it.

Thoroughly pissed off at having to negotiate six hundred unnecessary, wasted, frustrating kilometres through some of the most unpleasant weather I have ever ridden through, I turn the bike and begin the long journey back.

Welcome to Siberia. If this is what it's going to be like for the rest of the trip, I want to go home.

The gale now coming from straight in front of me, I lie on the tank while the wind peels my eyelids back and attempts to rip the helmet off my head. I curse myself for bringing an open-face helmet and light clothing to cope with the mid-summer, Siberian heat.

And so, for hours, I suck it up, absorb the pain, count down the kilometres and consider that there must be many more productive and enjoyable things a man of my age could be doing with his day, with his life, than this. When considering a long journey, days of this nature seldom feature in one's calculations. In the planning stage, the weather is always warm and sunny, the sky blue and puffed with friendly clouds, the locals tame and your bike doesn't break down; rain doesn't insert rude fingers down your neck to soak your chest and work its way through your trousers to grip your unmentionables with cold, clammy fingers.

The afternoon slowly wanes and darkness begins to settle over the land. The wind still rages and rain hammers down. And as exhaustion and the loneliness of the road come upon me, I find myself thinking: I miss my children, I miss my grandchildren - and then, before I can think, I say aloud, "I miss my wife -" and, unconsciously echoing Othello, I cry out against the wind and the rain, "My wife... my wife? What wife? I *have* no wife -" and I burst into tears borne out of a deep sense of aloneness in this wide, cold and confusing world.

Later the road turns to dirt and then, suddenly, as the rain increases, my engine dies. Fuel? I check and I have enough. Not for the last time on this journey I find myself standing next to my bike, the engine dead, surrounded by a sodden, empty land. Of course I am afraid. There are no vehicles on this road, no people or buildings - just wildly scudding clouds, rain and rapidly approaching darkness. At least I have a tent. I strip off my luggage, prod about hoping to find the cause, then turn the key and give the starter an experimental push. The engine fires. The DR just doesn't like water and, throughout the trip, the engine would die on me in the worst of conditions, leaving me wet and cold on the roadside wondering whether it might be something more serious this time.

I load up and press on again, close to the limit of my endurance; I need to find a place to sleep. At last, a small town appears through a veil of horizontal rain. I stop at a petrol station, shivering, and struggle to remove my helmet and gloves with hands so frozen they refuse to obey my commands. And here, at a very low moment, the kindness of a stranger reaffirms my belief in the innate goodness of humankind. A large Kazakh man approaches me, asks the usual questions. I mumble my answers with numb lips. He turns away and, when I go to the small window to pay for my fuel, the lady tells me that the man has already paid. In the meantime, a thin petrol attendant, shirt hanging outside his trousers, has entered a small shipping container, fired up his gas stove and put on water for tea. He beckons for me to enter; inside, the room is warm and I sit on a wonky chair amongst a pile of garage stuff and we drink hot, black tea together. While we are drinking, he looks at my thin gloves with a curl of his lip, roots about in his belongings and gives me a pair that, he assures me, using gestures, will be warmer than mine.

The large Kazakh man, whose name is Akan Alzhanov, joins us, asks me what I plan to do now. It is almost dark. I tell him I am looking for somewhere to sleep.

"Follow me," he says and I do. We wind our way through narrow streets to a small hotel. He enters ahead of me, talks to the receptionist, takes out his wallet and pays.

When I thank him, he tells me with a smile, "I am a Muslim. We are required to help a traveller..."

Often people express concern for my safety when they hear of the far-away places through which I travel. In my experience, though, it is kindness and goodwill that I have come to expect from strangers with thin arms and calloused hands; and poverty and lack of opportunity are never the arbiters of generosity from those least able to offer it.

Chapter Five

We don't say minus in winter

"And you raised us to be freaks just like you! What did we hear from you our whole lives? You have to live for others... for a higher purpose... throw yourself under a tank, go down in an airplane for your Motherland. The rumble of the revolution... Heroic death..."

It is only when I finally turn east onto a ratty little road that I finally feel I am reaching the start point of my journey: the Russian border, some 150ks away. And, as if to give a seal of blessing on the trip, the sun appears briefly to cast a pale, golden light over a sodden land.

The day has, again, been cold but not Arctic and, thank goodness, the rain has held off. I seem to have made slow progress despite riding for nine or so hours. The highlight of the day? Stopping for coffee at a small roadside place, shivering and trying to get my fingers working sufficiently to enable me to peel back the lid of a small, plastic punnet of milk; the lady who served me calls me to where she is sitting on the far side of the room. I assume she wants to talk but, as I reach her, I see (and feel) a wood fire blazing in an open hearth. Such are the innocent joys of long-distance travel.

Slightly warmed, I continue on across a swampy land, the deep trenches on either side of the causeway filled with water; even some fields are too flooded to plough, the dark earth waterlogged and smelling of amphibious creatures unused to the sun.

Then, at last, the border. A bus has arrived just minutes before me and I wait in the wind, revelling in the fleeting moments when the sun emerges bright from behind a heavy covering of cloud. At last the barrier lifts, the uniformed guard wishes me *Dasvedanya* and I say farewell to Kazakhstan. It has treated me harshly with its aberrant weather, causing me on many occasions to wonder whether there could just possibly be better ways to spend my retirement - but that isn't the land's fault or, for that matter, its people. They have, without exception, been generous, welcoming and gentle, a proud people engaged in building a new nation free from the Soviet yoke.

The land itself is beautiful - starkly empty, strangely flat, exposing its horizons. The contrast with Kyrgyzstan is dramatic and defining, especially when one travels across one country and then immediately into next: mountains and plains; rock and sand; high and low; vertical and horizontal. The one lies peaceful as if unchanged for millennia; the other roils upwards as fault lines form and tectonic plates collide and compete. In Kyrgyzstan one tends to look upwards; one is awed by the height, the weight of the mountains that bend the earth's mantle with their enormous mass; in Kazakhstan one cannot but sweep one's eyes from horizon to empty horizon and feel diminished by the vastness of infinite space, the enormity of sky.

Kazakhstan is ripe for development. Except in areas where semi-desert predominates (and even here sheep could be grazed if the stocking rate were low enough), the land is fertile, the soil dark black and deep; it has a look of fecundity about it and gives the impression that if you prodded any seed into its dark womb it would sprout and multiply as God intended. The tiny fraction that is being cultivated further north, closer to the Russian border, yields well and single fields the size of English counties are being prepared for a second planting after the first has been harvested. Here, a single ploughed field reaches the horizon without break or interruption - no hedges, fences, rocks, hills or trees - just gentle undulations the only indication that this is a natural expression of the land as it probably always has been.

This land needs the experience and expertise of the South African Karoo sheep farmer, the stockman of the Australian outback, the Texan cattle rancher. With this, Kazakhstan could feed the world.

*****

By late afternoon I am bumping my way over the potholes of Omsk, my GPS leading me towards the coordinates of the apartment of Rimma and her husband Sasha. I first met Rimma, director of a private language school in Omsk, when I visited the school eight years ago. Even then I knew that one day I would return, would ride my bike here, and I kept in touch. She and Sasha have offered me a bed for a few days, a breathing space, until I press on east.

I find the apartment with difficulty. It is one of a number of nondescript blocks known as *Khrushchyovka* because they were built during the Khrushchev era, hastily and sloppily constructed, characterless, architecturally bare, spiritless and starkly utilitarian. My GPS tells me *Here* - but where in this maze of identical high-rise blocks is *"Here"?* In front of me, to the left and the right, rectangular blocks of concrete with unseeing windows observe me; rows of trees rustle in the wind and, behind, massive steel pipes with ragged lagging straddle the road. Each block has thick, tight-fitting metal doors sealing the occupants inside (or the bad people out) and seeming to dare the burglar or thief to enter.

I approach a group of old men sitting on a bench and they point towards a door set into a wall covered with graffiti - just the same as twenty other doors set into identical graffiti-covered walls. Outside the grim facade are small touches of ownership: painted car tyres used as plant pots; small flower beds beside the rutted, mud-pooled road. Tall, pale-green trees soften the blocks of concrete and without them it would be a grim spectacle indeed.

I press a button and enter a dark stairwell. The metal door clangs shut behind me. In the dim light of the entrance I can just make out a flight of crudely fashioned stairs with banisters roughly welded from flat-bar, angle iron and reinforcing rod in the Soviet way, held together by weld splatter and a prayer. The walls to head height are painted bright blue and, despite the steel door keeping the vandals at bay, someone has sprayed graffiti all over one wall. There is no lift so bad luck to the old and disabled.

On the first landing electricity junction boxes dribble wires, the doors held closed with wire. One of the tenants, I assume, has attempted to raise the tone and screwed a series of Old Master reproductions in a wooden frame to the wall by the post boxes but some yob has added beards and moustaches so as I climb, a bearded Madonna and child look down on me and a moustachioed nude looks coy.

I drag myself up three flights of stairs and reach apartment sixteen. All apartments leading off each landing are protected by another massive steel door with heavy-duty, five-bolt locks. Just inside this outer steel door is the inner door that opens into the apartment.

And instantly I am translated into another world: culture, order, sophistication. On shelves, collections of early mechanical calculators, ancient wooden artefacts, old car number plates, books, antique clocks and radios. On one wall hangs an original oil painting of Lenin. (Sasha informs me later that he saved it from being used to seal a broken window at the local primary school. I find it telling that he feels he needs to explain, almost apologetically, its presence on his wall.)

Outside the wind still blows cold and an old woman in shapeless dress and headscarf sits on a painted bench in front of another steel door and watches the people passing by.

This apartment, I think to myself, reflects in some way the cliche of our Western conception of Russians: outwardly rather rough and work-worn, weighed down by life, unsophisticated and gauche but inside - ah, inside is the soul of a Pushkin, a Rachmaninoff, a Chekhov, a Nureyev.

I remind myself never to forget that despite the concrete insult to architecture and the bad workmanship that seems endemic to Russia, despite the unfortunate history of repression and purges, of murder and the Gulag, the Russians put the first man into space, produce still the greatest ballerinas in the world, have a legacy of literature and art and music that few other countries can lay claim to. And perhaps it's that legacy that makes all Russians love their Motherland with such a visceral passion despite the horrors she has perpetrated on them over time.

*****

"Twenty degrees," Sasha tells me later that evening when I ask him what temperatures they experience here in winter.

We have just completed our meal of soup and sliced tomato with sour cream and cucumber and bread and watermelon for afters. Sasha has opened a bottle of something strong - not vodka - and we toast each other and my journey. He is quietly spoken, his English hesitant but essentially good.

"Impossible!" I tell him. "That's too warm!"

"No," he insists with a tolerant smile, "twenty degrees -"

"Centigrade or Fahrenheit?"

"Centigrade."

"*Can't* be," I assert. "You get snow?"

He looks at me as if I am stupid and holds his hand about three feet above the floor.

"If there's snow," I assert logically, "the temperature must be at *least* zero."

"Yes, twenty degrees," he repeats and I shake my head, frustrated.

We decide to ask the lady who serves as the universal arbiter of all arguments - "OK, Google," I intone, "what is the average temperature in Omsk, Siberia, in winter?"

"The temperature in Omsk in January," she intones, "is minus 16 to 20 degrees."

"I *told* you so!" I whoop.

"See," Sasha insists, not understanding, "16-20 degrees -"

"But it said *minus* 16-20 degrees," I insist. "You said 20."

He looks at me with good-humoured contempt. "In Russia," he explains as if to a child, "we don't say 'minus' in winter because minus is..." he searches for a word, muttering to himself in Russian. He looks to Rimma for help.

"Assumed -?" she offers.

"Yes," he says. "In Russia in winter is always minus so we don't say..."

I ask him how warm the apartments are in winter. He tells me 22-23 degrees. "That's *hot!*" I exclaim. It turns out that the state or someone in local government decides what temperature the apartments are to be heated to. Instructions are given to the heating company and hot water is pumped through the massive pipes bleeding rust and flaking insulation that line most of the streets above ground into all the buildings where clunky, cast-iron radiators provide heat. There are no thermostats; the temperature cannot be regulated, except by opening a window.

Ah, the Soviet state - all must be equal in every way, even to the temperature of your home.

"*But, Comrade, our apartment is too hot -*"

"*Comrade, is the hot water that the State gives you for free not good enough? Maybe you would like it a little colder - like minus 48 in the Gulag, perhaps?*" (Although he probably wouldn't have needed to say "minus", obviously.)

"*No, Comrade, as I was saying, this temperature is just perfect. It's the temperature we've always wanted. Lena, open the windows a little bit to let some cold air in.*"

"Rimma and I sleep in the winter with the windows -" and he holds two fingers about half an inch apart.

*****

Omsk, established at the confluence of the Irtysh and Om rivers that flow slow and dark beneath its bridges, is a city that seems to be trying to drag itself into the twenty-first century but is being pulled back by the remnants of its Soviet past. So MacDonalds outlets rub shoulders with plaster-flaking, clunky buildings; modern cars jostle along pot-holed roads with rusty buses still tethered by long metal rods to dipping electric cables strung above every main street; modern office blocks and retail outlets stand cheek by jowl next to narrow, muddy streets where wood and tar-paper houses lean at alarming angles as their supporting beams rot away.

In evidence here, too, is the incompleteness, the sloppy, inadequate workmanship that is so characteristic of things ex-Soviet: if there is concrete, it will be lumpy, unfinished and cracking and, always, if you look, there will be bits of reinforcing rod sticking out and beginning to rust; if there are tiles, somewhere they will be falling off and cracking. Expanding foam bubbles untrimmed from around window frames; streets are pot-holed and drivers swerve about to miss the worst of them or attempt to spare their suspension by not hitting the partially exposed manholes that threaten with their sharp metal bits exposed. Anything welded will be covered with splatter, that lumpy hit-and-miss welding that identifies the incompetent artisan. Stairs will lean because the shuttering was erected without paying due regard to a spirit level. Parks are mostly weedy and overgrown; road verges muddy and crumbling.

This seems to be the Soviet way and, when travelling in Russia, I always struggle to understand how a country with the technological expertise to launch satellites into space should have such difficulty with basic construction. I get the impression that it's not a matter of not knowing, but not *caring*, not being held to account.

Later in the day, I speak to a small group of Rimma's students, fourteen- and fifteen-year-olds, eager to learn English and better themselves. And it is the young who have it in their power to change repressive countries and introduce the freedoms they so crave. The Internet has opened their eyes to life in Europe and America and it's a life that they want for themselves. Without prompting from me, one tells me he wants to live in America or Britain because it is free there. The lads speak about being careful what they say about political leaders because they could be jailed; that money was allocated by Central Government to Omsk to build an underground rail system but in the end only one station was completed. "Where did the money go?" one lad asks rhetorically, his face twisted with frustration.

It's the earnest, enthusiastic young who will eventually bring change; it's inevitable. They have seen the freedoms they so crave on the Internet and, try as they might (and they have), central government in Moscow cannot entirely block the free flow of ideas. And so they wear their *No Fear* and *New York* and *Star Trek* and *I Never Liked You Anyway* T-shirts with bravado and yearn for the new, free Russia that will one day come.

Chapter Six

Dalnoboyshyky

"After Stalin, we have a different relationship to murder... We remember how our people had killed their own... The mass murder of people who didn't understand why they were being killed... It's stayed with us. It's part of our lives. We grew up among victims and executioners... Human life – you can just spit and rub someone out. Just like in prison..."

Bike checked and loaded, I say farewell to Sasha and Rimmer, promising to call in on my way back (if the bike and I survive), fire up the engine and take the road east. At last, I feel, I am on my way; now, all I need to do is point my front wheel towards the rising sun and keep riding until I reach the Sea of Okhotsk 8000ks away.

As I leave the city behind, the land opens up - the lush grass, flowered with daisies, looks so soft and inviting one could fall asleep on it; ponds and small lakes soften the landscape even more, blue and calm, reflecting a clear sky. The land here has been partially cleared of trees, and wheat fields, all curves and sweeps between the lakes and shady clusters of white-barked birch trees, have been recently harvested, the black earth left exposed.

The day is hot and I make steady progress along a good road mostly used by trucks. Mid-day and I need fuel. I take a side road towards a small town. There is no fuel, despite a sign telling me there is. The town is dying and it reminds me of something Sasha said the previous day: *Small towns and villages in Russia are dying; the young are leaving for the cities and the old struggle to keep things going.*

I knew I would encounter dying settlements and ghost towns further east, especially along the Kolymer Highway towards Magadan, but it is something of a shock to come across a town in its death throes so close to the second largest city in Russia east of the Urals. Crumbling concrete shells, the windows and doors open to the elements; rotting, boarded-up wooden houses; the rusted wrecks of vehicles; a pile of scrap metal; an abandoned factory.

I stop alongside a group of young men. They are small in stature and their bones seem too large for their skin. One has a scar from his left eye into his hairline and a large dent in his skull. They look at me with the eyes of trapped and suspicious things. I ask them whether there is any fuel; they shrug and shake their heads.

A thin woman, her back bent with the strain, drags a milk churn along the dirt road strapped to a small cart. She has collected water from the communal well. Ducks paddle in a stagnant pool that laps the wooden pilings of a house leaning to one side as if weary of life.

I ride on and, when the engine dies, I top up with the fuel I have been carrying in my spare container. And then I remember I haven't had my visa registered with the police. (The Russian authorities give visitors three days' grace.) I check the dates and am relieved to see that I still have 24 hours before I am liable to be fined or arrested.

At a roadside cafe I pull up next to two large, clean touring bikes, 1000cc. The Russian bikers saunter over and ask me where I'm headed.

"Magadan," I say and they laugh at me.

My bike next to theirs looks so very, very small and tired and travel worn even though I have, really, just begun my trip.

Later I share a room with three truck drivers. They are friendly; one looks strangely like Novak Djokovic; another has gold teeth and the third wears a moustache. The man with gold teeth points under his jaw towards his jugular and beckons with a jerk of his head. I think they're inviting me to share a drink; it's a gesture I haven't come across before.

Downstairs, Anatoly, the one with a moustache and who used to be a member of the Russian navy on the Kamchatka Peninsular, orders four beers and a bottle of cognac. He points to each of us in turn, holds up four fingers then indicates the bottle. Looks like it's going to be a quarter each.

Oh, dear...

The Djokovic look-alike's name is Reddjup and he comes from Dagestan. Igor - with the gold teeth - lives in Tomsk. We communicate using Google Translate and I explain that I don't drink much. Contrary to expectation, they understand and only partially fill my glass each time we toss one back. Other truck drivers in the room look as if they are on day release from the local prison - heads shaved, thin, muscular arms covered with tattoos, they hunch over their tables and drink spirits until the bottles are empty. (Anatoly tells me that Russian truck drivers are often called *"Dalnoboyshyky"* and when I ask why, he types, "Del Boy.")

I finish my fourth half-tot and feel my lips begin to numb. I turn my glass upside down on the table and my friends nod their understanding. We share photographs of our families while they finish the bottle. I've just realised that my beer is 10.4% proof. No wonder my lips are numb. None of this namby-pamby 4% beer in Russia.

Later, strangely, the drunker they get, the better billiards they play. Igor, who has short-cropped blond hair and blue eyes, typically Russian, gestures at Reddjup with good-natured contempt, makes copulatory gestures and says dismissively, "Dagestan -", expressing light-heartedly the very real contempt felt by ethnically pure Russians for their ex-brothers in the 'Stans. Reddjup smiles, his darker skin and hooked nose marking him as different, accepting the gentle verbal slur that he has clearly heard many times before - that inhabitants of the 'Stans are, somehow, endemically rather backward.

When it is late and I make noises about laying my head on a pillow, Igor cries out, "Drink, not sleep!" and downs yet another beer.

*****

I leave Igor sleeping off the rigours of the night before and breakfast with Anatoly and Reddjup who have been more circumspect with their liquor consumption. Reddjup waves his hand in the direction of our shared room above, prods two fingers into the side of his neck, shakes his head and offers a resigned smile.

(Later in the trip I discover the origin of the gesture, which, I feel, is worth relating here: Long ago, during the reign of Peter the Great, it is said that a talented carpenter impressed the king with his work. As payment, Peter gave the carpenter a signed letter which permitted him to drink anywhere in Russia, free of charge, for the rest of his life. Unfortunately, the carpenter lost the letter so he asked the king to have the

Royal seal tattooed on the side of his neck. From then on, every time he entered a bar, merely pointing to the tattooed royal brand would qualify him for free drinks.)

This gesture used to be understood as an invitation to share a drink or two but, over time, has changed to mean someone who drinks to excess or who is, or is about to become, puke-in-the-gutter drunk.

******

You could draw a straight line with a ruler and pencil across a map from Omsk to Novosibirsk and that would pretty much describe the route for the next 650ks. And that's probably what they did. No reason not to, I suppose: there are no impediments in the way - no stony outcrops, hills, valleys, mountains; nowhere where the sandy surface has been wrenched or torn or penetrated by elemental forces - just sand and trees and flat land that doesn't encourage run-off, doesn't *slope* anywhere, so that water collects and pools in thousands of small lakes throughout the forest.

The road is good, the sun shining from a clear sky and the air still cool. My progress is slow, but then, as someone said before I left, "Slow is fast in Russia". I need to nurse my little girl along in preparation for what lies ahead.

Then things change and I bump my way along a battered road that has been heavily striated by some massive machine - in preparation for re-surfacing, I assume, and the excoriations make my front wheel behave like a drunk person for a while. With the bad road, suddenly the passing land doesn't seem quite so friendly; the trees seem to press in a little more. Once the civilizing influence of smooth tar is removed, the bare bones of a land are exposed and things become more elemental. One begins to feel the land as the early settlers and travellers did in all its rawness. Of course, here, on this road, we are still far removed from that, but as I travel east, the elemental nature of the land will become more apparent and the civilizing influence of people - and people themselves, in fact - will become less in evidence.

The thought fills me with both excitement and fear.

Chapter Seven

Please do not be offended

"Born in the USSR is a diagnosis..."

I pull into a truck stop and park my ratty-looking bike next to an equally ratty-looking Yamaha 250, travel-stained and loaded. The rider is Dema, a young lad from Belarus. Both he and his bike have that look about them that only many hard days on the road can produce. It kind of seeps into your eyes and skin and won't wash out. No polished chrome here; mud and dirt and oil splatter; a half-full bottle of water and a litre can of oil strapped to the load with bungees tell their own story. Rope and tie-down straps hold other bits on. I look closer and see that it's not *things* that the ropes and straps are holding in place: it's the whole aluminium rear frame, sheared off on one side. He's made the most basic error most first-time motorcycle travellers make: too heavy a load on the sub-frame.

I catch his eye and smile my understanding. That close bond that pulls long-distance bikers together in dusty places all over the world draws us to each other. It's more than a Brotherhood of Bikers thing - save that for the tasselled leather and the club patches, although I'm not knocking that. (Well, not much.)

It's deeper than that.

His face is sunburned and his lips cracked; he has a look in his eyes beyond tiredness. His leathers, and the shirt I can see underneath, are dirty and creased.

We share the usual: *Where ya from, Mate? Where ya been? Where ya headed? What's'a road bin like? How's'a' bike goin'?* - and then a closer look at the bikes. He's coming from Monglia, he tells me, heading home to Belarus.

"The roads are no roads," he says, shaking his head and showing me a picture on his phone. He points to his broken sub-frame and grimaces. "Six days - maybe seven -" he tells me, then adds, "- my family."

I can see that he's lonely and longing to be home. I know the feeling.

He straddles his bike and fires it up. It sounds smooth, the two-cylinder engine quieter than my single-cylinder's clatter. He's done well on such a small bike, alone and, dare I say, ill prepared. Next time he'll reduce his load and weld some struts to the sub-frame, spread the load.

And there will be a next time: I can see it in his eyes.

Perhaps a brief aside here for those of you planning your first trip:

Sub frames are flimsy things at best and only designed to carry a light load along good roads. Lump together tools and spares and water and fuel and oil and camping gear on an un-reinforced sub-frame and then bash it along bad roads for any length of time and it will break - as do many of the off-the-shelf pannier frames. They just can't take the stresses imposed on them by the abuse that a bike suffers in terrain where tar roads are a luxury.

Gareth and I have always designed and welded our own pannier racks and, where necessary, strengthened the sub-frame with welded gussets and added load-bearing struts bolted to the main frame. The load needs to be carried as low as possible and spread evenly, using as many mounting points as can be found or tweaked. Always over-engineer the frame: slightly thicker tube, extra metal around mounting points, added straps to tie it all together onto the bike and take some of the strain off the mounting points. This might add the extra weight of - what? a pint of oil - to your load but it beats picking up your luggage out of the stones when your frame cracks hundreds of kilometres away from anyone with a welder. (And if your frame is aluminium - good luck!)

*****

I attempt to leave the polluted, soulless, concrete environs of Novosibirsk faster than I entered it. The name itself shouts *Russia!* (Speak it aloud, roll the r, and you'll sound like a pantomime villain). Capital of Siberia and third largest city in the country, it occupies the geographical centre of Russia; so, whichever way I turn, left or right, I will have the same distance to travel to a border.

My expensive hotel of the night before - which I needed to get my visa validated as per strict instructions from those who must be obeyed - was, as expected, perfect and clean and efficient... and soulless, as all such establishments are. No one spoke to me, touched under their necks with two rough fingers, offered to share a bottle of something lip-numbing with me, enquired after my journey (except for two South Korean businessmen who wanted to share selfies with me next to my bike. Perhaps they hoped to absorb something of my adventure into their predictable lives by capturing us together in a photograph, I don't know, but it made them happy and stroked my ego).

Whilst paying the same for my evening meal as I paid for my room shared with three truck drivers the night before, men who kept me awake late into the night with their talk, and whilst the food, as expected, was good, I would have swapped it in a moment for a plate of indefinable meat and rice and the company of men with rough skin and tattoos who hold up a bottle, point to each of us and indicate that we will share.

The road out of town is good, the land undulating, mostly covered with birch and pine trees but also with patches of cleared forest newly planted with wheat. This is the domain of the truckers who pilot their great, lumbering beasts with skill and consideration. I see none of the typically Russian, mad-dog driving one has come to expect in this country after viewing dash-camera footage of Russian drivers killing each other and themselves in alcohol-fuelled stupidity. Perhaps I'm just lucky. They seem to travel at about 80kph - I say "seem to" because I have no speedo.

Thoughts for the day:

- Why do dogs tend to chase motorcycles instead of cars?

- Is there, perhaps, a national competition in Russia to see which car can overtake a motorcycle the closest without knocking him over?

- Surely Donald Trump has to be aware of what a pillock he looks with that hair?

- How long can I ride with my eyes closed on an empty road before I lose my sense of direction?

Near mid-day, I enter an area of some significance to myself, although most would find the meaning obscure: after passing through the town of Kemerovo, the road changes from double to a single lane; the woods nudge a little closer, the road surface shows signs of wear and I begin to dodge potholes. I notice, looking at my rev-counter, that I have reduced my speed - not because of the road surface, but because of a sudden feeling of isolation and the need to protect the only thing that stands between me and an unthinkable amount of angst: a serious engine malfunction.

But I am happy too - large, smooth highways might be convenient to ride along but, like my hotel the night before, they are bland and unremarkable; they lack character. I prefer the roads whose lives I share, like the people I meet along the way, to be somewhat worn by life's trials, to expose their wrinkles and bumps and bits broken through.

Later I meet Zema and his girlfriend stopped next to their Yamaha cruiser on the side of the road. I stop because I think they need help but they are just taking a break. I notice that Zema is sitting on a partially-filled hot-water bottle - not for the warmth, he assures me, but for the softness of the water. They are heading home from Lake Baikal. We share the usual biker pleasantries then continue on our respective journeys, they to the comforts of home, me to the uncertainties of the Russian far east.

Hot and tired from along day in the saddle, I come to a small town and decide to look for a place to spend the night. I wander aimlessly about but can find nothing. Then I remember my carefully translated message (like the one I have as a defence against excess consumption of alcohol) tucked inside my wallet. It says something in Russian like: *Please can you help me? I am looking for a place to spend the night - a hotel or guest house or even if someone has a spare room.*

I stop outside a cafe. Inside are two women, talking. They look up as I enter and regard me with suspicion or, at the very least, annoyance - as if my interrupting their private conversation is an affront. It's a look perfected by a certain type of Russian woman, usually middle-aged, overweight and dowdy, resentful at life in general and foreigners in particular. I put on my most winning smile and hand them my piece of paper. They peruse it for a long time - longer than I would consider necessary to grasp its meaning. Then they both look at me with a mixture of puzzlement and contempt; one hands my piece of paper back to me as if it were covered with shit. They say nothing; just stare at me blankly until I leave.

I am upset and annoyed at their rudeness, tired, frustrated at not being able to communicate effectively in this foreign tongue, looking forward to a restful place to stay and saddened that I should be treated, without cause, with such undisguised contempt. It is only once I have begun riding again, wondering how many hours it will be before another town appears, that it dawns upon me: *I gave them the wrong piece of paper!* I have two translated messages in my wallet; one asks for help in finding accommodation; the other says this:

Dear Sir, Please do not be offended. I have a serious medical condition and cannot drink much alcohol. If I drink too much I will become very ill and might die. Hope you will understand. Thank you.

No wonder the two women looked at me as if I'd escaped from a mental asylum!

*****

In the late afternoon, as the shadows lengthen, it seems as if the trees have crept a little closer to the road. Darkness falls and I stumble upon a roadside motel where I share a room with another trucker. As I begin to unload my bike, I am approached by two bony youths with that hungry look about them, the rodent-like eyes that speak of dissolute living. They stink of alcohol and speak to me loudly; it seems they are asking for something. I respond with a smile because I don't understand what they are saying and, as my parents taught me, a gentle answer turns away wrath. They stand about and watch me, sucking on cigarettes and spitting. Eventually they leave.

Later a man pulls up a chair next to me. Learning that I am travelling to Magadan, he tells me he's a seaman and has been there many times. "You are going too early," he informs me. "It will be too cold. You are alone?"

I nod and he shakes his head. It's a gesture I have come to expect, usually accompanied by a patronising smile.

"You can only do that road in a good 4X4," he tells me. "You got a satellite phone?"

I show him my phone. He shakes his head again. "That is a mobile phone. You got a *satellite* phone?"

I shake my head and he does too, as if deeply saddened at my stupidity.

He tells me that on my bike - he flicks his head in the direction of my road-weary DR, parked up for the night - I won't even make it to Yakutsk (the beginning of the Road of Bones), let alone Magadan.

"The road is a Russian deception," he tells me, "and is only passable as an ice road in winter; anyone who travels it does so with two or three 4X4s, together."

I'm not sure whether this information is given in ignorance but he seems genuinely concerned - about the road, the availability of fuel, the *isolation* of the place. He asks to see my map, points to a small town called Chernyshevsk, about 400ks west of Never (not a typo - that's its name) where the road divides, the south-east fork leading to Vladivostok, the other turning north towards Yakutsk.

"Here," he tells me, his voice lowered like a navigator of old intoning *Here there be monsters,* "is the last of civilization. If you see petrol anywhere, top up your tank." He continues to scan the map, pondering, then lays his finger on Never and says, "Joining to hell."

His somewhat melodramatic attitude has rather spooked me, I must admit, but I'm sure he's wrong.

We will see. There's not much else I can do.

"I'll give you my telephone number," he adds as an afterthought. "I'm going the same way as you for the next three days. Just in case you have any problems."

His name is German, he tells me, and he offers the kind of friendship and support I've come to expect on this trip even though his information about the road ahead is, as I find out later, wrong.

Later, in my room, I take out the map and do some rough planning. I have my notes in front of me as I type this:

Irkutsk - Ulan Ude 485ks

Ulan Ude - Chita 713ks

Chita - Erofei Pavlovich 774ks

Erofei Pavlovich - Nerungri 529ks

Nerungri - Aldan 274ks

Aldan - Yakutsk 541ks

Road of Bones:

Yakutsk - Khandyga (petrol) 419ks

Khandyga - Ust Nera (petrol) 556ks

Ust Nera - Susman 390ks

Susman - Magadan 590ks

Total: 5,244ks - 17 days @ 300ks/day

Chapter Eight

Is "successful, honest Russian businessman" an oxymoron?

"The men of yesterday reek of poverty."

The small town of Mariinsk is still wreathed in mist as I ride through early in the morning. A lone dog makes his way home along a weed-grown path next to the road after a night out chasing women. The wooden houses are still. They look quaint in their smallness, like chocolate-box houses or children's toys, the pretty wooden fretwork around the windows painted the same colour as the shutters, mostly blue; piles of newly-cut wood already being stacked in preparation for the long, cold winter - these things on the surface are attractive but they hide the harshness of a life lived out here in Siberia, the winter cold and the darkness and the poverty; for many the hopelessness of the future offers nothing more than what they have endured in the past.

Some of the little wooden homes are either rotting away or slowly sinking into the earth, evidenced by the alarming lean to their walls and windows that are no more than a knee's height above the ground.

I ride on into the day. The sun rises and the mist melts away. On either side of the road, deep in the dark shadow of spruce and pine and larch, sudden still ponds, mirror-smooth, reflect the sky; bright splashes of colour as plastic flowers mark the scenes of fatal accidents; fork-tailed kites wheel and weave in the light wind. A man sells eggs on the roadside from the bonnet of an old Lada. I buy sugary coffee from a kind lady with pink lipstick that extends beyond the natural confines of her lips. Yellow and purple and white flowers follow the roadside with their blooming and fluff from wind-stripped puff-balls hangs in the air like clouds of pale insects. In the afternoon, I race a long train of wooden wagons across flat land. I win.

And the trees... always the trees.

The day settles into a long counting down of the miles. The bike is running sweetly - just a worrying, rhythmical vibration coming from the front wheel. It's been there for a few days now and is becoming more pronounced.

At a truck-stop cafe, a Lithuanian biker approaches me. We chat briefly; he doesn't have much English. He is on his way to Mongolia and Vladivostok. His bike, I notice, is grossly overloaded (I mention this because of what happens a few days later when I meet him on Olkhon Island, Lake Baikal); the load on the back of his bike is a good 5'8" high. He's an experienced rider, though, judging from the destination stickers pasted all over his panniers, so I wonder at the weight he has imposed on his bike.

We part and I ride on. About twenty minutes later the vibration gets worse and I stop to check the front wheel - loose spokes, damaged tyre, worn bearings, bent rim, snatching brake calliper, something else more sinister? Whatever it is, I can't continue like this - it will shake my bike apart.

Within a minute of my stopping, the Lithuanian biker - his name, I discover, is Zhedrunatz - pulls over next to me. Now, to explain the delightful serendipity of this anecdote, I need to relate the following: Zhedrunatz was riding a BMW80S and travelling fast; had I not stopped when I did, within minutes he would have overtaken me with a toot and a wave and nothing of the next 24 hours would have happened. (The fascinating *Sliding Door* concept - what would have happened in my life if I hadn't spoken to Carol Beaumont, for example, that night when I was seventeen and she invited me to a Youth for Christ club where, later, I met the girl who would become my wife? But for that invitation, my son would not exist, nor would my daughter or my three grandchildren. Instead I might have met... Goodness, the thought is terrifying - and is a recurring theme of my ruminations during the long day's riding. *What if?* The infinite malleability of life, dependent on a thousand mundane choices we make every moment of every day. An accidental meeting... a chance turn in the road... a random decision...)

Anyway, I digress.

Zhedrunatz pulls up alongside and asks what's the problem - as bikers do. I tell him and say I need to find a workshop to balance the wheel.

He takes out his phone and makes a call. Now bear in mind that this is a random meeting in a random place along a Siberian road with a guy who approached me at a truck-stop cafe a few miles back. It turns out that he has a friend in Lithuania who has a social media contact through some biking group who just happens to live in Russia - the next town, in fact, ten minutes away. He's never met this guy before but he makes the call and they speak briefly. He waves his arm and I fire up my bike and follow him. We ride into the large city of Krasnoyarsk and, after another telephone call, we meet Sergey and his wife, Katya, who speaks perfect English.

They lead us (in their V8 Land Cruiser) to a posh BMW dealership. Everyone, including the mechanics, is dressed in white shirts and ties, and there is that atmosphere of quiet intensity about the place one associates with wealth. I feel out of place: my clothes are dirty; my old, worn Suzuki, with strapped-on, Easy Rider foot pegs made from a branch, smeared with dirt and oil, looks like it has just been dragged from a scrapyard.

Sergey takes over, speaks to the manager. I can imagine what he is saying: *Look, I know this is a posh BMW dealership and you're wondering what this shitty-looking Suzuki is doing cluttering up your forecourt, but please, mate, do me a favour? The guy's travelling to Magadan... Yes, I know he'll never get there... and, yes, I know he should be riding a BMW, but don't tell him that. Could your guys balance his front wheel for him? As a favour... please?*

The manager nods. It'll be ready in half an hour.

I am about to suggest that I remove the wheel myself and then re-fit it afterwards to cut down on cost but I don't think it appropriate. I'll just pay up and chalk it down to experience. My usual garage doesn't look like open-heart surgery is conducted in the workshop by mechanics dressed like surgeons so I know it's going to be expensive.

Katya asks whether we've had lunch. I shake my head. We climb into the air conditioned Cruiser and the tactile Katya lays a cool hand on my forearm each time she makes a point. The restaurant is posh, of course, and after we've eaten, Sergey pays with cash after Katya offers him a selection of credit cards a centimetre thick.

Back to the BMW dealers. My bike is done. I go to the office to pay, clutching my wallet protectively. And the total cost of removing the wheel, balancing it and replacing it? £6.50.

I could live in a place like this.

Do we need somewhere to stay? Katya asks. Yes, please! A phone call and Sergey leads us to a hotel; he'll pick us up in two hours for a tour of the city.

Later, showered but with my dirty clothes still on, we are picked up by Katya in her new Lexus. Sasha meets us at the ski centre on his Harley. With him is another Sergey, also on a Harley. Sergey One has three bikes, he tells us: the Harley he is riding and two BMWs - a street bike and a GS1200; Sergey Two has four bikes: two Harleys and two BMWs. Sergey Two looks more than a little like a hit man. I don't ask their occupations or from where they get their money in case they mention the words ..."oligarch", "friend of Putin" or "Mafia".

Into my mind comes the thought: *Is "successful, honest Russian businessman" an oxymoron?*

I reprove myself for my suspicions and concentrate on their openhearted welcome and generosity. Who am I to judge?

Both Sergeys wear everything Harley: jeans, shirt, belt, jacket, helmet, cap, key ring. (Underpants?) I have no doubt that when they ride their BMWs they wear everything BMW. It's what rich people do, I suppose. I wouldn't know. Designer stuff is not my scene. If you've got it, flaunt it, so they say. But three and four bikes when the riding window in Siberia is just a couple of months at best? Both Sergeys keep one bike in Moscow, though, for ease of travel into Europe, they tell me.

Katya ferries us around, showing us the sights and taking us to a war memorial where Zhedrunatz sits quietly, deep in thought. Later I find out that he spent two years in Kandahar, Afghanistan, where he lost several of his friends. It is a sombre moment and one that I don't want to intrude on.

Back in the Lexus, Katya tries repeatedly to discourage me from riding to Magadan: "It's *dangerous!*" she insists, touching me solicitously on the arm with her warm little hand. "There are *bears!* Now it's still covered with *snow*," she warns me."People *die* going there. You must not travel alone - maybe in a group of three or four only."

I am touched by her concern but later wonder whether I'm being patronised as an old man. Perhaps not. I don't feel old, although I suppose I am. When I meet fellow travellers on the road, I stop and greet them as a biker, an equal, not as an *old* biker; age never comes into it or into my thoughts. They, the younger ones, might see me as old but it's never how I see myself. I'm just me - a guy who enjoys the adventure of motorcycle travel. No more, no less. Age shouldn't come into it.

Anyway, finally Katya drops us off back at our hotel and wishes us *bon voyage*. Zhedrunatz and I find a restaurant. Sadly Zhedrunatz has not been able to escape the alcohol trap that snares so many Russian and ex-Soviet men. I notice him limping and he tells me it's from a recently broken leg. "Bike accident?" I ask, using sign language.

He shakes his head, points two fingers into his neck and says, "Stupid."

We order beers but he wants vodka too. The waitress brings a carafe of about 150ml. I accept one large tot (probably three normal spirit measures), we toast each other and drink. I refuse another. Zhedrunatz finishes the carafe and orders another, which he quickly drinks.

On the way back to the hotel, he stumbles a little, becomes garrulous and asks me if I want a Russian woman.

I tell him no...

We chance upon each other the next day when he catches up with me after 500ks of riding apart. "You OK?" I ask him. "Bike *garashor*?"

He shakes his head and pokes a finger into his neck.

*****

It saddens me when I come across young men who are snared by the demon drink. In Russia, whilst the problem is easing, alcohol still adversely affects the lives of many.

A glance at the statistics is sobering:

In Russia, the life expectancy for men is now 58 years and, according to the World Health Organization, alcohol abuse here is linked to 75% of murders and 40% of suicides. Government figures state that alcohol can be directly linked to the death of between 550,000 and 700,000 citizens each year and, of these, at least 20,000 are poisoned from lethally toxic, bootleg alcohol distilled from whatever comes to hand including household cleaning products, medicines and liquid industrial waste.

Russian men and women are five times more likely to be killed by an "external" cause - murder and violence, smoking, suicide, alcohol poisoning, AIDS, road accidents - than someone living in Western Europe and, in a large proportion of these, the underlying cause is alcohol. This country has the dubious privilege of having statistics for violent death comparable to some of the more insalubrious countries of Africa.

Under cover of the soccer World Cup this year, Dmitry Medvedev, the Prime Minister, signalled his intention to raise the retirement age for men in Russia to 65 by 2028 and 63 for women by 2034 - this would mean that, unless things change, two fifths of Russian men will not live to get their pensions.

Seen on the 'Net: "Russia can be summarised in one sentence: 'Apart from drinking, there is nothing to do here'." So Russian men and boys drink to obliterate the life that surrounds them, the poverty and the lack of prospects, the crowded living conditions, the cold and darkness of winter.

And here, the amount of alcohol you can put away is an indication of your masculinity, your comradeship: "If you won't drink with us today," a soldier said, "you'll betray us tomorrow." An officer commented, "Without a hundred grams of vodka, the Russian soldier won't make it to victory. If you leave one of our men in the middle of the desert, two hours later, he won't have found any water, but he will be drunk. They'll drink methyl alcohol, brake fluid..." and another said, "They're proud that a Russian can drink a litre of vodka without going cock-eyed. The only thing they remember about Stalin is that back when he was in charge, they were victors."

And, perhaps, just as worrying is that the population in Russia is declining at an alarming rate. A century ago, Russia's population was 220 million; today, it is 150 million and will fall, if current declines continue, to 120 million in 2050. And this ever-diminishing population is on the move. Just a century ago, the majority of the people lived in the countryside, tending the land. Today three quarters of Russians have moved to the towns and cities, leaving rural communities to wither and die.

Chapter Nine

Two lads and a Ural

"Few of us remain unchanged. Decent people seem to have disappeared. Now it's teeth and elbows everywhere..."

It is cold in the mornings now before the low sun warms the air. Increasingly thick boreal forest casts deep shadows across the road. Old men sell honey from the bonnets of their battered Ladas and tea from crude roadside stands, the smoke from their samovars hanging still in the early morning air.

At a truck-stop cafe I drink black coffee, thick as syrup, and fill my stomach with the warm, fatty, doughy things called *Piroshki*, always available on the side of the road throughout Russia, poor man's comfort food for 45p shared with the earthy company of truckers.

Later, passing an interesting-looking village in the middle of nowhere made up of a few dirt roads lined on either side with unpainted wooden houses, on a whim I decide to pause in my headlong dash east, slow down and experience something of the reality of life lived in rural Russia. And within twenty metres of leaving the main road onto the narrow, muddy track between the houses, I come across two young men, early twenties, working on a battered green Ural and sidecar under the shade of a tree. And with a deep sense of shame, it strikes me: In every village and town I have passed so far, mindlessly focussed on the straight road in front of me and unconsciously counting down the miles, there is real life being lived on every corner, in every home - and I am missing it all.

I pull into the long grass on the verge, switch off and remove my helmet and gloves, get off the bike and greet them, shaking their greasy hands. Because of the heat both are shirtless, their torsos pale and milky white, their forearms and heads burned dark brown from the sun. One lad has crudely drawn tattoos on the milky flesh of his upper arm and shoulder. They have that tough look about them that marks the bodies of people brought up hard, but there are none of the indelible marks that substance abuse or a villainous spirit etches into the contours of a face.

After a brief handshake, they turn back to the Ural - they are not here to entertain me and there is work to be done, but they are quite happy to allow me to stand and watch. The Ural's gearbox has been replaced with another, the old one lying in the grass covered in oil. Like the young lads, it has clearly lived a hard life - amongst other bumps and scrapes, something has come loose and scored away the casing in a deep circular pattern. I notice a heavy truck leaf spring, about two metres long, bolted onto the fixings between the Ural and its sidecar. On one end a thick piece of flat bar has been welded, a hole cut through it with an oxyacetylene torch and I realise that it is a roughly fashioned tow bar for a trailer. Tools, nuts and bolts and greasy spares are scattered on the floor pan of the sidecar.

I turn my attention back to the lads. One is whacking at the rear spindle with a large hammer; eventually it comes free and he pulls it away, releasing the back wheel. Both tyres are smooth, the edges heavily ridged like those you find on tractors.

I so want to talk to these young men, ask them about their lives - do they have jobs? What do they use the Ural for? What is it like living in this village so far from anywhere and how do they cope in the winter? Do they have girlfriends or wives? What do they hope for in the future?

But, of course, I can't, and it frustrates me. *This* is the real Russia, not a ribbon of tar and truck-stop cafes; not a mad dash across umpteen thousands of kilometres in the vain pursuit of a random point on a map.

In the end, all I can do is thank them and ride away, knowing that I am missing some elemental thing here. I ride slowly up and down the narrow dirt streets: wells surrounded by low palings on street corners for those houses without running water; a man pulls a large milk churn full of water down the road on a small, two-wheeled cart; wooden duck-boards have been laid along both sides of the roads, rotting now and with weeds and long grass pushing through; an old woman, her back so bent that her head faces the ground, carries four brightly-coloured plastic buckets in her arms. As I pass, she looks up with difficulty to reveal, momentarily, a large, bulbous growth across her lower jaw. Quickly, she lowers her face again, hiding the deformity in the folds of her jacket. A broken-down truck with opened bonnet and flat tyres stands amongst engine parts in the grass. Small children play on the street verges; ducks paddle in a pool of muddy water; a woman enters a small, dark shop about the size of a double bed. The air smells of cow dung and the sweet smoke of fires. Rough piles of wood, still yellow from cutting, show early preparations for the winter cold. The duckboards suggest that they must have a snowy time of it here.

And then there are the pretty wooden houses, always with brightly painted window surrounds, carved and shaped into geometric patterns, and matching wooden shutters, small touches that reveal a pride in ownership no matter how crude or basic the construction of the houses; and these touches are to be found too in the pretty flower beds and window boxes and neat rows of potatoes and beets and carrots cultivated in small back gardens. Outside, between the houses and the street, rusty cars, tractors in various states of disrepair, farm implements; cows mouth the long grass, picket fences lean...

And it is with a sense of shame that I come to the realisation that this journey has become an end in itself; that the goal of reaching Magadan, the compulsion to put miles beneath my wheels, has taken over the initial concept of this trip, whatever that was. What, I wonder, has happened to the dictum that the journey is of greater importance than the destination? Each day I fire up the engine, put my head down and ride, the comforting sound of the engine in my ears (and the lurch of the heart when it hesitates), feeling the vibrations through my body, the road a black ribbon ahead of me undulating through endless taiga as I count down the seemingly endless kilometres that creep with frustrating slowness across each fold of the map.

And getting off the main road to explore this small village has enabled me to pause a moment and reflect: Why am I doing this? Why has Magadan taken upon itself such arbitrary significance? Yes, I want to claim that I have ridden alone across Russia; and the more people that I meet along the way who tell me I shouldn't do it, has turned the journey into a personal challenge; that to fail would be tantamount to an admission of inadequacy.

Am I trying to prove something to myself? To impress others? Perhaps it is all of these things. I suppose I am doing it because I'm doing it. I do it because it defines me, who I am. And not to do it would negate something of myself.

Perhaps.

But meeting the two young lads working on their Ural has revealed to me the essential falseness of my journey. I have come to realise that I am riding *over* this country and not *through* it. I am, essentially, passing by the people I ought to be meeting, allowing their lives to become part of my own. My journey through this world has become the tableaux of my own little drama.

D.H.Lawrence was right when he wrote mockingly about us stepping out of our own self-centred, imaginary little lives into the real world of bar tenders with thin arms and tired eyes whom we ignore because we are so immersed in ourselves. And my experience of Russia has become little more than a narrow track of tar between trees, of sleeping in truck-stop motels, drinking coffee in roadside cafes, all conveniently situated along the route. I don't get to enter the villages, interact with the real Russian people and my tar-road, trucker's perspective of this vast country is, essentially, a false one.

Reluctantly, I leave that place and, once again, take to the road, heading east.

Such a long way to go; *got* to make progress...

Chapter Ten

Roller coaster ride to Lake Baikal

"They've swapped socialism for bananas. Chewing gum..."

This is not a normal place. Travel 1000ks in any other country - the UK, for example - and you move through England and into Scotland or Wales or Ireland, each totally different and distinctive; even travelling 100ks within a single country will usually reveal some regional difference, idiosyncrasy, particular characteristic of geography or culture. And when travelling across Europe, it's not uncommon to enter and leave two - or even three - entirely separate countries in a single day.

they were traitors...

But in Russia, I feel as if I am riding in a loop, seeing the same piece of lake-pooled, boreal forest every day. A thousand kilometres here in Siberia is pretty much the same as any other 1000ks in Siberia: a flat, slightly undulating landscape covered with spruce, pine and birch trees, small lakes and occasional villages, all alike. The only indication that I am actually making progress is the track I am able to mark in inches across my map and the fact that, occasionally, my GPS tells me that I have entered yet another time zone and need to adjust my watch.

The Russian writer Gorky felt that there was an insidiously destructive element in these endless horizons. He wrote: "The peasant has only to go out past the bounds of the village and look at the emptiness around him to feel that this emptiness is creeping into his very soul" and Guy Sajer in his book "Forgotten Soldier" wrote: "The hostile indifference of nature here seems so overwhelming it is almost necessary to believe in God."

For me, life on the road, alone, especially in the evenings, is very lonely. Whilst riding within the confines of my helmet, the words of songs often come to mind, many of them speaking of the loneliness of travel, and have taken on a new depth of meaning for me, especially the remarkable poetry of Paul Simon:

When I left my home and my family I was no more than a boy in the company of strangers, in the quiet of the railway station, running scared, laying low, seeking out the poorer quarters where the ragged people go, looking for the places only they would know. Asking only workman's wages I come looking for a job but I get no offers - just a come-on from the whores on Seventh Avenue. I do declare there were times when I was so lonesome I took some comfort there.

and:

Every day's an endless stream of cigarettes and magazines, and each town looks the same to me, the movies and the factories, and every stranger's face I see reminds me that I long to be homeward bound.

and:

Cathy, I'm lost, I said though I knew she was sleeping - I'm empty and aching and I don't know why...

With the emptiness in my life that used to be filled by my wife, I find a deep sense of empathy with the feelings expressed in these songs, the loneliness of the open road where strangers speaking a foreign tongue are one's only contact with humanity. And many were the times when I asked the question: *What is this thing called "life" all about? What does it mean and how do I fit in to its complex convolutions?* And as I ride across a land as endless as the sky itself, a land that seems, at the same time, to stand still, I cling with bleeding fingernails to the only anchors I have left in my world: my faith in a God who loves me, the constant love of my children, and my home.

*****

We all have expectations; some are met, some lead to disappointment. Sometimes it's not even an expectation, just a hope - like my dear little bike making it to Magadan and back to the UK. Before I set off, the closer I got to the start line the more I realised just how much I was asking of a small bike, unprepared and unused for two years in a shed, and then being expected to keep going without falling apart for 20,000kms. The circumference of the world at the equator is 40,000ks so that would make it half way around. For me, this was more of a hope than an expectation - and yet, as each day passes and she continues to putter along manfully (I think I've mixed up my sexes here, but "womanfully" just doesn't sound right), I am beginning to trust that she just might be able to do it. I hope so.

I was wrong in my expectation that Russians would treat me with aggression - or, at the very least, suspicion - for being British. Exactly the opposite, in fact. Still the same welcome; the amazement that I have come (and am going) so far; still the enthusiastic response, "Manchester? *Manchester United! Wayne Rooney!*" that I have come to expect.

But where Irkutsk is concerned, my expectations are badly served. I pictured, in my mind's ever-hopeful eye, a small town nestling in a picturesque bay on the western corner of Lake Baikal. What I experienced, instead, was the kind of concrete sprawl that epitomises everything I dislike about large cities. Pollution blurs all buildings except those in the foreground; the air tastes of acid and I have difficulty breathing. But, fortunately, I had decided, on Zhedrunatz's advice, to head straight for Olkhon Island, supposedly the jewel of Lake Baikal. But it takes me a good ten kilometres before I can breathe easily again without my mouth tasting of copper coins.

And then the world changes and becomes beautiful. I ride for 200ks along an undulating flood plain, three to four kilometres wide and covered with close-cropped, green grass. Sleek-skinned horses and cows make their home here, watched over by small-boned herdsmen on horseback who look more Cossack than ethnic Russian. The sky is egg-shell blue, cumulus clouds hang in the still air, and I ride in that Goldilocks zone loved by all bikers everywhere: the tar-smelling warmth from the road lifts itself off the surface while my body is cooled by the fresh breeze of my riding. The road is narrow, lumpy and nearly car-less, stretching out across this wide plain in gentle dips and curves until it disappears into the blur of the horizon.

Yes, this is why I came; it is for times like these that I am able to put aside all the pain and discomfort that is often the biker's lot.

At the small town of Bayanday I turn southeast towards the lake with 100ks to go. The road begins to climb into a range of low mountains covered with pine forest and, as I crest the final ridge, a cold blast of air hits me rudely in the face. Off to the left is a higher mountain range, snow-capped, overlooking the lake, astoundingly beautiful, mist-wreathed and clear with heavy, dark clouds threatening rain. This is everything I have expected of Lake Baikal and more - the kind of isolated, unspoiled beauty one finds in the Outer Hebrides and the more remote islands of north western Norway.

With the cold wind comes, not rain, but sleet and I quickly stop to drag on my waterproof trousers, the only protection against extreme weather, other than my riding jacket, that I have brought. With my hands freezing and the icy wind tugging me about, I descend to the lake edge where a small settlement of wooden houses cluster about the ferry docking station.

The ferry, a tubby craft able to carry about six cars, is already docked and boarding. I ride up the metal ramp and tuck my bike against one gunwale. Within minutes we have cast off and are making the short crossing to Olkhon Island over the dark blue, wind-whipped waters of the lake.

Remotely beautiful, Lake Baikal is unique in so many ways that it is worthy of a few lines here. Its very name conjures up images of a place of unspoiled purity, isolated by its very distance from anywhere in the heart of the Asian continent. Its very isolation, fortunately, has preserved its almost primeval state and, unlike many sites of similar beauty throughout the world, the difficulty of reaching its shores has kept it relatively free from the sullying influence of tourists and commercial exploitation. Fortunately, also, the Russian government has recognised its importance and have resisted the all too common impulse to treat it as an expendable natural resource.

A UNESCO Natural Heritage site, its statistics are enough to inspire awe. In this, it is just like the rest of Russia: larger than life, impossibly huge. This *one* lake, for example, contains the world's largest concentration of fresh water - 23,000 cubic *kilometres*, one-fifth of all the fresh water in the world - more than is contained in all the American Great Lakes combined. The lake's superlatives continue: with a maximum depth of 1,632 metres, it is the deepest lake in the world; originating 20-25 million years ago (some scientists say 35 million), it is also the oldest freshwater lake in the world. Its water is believed to be the purest body of water on the planet and, on a clear day, one can see up to forty metres beneath the surface. In fact, with surface dimensions of 636 by 79 kilometres and with a coastal circumference of 2100 kilometres, it could be referred to as an inland sea rather than a lake.

Some fifty million years ago India ploughed into Eurasia, thrusting up the vast mountains of Central Asia and ripping other sections apart. Lake Baikal is, in fact, the remains of an ancient rift valley, similar in shape to Lake Tanganyika, being at the edge of two massive tectonic plates that are still being dragged apart and causing the land between to collapse. As a consequence, the whole area is still unstable and it experiences about 2000 earthquakes a year; the surrounding mountains are still in a state of motion, both rising and falling. The rift valley is constantly being filled by over three hundred rivers and streams (one source claims 544) with only one outlet, the Angara River, that runs through Irkutsk then joins the Yenisei to flow 1,779 kilometres north to the Arctic Ocean. The bottom of the lake is 1,186 metres below sea level but below this lies some seven *kilometres* of sediment, the deepest sediment anywhere in the world. Remove that which has been deposited into the lake over the millions of years of its life, and the floor of the original rift valley is some eight and a half kilometres below the earth's surface.

But enough of that. It's a very special place and one that I feel honoured to have visited.

The ferry nudges against the Olkhon Island shore and we disembark. The light is fading and the dark sky is whipped with cloud. Ahead of me a dirt road winds over steep-sided hills and, as I begin the thirty-kilometre ride to the small settlement of Khuzhir on the northern shore, a light rain begins to fall, the first fruits of a deluge. I begin to climb the first hill and the sandy track divides and divides again, each seeming to find its own way up the steep, grassy slope as drivers, over time, have abandoned one and selected another that seemed less corrugated, rutted or disturbed by muddy potholes or loose stretches of soft sand. Over the first hill and the land drops into a steep-sided valley, the tracks fingering their way up the other side, no sign of habitation anywhere. Despite the muddy track, my tyres grip well and I begin to enjoy myself. Thunder crackles across the dark sky; fingers of lightning flicker amongst the surrounding mountains and the clouds release their burden of rain. The track turns slippery but the DR is light and responsive; I stand on the pegs and fly along, using the raised road edges as berms, my spirits lifted despite the rain, dodging rocks and deep puddles, sashaying through patches of sand, skimming across smooth, wet stretches of black earth that should have been glass-slick but wasn't. What fun!

And it is then that I notice a large, heavily laden adventure bike approaching from the opposite direction being followed closely by a Lada with two young lads in it. As it nears, I realise it's Zhedrunatz, my Lithuanian friend on his BMW. We both stop and dismount. Clearly, he is not a happy camper. The two lads get out of the Lada and approach and, while Zhedrunatz vents his frustration, one of the lads translates. In brief, he's fed up with these tracks, the high prices being charged in Khuzhir, the rain and the mud. He dropped his bike in some sand a while back, he tells me, and couldn't pick it up. These two lads in the Lada appeared and helped him. Now they ride behind him in case he drops the bike again.

"This road is *bloody* awful," he insists, "and not fit for any self-respecting biker to have to cope with." (Well, that's what I imply from the translation.) He seems almost angry, as if the condition of the road, the weather and his dropped bike are somehow a personal slight. He's leaving, he adds, going back to the mainland and getting off this pestilential island.

Strange, I was rather enjoying myself. Perhaps, I think, it gets significantly worse further on. "How far to Khuzhir?" I ask him.

"Thirty kilometres," he tells me, shaking his head at the enormity of it.

Press on or turn back? It's getting dark now and the rain is drumming down and blurring the hills about us. I know there are places to stay just before the ferry landing, a few kilometres back, but I decide to continue on. We say our farewells and part - he, still being followed by the Lada, towards the ferry; me to face the thirty kilometres of muddy tracks before I can hope to find somewhere to stay for the night.

And as I continue to revel in the exciting roller coaster of tracks threading their way up steep hills and into narrow valleys, thunder echoing off the mountains and lightning arcing through a sky brooding with cloud, I reflect on how perceptions differ. These tracks were one of the highlights of my entire journey. *Slow is fast in Russia* - I keep trying to remind myself as I fly along, faster than is wise, muttering into my helmet, *Don't break the bike... Don't...* But I'm having too much fun to listen to an old man's words of caution.

In this life, I try not to be unnecessarily critical of others: live and let live, each to his own and so forth - especially towards a lovely man who befriended and helped me on the roadside. But, surely, a biker with his experience - and he *was* experienced - ought to know certain basic rules of long-distance travelling. Rule One: Don't overload your bike.

I know I've said this before somewhere, but it bears repeating: An overland biker, especially one travelling alone, ought to be able to pick up his bike unaided. If not, spend more time at the gym, reduce your load or ride a smaller bike. For me, the ultimate indignity for any biker would be to have two lads driving behind in a car in case he falls over and can't pick up his steed.

Just saying...

And the high prices? I reach the small town of Khuzir in the darkness and stumble upon a delightful hostel run by blond Olga, middle-aged, round as a medicine ball, welcoming as a mother hen. Cost? £10 a day with all meals included.

Whoo, boy! How could Zhedrunatz have got it so wrong?

Chapter Eleven

I'm going to be *so* in jail

"My generation grew up with fathers who'd either returned from the camps or the war. The only thing they could tell us about was violence. Death. They rarely laughed and were mostly silent. They drank... and drank... until they finally drank themselves to death."

Gaunt and taciturn, our Chinese-looking driver wearing a Chairman Mao cap drives his UAZ at a rapid pace through the back streets of the town. All he needs are wire-framed, round glasses to complete the caricature. Fortunately grab-rails are fitted for us - Petra, Max, me and four Russians who are accompanying us to the northern cape of Olkhon Island. The heavy reek of petrol permeates the cab and a rat's nest of wires dangles from under the dashboard. Clutch and brake pedals are strapped together with a bungi cord, presumably to stop them rattling.

Petra is German, Max, Spanish, both mid-twenties and riding the trans-Siberia railway to Mongolia. They, like me, have nudged together as our trajectories briefly coincide before we separate and head off somewhere into the world again. And, strangely, as I have found many times before, age has no effect on our brief bonding. We communicate, as most random travellers do, in English, and are drawn together by a love of travel and a shared culture in a foreign land that transcends the normal social rules usually predicated on age.

We grind our way through pine forest across deeply rutted sand tracks knotted with exposed roots, then break free onto a grassy plain furrowed by raw, erosion-cut ditches, the ancient UAZ stuttering and groaning as we cling to our panic handles. The land is shrouded in mist and even when we pause at prominent headlands overlooking the lake, the view is mist-obscured except for the snow-covered peaks of far mountains. Then for a spell we drive along the beach just above the waterline, clear and clean with little fish swimming.

By mid morning the sun has burned the mist away to reveal the purple-blue waters of the lake, headlands dropping steeply, the lake waters disappearing smooth into the soft haze of distance on the far side.

We walk the kilometre or so down a steep path to Cape Khoboy in the north, wind-bent pines and carved poles festooned with colourful ribbons and pieces of cloth in the Buddhist tradition, this area being regarded as sacred to the indigenous Buryat people of the region.

I would so love to report that the lonely drive to Cape Khoboy with our Chinese-looking, silent driver and his Chairman Mao cap was achieved in splendid isolation, allowing us to commune with nature and immerse ourselves in the emptiness of this lovely place - but, sadly, no. It was not to be. We share the experience, beautiful though it is, with twenty-seven other UAZ 4X4s, each with its load of mostly South Korean and Chinese tourists who pose for selfies, taken with articulated, button-pressing selfie-sticks, and exaggerated *I was here!* V-signs and pantomime grins. Later, when we all pause for a late lunch under the shade of some pine trees overlooking the lake and our drivers light fires to heat pots of fish soup, from the interior of one vehicle the annoyingly repetitive abdominal punch of a sub-woofer pounds out some mindless beat.

I meet Russian biker Gennady wearing his leather jacket with club badge on his way to Vladivostok. He plans to transport his bike back to Moscow by train, the second biker I have met planning to do this. If I were clever, that's what I would do - ride to Vladivostok, put the bike on a train back to Moscow and meet it there. Done. Why break my balls trying to get to Magadan?

But I won't. I must give it a go. If I find that the Never-Magadan road is a bike breaker, I can always turn back and head for Vladivistok. It's a fallback plan but not one I want to rely on. I feel that I must complete what I've set out to do or at least give it my best shot.

On our way back, we stop (alongside four other vehicles already beginning to disgorge passengers) and Petra calls out, "Quick, quick - before the Chinese!" laughing at her joking racism and she, Max and I run giggling like schoolchildren to get ahead of the crowd so we can take a few photographs unblemished by the crush of bodies.

And in the afternoon Max, Petra and I strip to our underclothes and swim in the icy waters of the lake, Petra's baby fat, smooth as a seal's, disturbingly white in the pale yellow sun that carries with it no warmth at all.

*****

It is day two of my rest break. The sun is bright in a deep blue sky but still the air carries with it the chill of the snow still visible on the surrounding mountain peaks.

I check the bike over, clean and oil the chain. The tyres are wearing badly and won't make it to Magadan. I can't risk the Road of Bones on worn tyres and will need to get replacements.

My body is recovering. I'm starting to feel the need to move on.

I take a slow walk through the village. Cows make their way along the main street and the dusty air mixes with the smell of their dung. Two out of three vehicles here are UAZ 4X4s; understandable, because the roads are all dirt and, outside the town, make their haphazard way over the island's steep-sided hills.

I am drawn again to the calm, deep-blue waters of the lake. The rusting hulks of beached fishing boats lean against each other alongside a pile of rotting logs from the pier that is being refurbished. Workmen sit about, smoking. I have learned that, a year or so ago, a ruling from Moscow outlawed fishing in Lake Baikal and all the fishing boats had to be dragged out of the water where they quietly rust away and provide handy canvasses for local spray-can artists. No quotas, just an order to stop fishing immediately. As a result, the entire Lake Baikal fishing industry and large fish processing plant in Khuzhir just died. What became of all the workers and the fishermen, I do not know. In Russia, Moscow issues edicts and the rest of the country must obey, something those living in the far east have come to resent.

On the shore, a man stands next to his old Ural outfit, lights a cigarette then tries to push it backwards to face the sandy track out. It is too heavy, even with the help of his small, shaven-headed son. I lend a hand and soon we have the heavy machine turned. While he answers a call on his mobile phone, cigarette still hanging from his mouth, he gives the kick-start lever a few desultory pushes. Eventually the engine fires but immediately dies. Still talking on the phone, he kicks a few times more until the engine takes - then dies again. He finishes his call, fiddles with a wire attached to a car battery resting unsecured on the floor of the sidecar, kicks again and the engine fires and putters away, blowing blue smoke. The little boy climbs onto the back, the man swings his leg over and they slither their way through the deep sand and onto the road.

A sunken boat leans against the old poles of the jetty. Fishermen cast their lines into the water. I walk off down the shore wondering why it is that rusted and patched-up things capture my attention more than the new and glossy. I'd much rather look at a rat-bike than a shiny Harley with all the bells and whistles, the tassels and look-at-me flashing lights. Perhaps it's because the old and the patched-up have a story to tell; the scratches and the welds, the bits bolted on and altered, speak of a hard life, of a struggle and an overcoming. I have a visceral distaste for the gaudy and the bling, the conspicuous consumption that attempts to tell the world how successful and wealthy the wearer/owner is but, for me, speaks rather of an inner emptiness, a too desperate desire to impress.

I'm sounding pious again. Sorry. Got to stop this.

I continue to walk along the rocky beach then up a headland towards five standing poles festooned with bright cloth and ribbons fluttering in the wind. The mud-hardened ground is paved with tarnished coins and grains of rice, all offerings to the Buryat gods. I sit myself on a warm rock overlooking a small bay separating a rocky outcrop - Shamanka Cliff, I understand it's called - one of the nine most sacred places in Asia, and suddenly I find myself asking: *Why am I here?* Not *here* as overlooking a sacred place, but here in Russia, alongside Lake Baikal, far from home. *What am I doing here? For whom? What is the point of it?*

I think since my wife died I seem to have lost that which centred me, the still point of the turning world around which I could roam, knowing she was always there, at the heart of me. Now, whilst the pull of *home* is strong, what now is "home"? An empty house? It comes upon me, with a deep sense of sadness, that my roots are loose in the soil and a big wind is coming; the anchor has pulled free and I find myself adrift in a new, strange place called *life* that I no longer fully understand.

The reason for my being cannot be my children or, for that matter, my grandchildren. Precious as they are, they belong in a different world, a different time; they have their own lives to lead and I am peripheral although, fortunately, closely tied. They are not, nor can they be, my centre.

So I turn increasingly towards God, that other rock, anchor, paraclete - one who walks beside, one who goes ahead of me, friend and saviour.

******

Later, back at the guesthouse, we meet Yava, a young Russian lass with the round face and slanted eyes that betray her Asian Russian heritage. She speaks fluent English (almost non-stop) and works for a travel company. Although negative about conditions in Russia, she is loyal and will not leave.

"The countryside is dying," she tells us. "Drugs, alcohol and sex problems all over. The problem with the Russian people, you know - they're just too lazy. In our village, we had the Internet but some man stole the aerial to sell for scrap iron. They're like that - they just don't care. The countryside is dying."

"What do you think of Putin?" I venture.

"Are you recording this?" she asks, noticing the phone in my hand. "I'm going to be *so* in jail tomorrow!" she laughs and glances around theatrically, then continues, "I don't like Putin. All he's interested in is Russia's name in the world; he doesn't care about the people. And the church is corrupt."

"What," I ask, "you mean working for the government?"

"Yes, of course working for the government. But also corrupt. All of them. There's been this big change. Once we were all supposed to be atheists; now, no one is allowed to be an atheist. The people are poor and there's no help from the government - except medical, but it's bad. I went to the hospital with a problem one time and they told me to come back at three o'clock. This was at *eight in the morning!* It's bad."

She takes out her ID document, a passport-sized booklet. "Look - we have to carry this *all* the time. It has *everything* about us in it. And these -" she takes two official-looking documents out of her pocket. "This one is for the medical - I have to show it if I want medical help - and this one is for where I live. There are a lot of homeless people -"

"Is there any help for them?" I ask her.

She shakes her head.

"What happens to them in winter?" I ask her, shocked at the thought of anyone living on the streets through a Siberian winter.

"They die," she says matter-of-factly. "The homeless drink a lot of..." She searches for the word, makes wiping motions on her skin.

"Surgical spirit?" I offer.

"Yes. And it's poisonous. Last winter in Irkutsk, three hundred homeless died from drinking that. The authorities said it was only sixty-seven but it was more than three hundred. And Ukraine. Why are we fighting Ukraine? We are the *same* people. It's stupid. And the army. When you leave school - boys - you have to go to army. And it's so bad that boys are killing themselves. They commit suicide because they can't take it, it's so bad there. Terrible things happen there."

"I've heard about that," I tell her and I mention the Russian author Svetlana Alexievich who interviewed many men - and their families - who went through the shockingly harsh twelve-month Russian conscription (called "Universal Military Obligation") imposed on all male citizens between the ages of 18-27. Avoiding this draft is treated as a felony and is punishable by up to two years' imprisonment.

"And here in Russia," Yava continues, unstoppable, "it's so difficult to get anything done. You need a form to get a form to get a form. You have to make a phone call to get permission to make a phone call. It's stupid. Our priorities are all wrong. We have terrible social problems - a few people very rich but most are poor. Old people who starve because the pensions are so low. Putin - I don't like him. Today it's crazy. The whole country is run by a hundred people."

*****

Later, I check the route on the Internet: The temperature in Magadan is four degrees and the mountain passes on the Road of Bones, travellers are warned, are snow covered.

What on earth am I doing?

Chapter Twelve

Flesh in the radiator grill

"War and prison are the two most important words in the Russian language. Truly Russian words. Russian women have never had normal men. They keep healing and healing them. Treating them like heroes and children at the same time. Saving them."

Olkhon Island is behind me now as I make my way towards the far western tip of Lake Baikal. The ride from Khuzhir, across the hills and meandering tracks of the island to the ferry and then 250ks back across the wide, near-wilderness flood plain to Irkutsk has been a delight. I feel rejuvenated and ready now for the long haul to Yakutsk.

Once the AIDS capital of the world, Irkutsk is softly beautiful with its avenues of pale green trees casting mottled shade onto the walls of old, log-built houses; pussy-willow fluff fills the air and collects in corners like snow-drift as I ride into the town centre on a hot, still afternoon. All the women walking the pavements seem beautiful, svelte and confident as newly preened cats. The smog-besmudged air that so distressed me three days ago seems to have dissipated; neat flowerbeds edge the sidewalks and soften the concrete with colour. And, of course, there is the river, wide, blue and slow flowing - one river out, over three hundred flowing in. Any city built near water is the better for it.

And I realise that it is the days of rest that have rejuvenated my spirit; that my exhaustion as I first entered this city just a few days ago tainted my experience of it. And it impresses upon me the subjective nature of travel, how, as one passes through a country, one can only experience a thin slice of its reality and perceptions are influenced by one's own state of mind.

On my evening walk-about, drivers, every one of them, respect pedestrians' rights of way. This (allied with what provisions are made for its citizens to evacuate their bowels) is a sure indication of its progression up the developmental ladder. I follow the "Green Line" - an actual green line painted on the pavement - leading visitors to the most significant features of the city, all with photographs and information plaques in Russian, English and Chinese. A great idea.

Irkutsk is clean and graffiti-free, the natives well behaved and beautiful. The buses and trams, however, seem to have been left behind somewhere in the nineteenth century. The trams are clunky, rusted things that trundle and wheeze their ponderous way about the city on death-trap rails loosely embedded in eroded tar trenches just waiting to hook a careless motorcyclist's front wheel.

I follow the green line to the Epiphany Cathedral; it looks like a gingerbread house with its brightly coloured walls. Inside it's all bling, gaudy and polished, its gold and brass reflecting the votive candles that flicker in front of gilded saints and the macabre bits of bone and flesh revealed through glass panels for the faithful to kiss. I think of Yava's comment: *The church is corrupt...*

When a church is state-sponsored, like the Russian church now, it becomes institutionalised and will begin to atrophy. Ritual replaces personal devotion; a mechanical penance takes the place of a deep, personal change; the *church* becomes associated with buildings instead of what it ought to be: the people.

In one corner sits a man, his face in his hands, praying: getting things right, sorting stuff out, keeping short accounts. I like to see people praying like this, *real* prayer, de-ritualised and honest. He wasn't *saying* a prayer; he was *praying*. There's a difference.

I look away from this man communing with God to the golden bling of the cathedral. There is something distasteful for me about such displays of opulence in a world where too many children go to bed hungry. And the paintings - Jesus looks like a wimp, limp-wristed and somehow supercilious, effete, as if we soiled humans are rather beneath his dignity. I want my Jesus to smell of sweat, laughing as a horde of snot-nosed children climb all over him; looking with soft eyes on the prostitute who washes his feet with her tears and dries them with her hair while the Jewish leaders look on with curled lips. Let's dump the bling and the smooth-faced, white-teeth-smiling, prosperity gospel advocates and their flash cars and big houses and the patriarchs in their dresses and gem-encrusted pectoral crosses and get back to *Whoever wants to be my disciple must deny himself, take up his cross... and For those who exalt themselves will be humbled... and What good is it for someone to gain the whole world and forfeit their soul?*

Just saying.

I leave the cathedral and the women worshipping wide-eyed in front of bright paintings of long-dead saints, lighting candles and crossing themselves and I leave, too, the man sitting hunched in a corner with his face in his hands and I am aware that my attitude is critical, judgemental, but I can't help it.

Time for a beer. With the World Cup hosted here, the Russians have gone football mad. Game 1: Russia 5: Turkey 0, and, as a consequence, it is a nation at peace with itself, if not with the rest of the world. Peter Tatchell has been arrested in Moscow whilst protesting for LGBT rights (not for the first time - I remember when he performed a citizen's arrest of Zimbabwe's Robert Mugabe in London. Probably would have been better if he'd shot him - Mugabe, that is, not Putin.)

Suddenly the sky darkens and lightning fizzes about the apartment blocks, thunder rattles the windows and then heavy rain floods the streets and washes all the snow banks of pussy-willow tails into the drains.

*****

If I have to watch another pouting, writhing, sexually provocative music video whilst trying to eat a meal, drink a cup of coffee, tie my shoelaces, whatever, I will be forced to eviscerate myself. Why, I ask myself, is it obligatory in Russia and ex-Soviet countries to force this slop on us? I know I'm sounding like my father and, believe me, I swore I never would, but it's all so *mindless*. The music (sorry, delete that: the - what? - *Noise*? *Sounds?)* just has no character; it's as if the fake arousal on the screen is there to make up for a deficit in the mediocre, repetitive, generic slop that passes for music here. I feel as if I'm watching re-runs of the Eurovision Song Contest every day.

And this morning a recent "friend" on social media who posed as a biker sent me a pouting, push-up-bra pic of herself lying on a bed and suggested that I "might be interested". I asked her please to go away. What's gone wrong with this bloody world?

I don't think I'm sounding like my father; I think I'm becoming my father.

*****

How's this for putting my insignificant little journey into perspective: along the Green Line walk yesterday, I came across a statue dedicated to "eternal friendship" between Russia and Japan, sealed when a Japanese captain, Daikokuya Kodayu, ran aground and lost his ship on the north Siberian coast in 1783. Looking for help, he and his two companions *walked from Yakutsk to Irkutsk* - just 3,400-odd kilometres - through the taiga (no roads then, I assume, helpful signs pointing the way, truck-stop cafes serving coffee?). Nine years after they'd run aground, in 1792, they made it back to Japan and, so the story goes, their return became the first step towards establishing diplomatic relations between Japan and Russia.

They must have been pretty tough buggers in those days.

*****

The day is heavily overcast; a cold wind leans against the trees and deep puddles from last night's rain lie on the street corners. There is a fresh cleanness to the air, rain-washed, and the streets smell of mud and wet stones.

It's time to hit the road again.

The land is steep that falls from the mountains which hug the south western tip of Lake Baikal, and deep shadows cast by boreal pine forest darken the road. To my left is always the lake, sombre now with the sun hidden behind heavy clouds, just a trace of the low hills on the far side, almost lost in haze. I ride slowly with no pressure to make progress and this makes it easier to observe, but not get involved in, the many suicidal Russian drivers who think it's quite acceptable to overtake trucks on blind corners at speed. Sometimes it's so bad that I notice even the imperturbable truck drivers shaking their heads in disbelief. I shudder as I watch them, and wonder how it is that some people are prepared so wantonly to play Russian roulette with their lives - and, more significantly, the lives of others. My mind turns to images of blood smeared on windscreens when two vehicles meet head-on at 80ks an hour; and then, for a while, I ponder the physics of two heavy objects coming to an instantaneous stop against each other and how that energy is dissipated through the release of heat, and what happens to a human body when it translates from speed to stop in a microsecond or, in a collision with a truck, from travelling in one direction to an instantaneous reversal of direction as the truck blunders on with flesh embedded in its radiator grill.

I suppose you've got to think about something on the long, long, solitary hours on the road and Juilus Mayer's Law of Conservation of Energy is as good as any. (And what about, when the vehicle and its driver hit the truck, the instantaneous translation from this life to the next?)

I ride slowly now, allowing the mad dogs to play with their mortality while I attempt to conserve my own energy in both the literal and scientific sense.

The villages become fewer, smaller and further apart, mostly populated by the little log-built cabins with their painted shutters and corrugated asbestos, iron or tar-paper roofs weathered to the colours of the earth from which they came and into which they inevitably will rot and rust when the people leave.

Finally the road descends from the snow-covered mountains that corral the lake on three sides, and skirts its eastern corner at the small town of Kultuk. I pull over at a collection of roadside booths selling fresh and dried fish caught from the lake, the air hazed blue with the smoke from charcoal fires. I drink cheap coffee amidst the stalls, holding the plastic cup in hands numb from the cold, and chat with difficulty to women in bright headscarves and cardigans standing behind their piles of fish smoked to the colour of old pennies.

Then on, following the southern shore of the lake. By late afternoon, cold and tired, I reach a ragged settlement called Tankhoy where I hope to spend the night. The dirt road that makes its way between houses is pooled with water-filled potholes and, with a sinking heart, I know that I will find no accommodation here. Many of the houses seem to have been built from old railway sleepers; cows graze on the road verge. Outside a convenience store - called a *magazin* in Russian - I see a massive man wearing camouflage gear (as so many Russian men do, as if life itself here is to be waged as a war) preparing to mount a motorcycle. I pull up next to him and ask whether there is anywhere in the town I might spend the night. He crushes my hand in his and tells me through missing teeth that there is nothing.

I reflect on the possibility that I might have to ride all the way to Ulan-Ude, two days' riding in one, grit my teeth and set off again. But my GPS tells me there might be somewhere to lay my head just off the road a few kilometres further on so, even though reluctant to waste my time, I follow a narrow dirt track towards the lake and stumble upon a rustic home stay that perfectly meets my needs: small, cosy hut, heated by a wood-burning stove, just a stone's-throw from the still waters of the lake. I am the only guest and it is perfect.

There is no food and, when I ask, the man says, "*Magazin* -" and points down the road, back towards the village.

I tell him (miming, of course), that I will go on my bike but his son, a twenty-something young man who has the appearance of a hooligan - thin as a stick, gaunt, home-made tattoos on his hands, dirty sweat pants hanging low on snake hips, red football shirt - insists he take me there in his car. We set off down a road so rutted it would have been faster if I had walked. The road verges are overgrown and populated by scrawny fowls as we scrape our way over hummocks and rocks. Each wooden house we pass seems to be rotting or falling apart, the underbrush reclaiming its rightful place between gaps in the logs. But the young man, despite his stray-dog appearance, is sweet. He digs out his phone, selects Google Translate while steering with his knees, and types: *Where are you going?*

"Magadan," I tell him.

He laughs, making a disbelieving sound. Then he speaks into his phone and holds the screen so I can see it: *Then where you go?*

"Back to the UK," I tell him.

He doesn't laugh this time, just shakes his head.

"Delico," I say, knowing this word. It is far.

"Delico," he agrees.

At the *magazin* I buy some provisions for my supper and breakfast (I ask the lady for eggs but the young man shakes his head - there are eggs at home, he tells me, and he will give me some). He buys two beers. I decide to buy one for myself but he stops me, gesturing that he has bought one for me. He then buys six litres of strong cider and I think, *Oh, dear...*

And now I sit, overlooking the lake, writing; a bird whose call I don't recognise sings in a tree above me; trains rumble and clatter by on the line just behind the house and I am at peace.

*****

A little later, I ride into the village to see if I can meet some of the locals and, as often happens, it is a drunk man who hails me, clasps me by the hand, embraces me like a long-lost brother and attempts to communicate with me in Russian. I discover that his name is Genius - but perhaps I have misheard.

We quickly establish the usual: Where you from... going... age... family? Then we salute the Russian flag that flies in front of a wooden building and agree that the Russian football team is, without doubt, the best in the world. He then leads me through long, wet grass and the rusting hulks of cars to a woman in her fifties who sits outside a small log cabin next to a vegetable garden. A plastic chair is brought for me, tomato and radishes sliced with a wicked-looking clasp knife, and a bottle of vodka appears, seemingly from nowhere.

"Russian water!" Genius slurs and points to a half drum next to the old woman who, I learn, is his mother. In the drum are five large, empty vodka bottles. The mother, whose face has been burned to leather by the sun and who wears a red headscarf, slippers and a faux cheetah-skin blouse, fetches two rather dirty glasses and fills them with vodka.

She downs hers before I have even picked mine up; I sip at it, tentatively, like a wimp, and my voice immediately becomes husky. She laughs and pours me some orange juice.

The garden looks well tended despite the vodka, with onions, radishes, potatoes, tomatoes and pumpkins growing well. I ask whether I can take her photograph but she demurs. "Not beautiful," she says and I assure her she is. She lights a cigarette and coughs wetly into her hand.

When Genius, in his vodka-numbed state, becomes over familiar, she orders him away like a five-year-old and, smiling meekly, he obeys.

Chapter Thirteen

Tormenting a dwarf

"I never wanted to be a hero. I despise them! Heroes either have to kill a lot of people or die beautifully..."

I notice that a random biker has posted on social media words that, on the surface, sound kind of romantic - leaving the past behind, getting on your bike and heading into the future, the romance of the open road and all that stuff...

But he's wrong.

It's a great sound bite but on a long ride you carry your past with you - as close as thought and reminiscence, thin as folded paper but as heavy as a rucksack full of boulders. Within the muffled, hollow space of my helmet I take with me all the baggage of my dead wife and my living children; all the stupid things I have said and done that I so wish I hadn't, the mistakes I've made. And the good things too, the special moments. Long-distance travelling allows a barrel full of empty time for reflection, especially in Russia. I take them all with me, gnaw on them to the bone, try to balance the bad with the good. On the open road, there's always time enough to ponder...

*****

Eventually I leave Lake Baikal behind, turn east and then south towards Ulan-Ude. And there is a palpable change to things. I can feel it. The road is more isolated; most of the trucks seem to have disappeared and, with them, the roadside cafes and motels spaced at convenient intervals and offering succour to weary travellers. I seem to have stepped back into a previous age when I pass old women collecting water in plastic barrels from wells on village street corners.

In the mid-afternoon I approach and enter the busy streets of Ulan-Ude and find a cheap hotel. I am told that I must pronounce the final "e" in Ulan-Ude. And I learn that "Russia" is spoken using three syllables, not two, as we have grown accustomed to in the West, the second syllable elongated and stressed: Rus-*si*-a, the "r" rolled on the tongue. Two-syllable "Russia" is just so poncey and upper class. Say "Rus-*siiii*-a" aloud whilst holding up a full glass of vodka before quaffing it in one gulp and you get a feeling of the rawness of this place that is centuries deep. You can hear it in the chants of Russian football fans in the streets and bars when the national team is playing: "Rus-*si*-a! Rus-*si*-a! Rus-*si*-a!"

It's good to know these things when proposing a vodka toast or saying which team is going to win the World Cup when surrounded by a crowd of inebriated Russian men rekindling the spirit of death for the Motherland before betrayal. It creates a good impression and encourages men to hug you, especially if you make your voice gravelly. It also makes them want to buy you drinks.

My taxi driver is called Mergin. He tells me it translates as "archer" and that he is Buryat by birth. He seems proud of both. Judging from the statues around the city, the Buryats, who have a round-faced, heavy-set Chinese appearance (although I am sure they will feel insulted at my ham-fisted comparison), descend from the Mongols who survived as nomadic herders and hunters in this region long ago, living in yurts. They have occupied these eastern territories far longer than the Russians themselves, being assimilated into the Russian state in the 1660s. They now function as an autonomous *oblast* and are allowed a certain degree of autonomy.

Mergin's taxi is shot. In front of me, exactly where my head would strike the windscreen if we came to an abrupt halt, a spider web of cracks radiates from an indented centre. It doesn't inspire confidence. The roads are in a shocking state; Mergin points to a particularly ferocious pothole and shakes his head.

He drives me to a small motorcycle dealers in an industrial unit and I buy cheap, plastic rain gear and winter gloves that look as if they were meant for snowboarding, but at least I'll be a little warmer and less wet as I head north into that place that never seems to get warm.

*****

The concrete skeletons of dead factories stare out from the outskirts of towns; the few factories that still work pollute the atmosphere for kilometres and turn the air a sickly yellow. My spit tastes of battery acid.

During the Soviet era these factories were state owned and did not have to make a profit. Now they just die. Russia's greatest barrier to development and social rejuvenation is its size. Maintaining an infrastructure over 10,000 kilometres and eleven time zones, where most of the land is snow-covered for large parts of the year, would be draining for any society. Attempting to export manufactured goods (or even transport raw materials to somewhere in the country where they can be exploited) over these distances makes it impossible to compete against countries with more nimble economies situated close to international borders. In the past, these remote regions were viable only because the state deemed them to be so; a centrist, totalitarian, communist philosophy allowed them to exist. A capitalist system doesn't and so I pass the detritus of Soviet hubris, the ruined factories and rotting log-built homes and blank-windowed *khrushchyovka* apartment blocks and my thoughts linger on the tens of thousands of human beings who once breathed life and love and community into these sad wrecks of buildings, now gone - to where?

The road east from Ulan-Ude follows the wide flood plain of the Khilok River as it meanders slowly towards Lake Bakal. Then the road leaves the river and begins to climb.

Villages become fewer and those that do appear seem to cling to life with bleeding fingertips, the wooden houses weathered, the corrugated iron and asbestos of their roofs weathered and rusty. There is a poverty about them that is palpable. Again, as I have done many times before, I reflect on the long, dark, cold days of winter, how it is endured - *life* that is. What food do they eat, how do they fill the interminable hours of bleakness and cold; how does one make a living so far from anywhere and what prospects do the young people have? I know so little about these people through whose land and lives I pass with such fleeting touches.

There comes upon me suddenly a small pricking of fear - like the certainty that you feel between one breath and the next that there is someone other than yourself in the room. I try to analyse it; I think it is the wide-open spaces that surround and diminish me. When the trees close me in on both sides of the road, the endlessness of this land can only be imagined. But here there are few trees and the undulating, hilly plains stretch away from me on every side until they disappear into the hazy vanishing point of the horizon and I feel insignificant and vulnerable. It doesn't help that my engine has been cutting out intermittently - a few times each day now - for no apparent reason. It's not fuel and, after a little encouragement, it always starts again and rattles away as if nothing is wrong. I suppose I am experiencing something of what it must be like to live with a weak heart: you continue with your life as if all is normal because there's nothing much else you can do, but somewhere, behind everything, is that nagging thought: I wonder when it's finally going to pack up, perhaps far from help? The left-hand reserve tap in my long-range tank seems to be blocked, but it's not that. I will have to investigate this anyway, remove the fuel taps and clean them. I need all the fuel I have available for the Kolymer Highway and can't afford to have five litres still in the tank that I can't access.

At last I come across a small establishment selling coffee and pay 20p for a cup. The narrow hut is warm and cosy and empty except for me and the lady who stands behind the counter.

I don't remember ever paying 20p for a cup of coffee before...

I know it's naughty of me to mock others' honest attempt to provide a menu translated into English, but I notice this on the table as I drink my coffee and it raises my spirits:

MENU

Fat
Russian beauty
Munch munch
Meaty
Cutting vegetables
Wings of chickens
Tenderness
Juicy with cheese

Other than the first, I reckon any of these would go down a treat.

Again the road climbs and follows the edge of a wide, slow-flowing river that meanders across a treeless flood plain; far below me a rail line follows the river and, while I watch, a long train pulled by two diesel-electric locomotives makes its silent way. The increased height gives perspective to the endless boreal forest beginning outside the confines of the flood plain and continuing dark green to the horizon far, far away.

And to think that those Japanese sailors, long ago, *walked* through here. I wonder whether they clung to this river, hoping it would lead them to somewhere where people lived.

Then the plains are gone and the taiga comes close, pine and birch, hemming in the road. In places, large swathes of forest have been burned and the blackened trunks of trees cling to the hillsides like the shattered, branchless trunks left behind after the Somme.

The day is done; I look for a place to stay for the night. A small town beckons. My GPS assures me there is a hostel here; I do not believe her but decide to investigate - even if she's lying, as she often does in Russia, leading me through deserted streets towards promised accommodation that does not exist - and I ride through its narrow streets, ever hopeful. It's a large rail hub and a barrier comes down across the road while an engine shunts. I wait a long time. Eventually a man shouts, pointing to the left. I follow a small road that leads me through a tunnel beneath the tracks then past a tall, abandoned water tower that just cries out for restoration into a chic, modern dwelling; a police station and, finally, I stumble upon a home-stay/hostel patronised by a gang of road workers. They have finished work for the day and loll about, shirtless, their massive 6WD Kamatz truck parked outside.

The lady of the establishment shows me a pleasant room that I share with another man; the road workers occupy a large, open bunkhouse with attached kitchen.

After checking my bike, I make my way back past the bunk-house and am greeted by Victor, skin burned dark from exposure to the sun, heavy-duty camouflage jacket and no shirt, his chest pinched and thin. His friend Maxim joins us. We sit on wooden benches and they smoke. Maxim tells me he has family who live in a small village about 800ks away. I get out my map and he shows me. It's a hard life but they have to take whatever work they can get, even if it's far from home. Victor digs out his phone and shows me a picture of a prairie dog he has shot. "Big mouse," he says and they laugh.

Maxim produces a two-litre plastic bottle of beer and we toast each other while he and Victor blow smoke over me.

Later my roommate, Alexi, leads me to the local *magazin* and I buy food for my supper as well as some beers for my new friends. On the way back, a distressed cow bellows as she trots along the pavement; gusts of wind stir the dust in little eddies, cold and then warm, and I can see that it's going to rain. Snow-showers of pussy-willow fluff are whipped into the air and dark clouds mass in the west. On the street two drunken men square up to each other, shouting, but a woman manages to separate them, scolding them both roundly like children. They stagger off down the street, shouting insults over their shoulders as drunks do, becoming more confident in their aggression as distance lends them courage.

I make it back to the hostel just before the rain and it beats down on the small wooden shelter roof, the large drops leaving marks like pennies in the dust. Lightning crackles behind the clouds and the smells of ozone and newly-wet, warm earth rises about us. The Russian workers all crowd into the shelter and light up, the damp air hazing and blue with acrid cigarette fumes. As each squeezes himself onto a bench, he introduces himself: Zinka, Pauille, Zandra, Alexi, Alexandra... Their hair tends towards the shaven, tattoos loose and smudging under the skin; the atmosphere is thick with testosterone, working men's smell, their bodies sun-browned and rough, smokin', drinkin' men who, in the absence of women, scratch their crotches and hawk and spit and who welcome me into their presence like a brother.

And, later, do they invite me to share their meal? Of course they do. We sit on stools and benches, pressed together in the large kitchen with its gas stove and sink, its fridge and plastic tablecloth; some, who have nowhere to sit, stand shirtless with plate in hand, lean across to help themselves from a large pot of *borsh* made with potatoes and hunks of bony meat, sliced tomato and cucumber with sour cream, dry bread and what I bought at the *magazin*. They encourage me to eat, smiling and urging me not to hold back, offering me black tea to drink after the meal and then we retire to the shelter again to smoke and talk. Later, as we swig strong beer from a two-litre plastic bottle, they pass around a phone and laugh as they watch a video of men tormenting a dwarf - as you do.

Much later and my throat and eyes are raw from smoke; the men are still drinking and their tongues have thickened and slowed. A different plastic bottle is now being passed around. When it reaches me, having been warned never to drink spirits from an unlabeled bottle, I ask, "Wodka?" and they laugh and say,

"Peeva!" - beer. I take a swig. It is dark and strong.

Alexi points to a small man with a pleasant, open face, explores the unfamiliar words a moment with his tongue and then says, loudly and slowly, "I like wodka!" The small man smiles bashfully then points to his jugular, holds out his hands as if riding a motorbike, makes revving noises then mimes falling over. They all laugh. The plastic bottle is passed around again. I decline. One of the men attempts to tell me he has a motorbike and has ridden to... and he mentions a country in Russian.

"Ukraine?" I venture because that's what it sounds like.

As one, they whoop in derision. Maxim puts up his fists like and old-fashioned pugilist. Clearly there are no kind feelings towards Ukraine here. Eventually we work out that he means Poland.

I notice from their watches that I've entered another time zone. The plastic bottle is empty. Maxim attempts, I think, to encourage me to go to the *magazin* and buy more alcohol but Alexander, an older man with heavy features, swept-back black hair and a thick Stalin moustache waves him away. The men begin to slope back to the bunkhouse but Alexander stays with me, different from the others, older. When we are alone, he shows me a photograph of himself wearing dress uniform, his chest covered with medals. "Twenty years," he tells me.

"Afghanistan?" I ask him.

He nods and then adds, "Chechnia." His face is sombre. Then, in turn, he pulls up a shirt sleeve and trouser leg to reveal two large, ragged scars, each six to nine inches long.

I lift my arms, miming a rifle. He nods then waves his hands dismissively, as if it is of no consequence.

"Chechnia," I say, shaking my head.

"*Da,* Chechnia," Alexander echoes, his heavy features etched in sadness.

Chapter Fourteen

A woman in pink shorts

"What's next? A new Gorbachev or the next Stalin? Maybe it'll be the swastika. Sieg heil! Russia has gotten up off her knees. Now is a dangerous time because Russia should have never been humiliated for so long."

Outside my window is the rusting body of a truck. Crows squabble and peck at something dead in the long grass.

I say goodbye to my Russian workmen friends who seem unaffected by their alcoholic excesses of the night before. Back on the road, I am led remorselessly east, the road a straight line disappearing to the horizon across an undulating plain, coloured with purple and yellow flowers, wide and mostly undisturbed by trees. It could have been, in places, the tended grounds of an English country estate. With a wide blue sky, lumpy with clouds, doming this half-world of space, it is beautiful beyond the telling of it.

Along the way, I pause to explore a few isolated villages, often presaged by a small herd of cattle tended by a lone man on horseback. As usual, I am enchanted by the tiny, log-built houses with their blue-and-white painted window frames and shutters.

But the weight of distance keeps pressing on me like a malign presence. I measure my progress across the map in teaspoons when I want it to be shovels. I ride with one ear constantly listening for those tell-tale anomalous sounds coming from the engine that warn of an impending breakdown, worn parts rubbing together, losing their harmony. Can she possibly keep going 'till the end?

The vibration in my front wheel, despite the balance at the BMW workshop, persists and is a concern; this constant vibration for 20,000ks is bound to fatigue metal somewhere on the bike. I have a feeling that my front wheel is slightly oval and it's not a balance issue at all. Using my thumb as a micrometer to gauge whether it's true produces inconclusive results.

When, finally, I call it a day, I re-check the wheel but can find nothing amiss. But, during my inspection, I notice that the chain rollers on the swing arm are badly worn - so bad, in fact, that I am sure they will fall off soon. (They do.) And my front tyre is wearing badly. It will make it to Yakutsk, I think, but it will not take me to Magadan. Will I be able to find a replacement somewhere?

There is a workshop next to the motel, as there usually is, to cater for the passing truck trade, and I wheel my bike across and ask a young man, thin as a coat hanger and wearing filthy overalls, if he can balance a motorcycle wheel. He nods, his face, hands and arms smeared with grease and brake dust. I remove the front wheel and he places it on a workbench, studies it a while then shakes his head. His balancing machine is designed for the massive Kamatz truck wheels that thunder past as high as my shoulder every day; my tiny bike wheel simply won't fit. He suggests pouring some wheel-balancing beads into the tube but they soon block the valve stem and we give up.

He is apologetic; there's nothing he can do. I offer to pay for his time but he refuses - the typical response of working men who give up their time to help me in Russia.

I re-fit the front wheel. A feeling of concern sits heavy in my stomach. Tomorrow I will pass the town of Chernyshevsk and I remember that it was this town that the man described as "the end of civilization", warning me to keep my tank filled whenever possible because of a scarcity of fuel from then on.

There is no WiFi here and I am feeling isolated and concerned. If my bike keeps going, I can do this; if it packs up, I'm screwed.

*****

The man sitting at a desk in the motorcycle shop looks at my phone where the translated message says: *I need a 21-inch tyre - do you have one?*

He nods briefly, gets up and drags a knobbly out of a dusty pile of tyres in a corner. It's the only 21-inch tyre there - made in China, but who's complaining? These days, most things are made in China anyway.

On a whim, after setting off from a night disturbed by my worries, and just before reaching the turnoff to Chita, I decided to resist my dislike of towns, pop in and see whether I could locate a tyre. I rode to what looked like the centre of town, got off the bike hoping to hail a taxi. But within a few minutes, a motorcyclist approached. I flagged him down, pointing to my loaded bike on the side of the road and trusting he would recognise a fellow biker in need of help. He ignored me momentarily then I heard his engine hesitate and he pulled up about 30 metres down the road. I greeted him and passed him my phone: *Can you lead me to a motorcycle shop - I need a tyre?*

"*Delico -*" he said (It is far) then he waved for me to follow him. A quick u-turn against the flow of traffic, about two kilometres through town and he left me outside the bike shop where I got my tyre. From a random decision to take the turn-off into Chita, to holding my much-needed tyre in my hands had taken me no more than half an hour. Relieved, I was able to ride on, my new tyre strapped to one of my soft panniers.

All day I continue to head east along a straightish road, rising and dipping over a landscape that gives the impression of having recently emerged dripping from under a trillion tons of ice. There have been stretches of taiga but, mostly, contrary to expectation, I have ridden across an endless plain - the same endless plain I rode across yesterday and the day before. I sometimes feel as if I am on some continental treadmill and am, in fact, standing still.

And as one travels through this vast sameness, it is the small details that snag and catch at the corners of one's mind that end up defining the day: the little girl drawing water from a village well who looks up as I pass; a line of neatly-parked tanks behind a barbed-wire fence; a woman in pink shorts hoeing a small potato field behind her log-built house; a barefoot boy pushes an older boy - I assume his brother - also barefoot, on a bicycle, an inflated car inner tube held between his stomach and the handlebars, fishing rod held in one hand; sun glinting off a mirror-still pond surrounded by deep grass; a herder on horseback, tending his cows, raises a hand as I pass; a little boy catches my eye as he pees on the roadside and he waves, unembarrassed (after all, it's what men do); villages, devoid of colour, rise and subside as the road carries me away; stopping to check my fuel and becoming suddenly aware of the silence, and with the silence, a sense of deep isolation.

But then, unaccountably, there is a change: as the dark finger of my shadow crosses slowly from behind to in front of me, I reach Chernyshevsk and become aware that, in some subliminal way, things are different. Whether this is just a trick of my mind, my imposing a preconceived impression onto the landscape, I am not sure. Probably. As the last small wooden houses, that seem to grow organically out of the earth, pass behind me, people and the things one associates with them simply disappear. I ride on for another three hours through an empty world and, at times, small twinges of fear rise up in my chest, just little flutterings because the road itself is still good. I know that the isolation will be far greater the further north and east I travel and I will have to deal with that fear when I get to it. Feelings of vulnerability are very real to me out here.

And as I ride, leaving the plains behind and entering a long section of taiga, the hills darken and rain hangs in the air below heavy clouds that have been gathering all afternoon. As the first heavy drops begin to tap against my visor, filling the air with the sweet smell of water on warm grass, I think again of the Japanese sailors shipwrecked near Yakutsk who *walked* all along this way, all 3,400ks from Yakutsk to Irkutsk - and I think to myself *How?* What kind of men were they who could have endured such a journey? What did they eat? Were there tracks? Did they know there was a settlement at Irkutsk where help could be obtained or did they just keep walking until they met someone?

My small flutters of fear need to be put firmly into perspective when set against achievements like these.

*****

Mist veils the trees so that only the trunks of white birch are visible, pale and ghostly against the dark interior of the taiga; above, a translucent canopy of blue before the day warms and clouds begin to cluster like balloons, gather and darken in preparation for the usual late afternoon storm. The air is cool, my bike running sweet as a nut after yesterday's 8,000km oil change. I start to sing: *Oh, what a perfect day! I want to spend it with you...*and then I realise that the person I want to spend it with is dead and I cry into my helmet for a long time saying, aloud, *Oh, I should have loved you more; I should have loved you more...*

Yes, my dear wife, I should have spent more time with you when I knew you were dying, joked with you more, played *Remember When* games, looked with you through our photo albums...

But then, I tell myself, that's the secret cry of all of us, isn't it?

Later, purged of my grief to a lethargy, I ride all day through a boreal landscape, that mind-numbing canvass of green that seems to cover half the world - five hundred kilometres under my wheels of trees, trees, road, hill, trees, trees, trees, hill, trees, road, truck-stop with fried eggs, sweet coffee and Jackie Chan, trees...

And in the late afternoon the clouds, still bright on the edges, darken and coalesce and the panorama of them is beautiful. Veils of grey, like spun glass against the sky, reveal the rain; the road leads me away and only a few, isolated drops strike me in the face, the air suddenly cooling as if a fridge door has been opened.

Finally, as an evening calm settles over the land, approaching the small town of Never, I reach the crossroad.

The sign speaks of distance: to the east, from whence I have come, Irkutsk, 1056ks; Vladivostok to the south east, 1946ks and, to the north, Magadan, 3177ks.

And as I contemplate setting off tomorrow on what could be called the *beginning* of my journey despite the fact that it is already some 8,500ks long, I must admit to being somewhat fearful. It's the not knowing that conjures up feelings of self-doubt; also the aloneness. It would be so different if Gareth were here with me. But he isn't; I need to do this alone.

And I reflect on the fact that the decision to route my journey north to Magadan and the Road of Bones instead of Vladivostok was made on a whim, nothing more. A chance remark by Gareth that if I *really* wanted to ride across Russia, then I needed to reach Magadan. And that settled it. The last few weeks have made me realise that ending my journey in Vladivostok would be easy: the road is good all the way, it's a major rail and shipping hub so repatriating the bike to Novosibirsk or Omsk would be straightforward. Instead, I am faced with 1,200ks of unknown road to

Yakutsk and then the 4,000ks of dirt along the Road of Bones to Magadan and back.

And as I mull over the days to come, the sliding door that will define my future in so many ways as I make the choice whether to take the left or the right fork tomorrow, I am embarrassed to admit that there briefly crept into my mind the thought: *If I choose to ride to Vladivostok instead of Magadan, who will really know the significance of that choice? To most people, I will still have ridden across Russia.*

But *I* would know, I tell myself. I would always know, deep down, that I'd wimped out; that, when it came down to it, I didn't have the balls to see it through. And my kids would know that their dad wasn't up to it...

No, I need to do this. Anyway, I'm tired of the good road and long to feel the lumps and bumps, the wrinkles of an old road again, a road that's been around the block a few times and has the scars to prove it; I need to dodge some potholes again, to engage in the *craft* of riding rather than the mere *endurance* of it.

Later, showered and refreshed, bike checked and oiled and ready for the morrow, I set off on foot into the taiga, just to get a feel for it, to experience a little something of being inside the frightening, dark, greenness of it. And I find the going tough: insects bite my exposed flesh, spiders web me, broken branches block my way, trip me up, slap me in the face; the dense mass of trees confuse and crowd upon me; under foot it is soft and yielding, my feet sinking below the ankle into leaf-mould and moss. After a few hundred metres I am stopped by a wide bog smelling of stagnant water held long in damp places where no sunlight can reach; in the centre, open water, reed-edged and deep, clouds of midges hanging in the still, hot air.

A cruel land.

And again, I have to ask myself: *How on earth did those Japanese sailors?*

The die is cast: Tomorrow I begin to head north.

Chapter Fifteen

Travelling in the north country fair

"Stalin used to kill people, and now the gangsters do. Is that freedom?"

It doesn't take much to brighten the day of the long-distance motorcyclist: someone calling, *"Otkuda?"* out a car window and expressing amazement when you shout over the noise of the engine, *"Anglia";* a small patch of blue in a dark, rain-drenched sky; a stretch of good dirt after days of boring tar; a stretch of smooth tar after miles of bad dirt; catching a child's eye in a passing car and evoking a shy smile; a knife and fork sign on the roadside when you're cold and tired; a waft of hot air, tar-smelling, lifted off the road on a cold day or a sudden patch of cool air in the heat; the smile of a waitress when you give your order in English and she doesn't understand; the kindness of strangers; when your bike is going well...

Of course, things can change the other way just as quickly: the first, fat drops of rain falling from a darkening sky; an unusual sound or vibration coming from the engine.

Right from the start the sky threatens rain. I ride a few kilometres from my motel back to the crossroads and take the turning north - Magadan: 3177ks. The road is new and, as I settle into the day's proposed 385ks, I must admit to being a little disappointed: another boring, new, tar road. Will it be like this all the way? If this trip was supposed to be a challenge, an adventure, the only challenge so far has been one of fortitude, of perseverance. Where's the adventure in that?

Then, after no more than five kilometres, the road simply disappears. It is as if an avalanche has swept it away just after a large motorway sign telling me: Yakutsk: 1172ks. My GPS urges me to keep going. *Trust me*, she says, *straight ahead, you can't miss it...*

But straight ahead is nothing but forest. Trees and yet more trees. No sign of a track, let alone a road of any kind. I turn and ride around a muddy clearing, looking for, perhaps, a dirt track leading me around an obstruction, a section of road works.

Nothing - just trees.

A road worker comes by and I ask him. He points back the way I've come. I glance again at my GPS: *Straight ahead, mate,* she insists.

I take the map out of my tank bag, study it minutely. And then I realise that this is the *new* road, all five kilometres of it. Just a few thousand to go. Come back in twenty years.

Back to the small town of Solovyesk, turn left and I find the road. I glance at my GPS and am pleased to see that she now says: *Sorry,* this *is the correct road - my bad.*

Ah, just the road I had been hoping for: slightly distressed, narrow and winding, a few potholes, clear signs of character. I could come to like this, I think to myself, when *Wham!* I hit the dirt. It's bad dirt that rattles my teeth and punches my little bike in the guts. Now I am worried: there is no way my bike will be able to absorb this amount of abuse, this beating from rocks and corrugations, for the next 5,000-odd kilometres. Something will break and bits will begin to fall off. Then, just as suddenly, good tar appears - a stretch of new road. Yes, I could like this, I think in somewhat contradictory fashion, when *Bam!* bad dirt again - followed, after a few kilometres, by good dirt, smooth and comfortable. Yes, I muse, again, I could do a few thousand ks on this; piece of cake - when *Bam!* a long stretch of bad tar, the kind that disillusioned road engineers know can never adequately be repaired so they just spread a layer of sand over it, hiding the potholes and ruts and sharp edges until the trucks and the first rains expose it all again. After the bad tar, back to dirt, pale yellow and smooth.

Then it begins to rain. I stop to put on my wet gear, hoping to find a friendly truck-stop cafe soon because I left this morning without breakfast or coffee, hoping for civilization of some kind along the way ready to offer a warm cuppa and, perhaps, a fried egg, but all I am offered is forest. The truck-stop cafes ended way back where my purveyor of doom told me "civilization ends here". And the trees drip in the rain, the air smelling of mud and stagnant water and newly lifted, wet stones. The dirt road turns to slush and becomes slippery - which I rather enjoy because the give in the mud turns the surface silky, no bumps and lumps; smooth mud with an inch or so of slush on top, just enough to let me know that both wheels have very little grip and if my bike feels like lying down it will and there's nothing much I can do about it.

But, ah, what fun!

And then, when I least expect it, after passing a few dying villages with decayed buildings where the ghosts of long-gone inhabitants still watch the rain from empty window frames, a knife and fork sign appears - coffee, hot and syrupy, four fried eggs, a fatty-doughy *piroshkis* with mince inside - and I am a new man!

And so on for 385ks: good road, bad road, shocking road, slippery road, road with marbles - and a trillion trees.

Very tired (I must be getting old) and I reach the small town of Neryungri. On the outskirts I cross a river and notice something strange. I stop, take a small track to its banks and realise that, despite the supposedly balmy month of July, the river is still locked in ice, two metres thick in places. I wondered why I was feeling cold.

Both hotels in town are full. A nice lady asks whether, perhaps, I would like an apartment. *Apartment!* Yes, please, I say, but the cost? Less than the price of the cheapest hotel room so, here I am, clean and vaguely rested, in a two-bedroom apartment in the Russian style (fifth floor, no lift), happy as a sand boy - although why sand boys are always happy is beyond me.

The journey is living up to expectation: my request: *If it's tar, give me tar with character; if it's dirt, give me good dirt* - is being honoured. I don't want to be killed by boredom on the one hand nor have my bike beaten to death by feral roads on the other. Goldilocks roads, please.

*****

The next day we - my trusty bike and I - continue to make steady progress north through the taiga. I like the word *"taiga"* - it has connotations of deep snow and wild things in the dark spaces between trees and endless distances and cold that will kill you. It has a ring of adventure about it. *I rode north through the trees* doesn't quite cut it.

(But how could those Japanese?)

The sun is shining; the road lumpy and cracked and so very worn and I am intensely happy. I sing to myself:

> *If you're travelling in the north country fair*
> *Where the wind blows heavy on the borderline,*
> *Remember me to one who lives there*
> *'Cause she once was a true love of mine.*
> *If you're travelling when the snowflakes fall*
> *When the rivers freeze and summer ends*
> *Please, see that she has a coat so warm*
> *To shield her from the howling winds.*
> *Please see that her hair's hanging long*
> *If it rolls and flows all down her breast*
> *Please, see for me that her hair's hanging long*
> *'Cause that's the way I remember her best.*

- and, somehow, it just seems right.

The last 150ks is all good dirt and it threatens to rain in the afternoon but the rain keeps away so, there too, I am happy. I find I am talking to myself like Friar Lawrence to Romeo: *Thy Juliet is alive, for whose sake thou was but lately dead,* there *art thou happy. Tybalt would kill thee, but thou slewest Tybalt -* there *art thou happy.*

"*Aaiiii! Heppy, heppy, heppy!*" I shout into the passing wind, as the African women would say, clapping their hands.

*****

Aldan to Yakutsk is 530ks. I decide to run it in a day, eager to reach the iconic north Siberian city where my journey turns east towards the start of the Kolymer Highway, the Road of Bones.

The road...

What else is there to comment on - the scenery, perhaps? Trees. A little swampier than yesterday; more small lakes and rivers, but still the endless taiga. The sky, perhaps? Heavy and pendulous with cloud, mammalian in form with occasional - very occasional - rips in the fabric allowing the sky to break through, just like yesterday and the day before.

There you have it: above me, the sky; on the left and right, boreal forest. Same as the past few days... same as the past 500ks.

And so, back to the road:

It tracks ahead of me, always heading north; on the crests of ridges, a pale, ragged line ahead is revealed where trees have been cut to make way for the road, dipping and cresting across a dark green, undulating ocean of trees.

Where there is tar, it is good tar: worn, lumpy, cracked and potholed but comfortable in its age like a benign uncle who has lived a hard life but retained a kindness of spirit; where there is dirt, it's good dirt, 100kph dirt and I wonder to myself how it is that I have been so blessed to be riding for thousands of kilometres across this achingly beautiful land, so remote and pure that it heals the spirit.

And then, to crown it all, as the day warms I am graced with the presence of millions of pale yellow butterflies that carpet the dusty soil with the fluttering of their wings and snowflake the air through which I pass; butterflies in such numbers that bring to mind photographs I have seen in National Geographic where the weight of butterflies clustered in the cool of evening is such that the branches upon which they settle bend and even break.

And I find that there is no longer in me the sense of fear that plagued me earlier in the journey about facing this part of the world, the feeling of threat as the trees crept ever closer to the road like a malign presence. Now, here, as I press on further into the northern regions of Siberia, the trees *have* encroached on my personal space, the road *has* deteriorated to dirt - the tangible manifestation of remoteness and isolation - but the fear has gone. And the reason, I believe, is my bike; so far it's proved itself trustworthy and I have grown confident in its reliable (although disturbingly rattly) engine note. If it can make it, then so can I; if she falters, then I'm stuffed.

The Road of Bones is now just around the corner, I can almost smell it, and I'm feeling strong.

*****

I write this in a small truck-stop cafe; the TV, as usual, plays some mindless soap; around me, tired-looking, pot-bellied truckers drink coffee and eat *borsh* and omelettes. The middle-aged waitress makes eye contact with me and tries out her handful of English words. She asks my name and tells me she's Tanya. Yakutsk, she says, is a lovely city. I order what I see a trucker eating - pancakes and condensed milk.

The whole world is a happy place and I am content.

Before I leave, two Russian bikers on well-turned-out Suzuki 250s pull up. They have no English so I find, strangely, that it is I who speak Russian for a change instead of the usual practice that all English speakers worldwide adopt when meeting non-English speakers, expecting them to defer to our language. "What's the road to Magadan like?" I ask in pigeon Russian.

One pulls a face and makes a non-committal rocking motion with one hand then signs falling rain and makes sliding motions with his body while holding imaginary handlebars. His meaning is clear. I have heard that the Road of Bones is very slippery when wet.

Well, a *So-so* description of the road is not as bad as a *Shockingly bad, fall over and kill yourself* description, so I take comfort in that.

I check out their bikes and notice that one is carrying a rifle in a canvas case strapped to the back of his seat. I point to the rifle and make a questioning face. He lifts both arms above his head, fingers clawed, and makes roaring bear sounds.

Oh, dear...

When we part he does something strange - he gives me a hug. And when a big Russian biker with a rifle gives you a hug, *that's* what the brotherhood of bikers is all about.

*****

Finally, by late afternoon, I crest a rise and in front of me is the Lena River, wide and blue - so wide, in fact, that the buildings of Yakutsk on the opposite side look like Monopoly houses. Close up, the river is running strongly, at least 10kph, the sandy banks so deeply eroded that wooden houses built on the riverbank and their picket fences are collapsing into the water.

My GPS has led me onto the sand opposite three smallish boats that are loading foot passengers. Just upriver, small speedboats are doing the same. Clearly there is a demand for watercraft to transport passengers across the river to Yakutsk, but what about vehicles? I study the larger boats and can see no place where a motorcycle can be loaded, no ramps, deck space. These are for foot passengers only.

I look up and down the riverbank, hoping to see a jetty of some kind. There is nothing so I approach a man sitting in a UAZ and ask him. He points up the road, back the way I have come. "Two kilometres," he tells me in Russian.

Reluctantly, I turn in the soft sand and make my way back onto the road; I look for and eventually find a dirt track leading onto the sand and follow deep tracks towards a collection of trucks waiting on the riverbank. Out on the river, a huge ferry is approaching, large, cable-stayed metal ramps like extended gulls' wings extend outward, just above the water on either side. As the ferry approaches, I can see that she's an old lady, about as battered as some parts of the road up here. Her plates are buckled and dented; rust bleeds from scuffs and scrapes and her ramps hang askew. The ferry itself is little more than a large, flat, metal barge with a small superstructure at the back to house a toilet and provide shelter for the man collecting ticket money.

The ferry slows and nudges one of its ramps gently into the shingle. Where the sand has been ridged, a crewman with a shovel scrapes it away, filling any gaps; another crewman drags a heavy, rusted cable up the sand and attaches it to another cable, one of many random strong points littering the shore - old metal hoops bleeding rust, bits of railway line, blocks of concrete. The vehicles on the ferry - mostly 4X4s and trucks - disembark; engines revving, they plough through the soft sand and onto the road.

The man with a spade fills the wheel tracks and any gaps that have opened up below the ramp then waves us on. I tuck my bike into a corner, pressed closely by a truck that has been manoeuvred into position by a crewmember who directs the driver, making most use of the space available on the wide deck.

The deck plates are rusty and buckled; over time, metal bits have been welded on and cut off leaving sharp, protruding edges, the weld splatter revealing the shape of what had been cut away but not its function.

I reflect on this primitive method of loading from a sandy riverbank, the only way vehicles can make it across the Lena River to one of the most important cities in north eastern Siberia. The absence of any permanent loading jetties on the bank of the river, I believe, is because, this being the coldest place on earth, the entire river freezes over during the winter months and, come the thaw, the massive slabs of ice jostling and shoving their way down the channel would rip any man-made structures to matchwood. The riverbanks, too, must constantly be changing as the soft sand and shingle are eroded and deposited by both water and ice. The banks are not high, seldom more then ten foot, the shingle gently sloping so this method of loading from *ad hoc* ramps formed (and re-formed when necessary) by an old, rusty grader stationed permanently on each bank is a logical one.

The ferry fully loaded, the ramp is raised, the cable attaching us to the shore released, the old engine starts up and we drift into the current to begin what I assumed would be a quick trip across the river but what, in fact, turns out to be an hour-long journey around some islands before we bear left towards the western bank some ten kilometres down-river of the city.

With a feeling of relief and satisfaction at having made it to Yakutsk, despite all the dire warnings I have faced, I explore the ferry. Most drivers have reclined in their seats and are sleeping; others lean over the railings and smoke. At the stern, I find the engine room door ajar so, with no one around to deny me access, I creep in. The noise coming from a large, straight-eight engine below me is deafening. I stand on a walkway of perforated metal panels overlooking the exposed tappets fingering away, feeling the beat of the pistons beneath my feet, the smell of hot oil filling the dark engine room. To one side, covered in dust and oil, are spare piston sleeves and cylinder heads just in case the engine breaks down half way across and some engine maintenance needs doing before we are washed north into the Arctic Ocean.

Finally, with the sun now low on the horizon, we beach on the east bank. I negotiate the ramp and the soft gravel up onto the main road into Yakutsk. It is busy with trucks. The buildings I pass have that run-down look produced, I would imagine, from being deeply frozen and thawed out each year; all the larger structures are built on concrete piles five feet above the ground and, as is the case with many Russian cities, there is an air of decrepitude about the place, as if it is slowly falling apart and no one has the money or the will to build it up again.

In the city centre, I am directed to a small hostel and given a bed in a room I share with three other men. My bike I tie to the railings outside with all the tie-down straps and bits of rope I carry with me and hope that it will be there in the morning.

Two days' rest before the Road of Bones...

Chapter Sixteen

Tenacious little beggar

"Our conversations always end the same way: 'It's a mess out there. We need a Stalin'."

Yakutsk is in many ways a strange city and one that gathers to itself nearly as many superlatives as Lake Baikal. Most countries in the world would never have even considered developing a city in a place as remote and extreme as this, simply because its existence is economically illogical. It's just too cold and too cut off by vast distances and wide, temperamental rivers from the rest of Russia and hence the world. Many Russians feel that the drain on the country's economy trying to keep these remote settlements viable is an unwarranted burden, refer to it as the "Siberian Curse" and argue that it would be better just to allow them to sink back into the permafrost.

It was only after the 1917 revolution that Yakutsk developed from a small outpost to something larger as it started being used as one of the many open prisons for political dissidents and criminals throughout Russia (although it had been used as a prison for many years before that). The rich mineral deposits discovered here, especially gold and diamonds (twenty percent of the world's diamonds come from this region) coupled with unlimited slave labour provided by the Gulag led to Yakutsk's development and growth. Today, with a population in excess of 200,000, it is the third largest city in eastern Russia after Novosibirsk and Omsk.

But life in Yakutsk is a constant battle: it has the dubious reputation for experiencing the coldest winters of any major city in the world with average temperatures of just below -40C with its lowest temperature recorded at -64.4C. (The coldest temperature ever recorded on earth occurred at what is now known as the Pole of Cold, Oymyakon, just east of Yakutsk along the Road of Bones where a temperature of -71.2C was recorded.) In fact, Yakutsk has *never* recorded a temperature above freezing between 10 November and 14 March since records began.

Anton Chekov wrote about Yakutsk when he toured the Russian penal colonies here in 1890, describing it in grim terms: "They (the prisoners) have lost whatever warmth they once had. The only things that remain in life for them are vodka, sluts, more sluts, more vodka. They are no longer human beings but wild beasts." I take it he didn't like it much, then.

Because of the cold, all buildings in Yakutsk are built on concrete piles, sometimes up to 25 metres deep. (Permafrost covers 15% of the world's land mass but in Russia it is 65%.) And evidence of the massive forces unleashed by the repeated melt and thaw in this forbiddingly cold place is clear throughout the city even to the casual observer: roads are broken and shattered; great hunks of concrete and the blunt edges of ancient wooden piles elbow their way to the surface as if some large, living thing deep underground is trying to claw its way out. Such primeval forces must wreak havoc with buildings and infrastructure here. It is understandable why the massive pipes, heavily insulated, that carry heated water to every building and apartment are laid above ground; without this heat, life, as the inhabitants here know it, would cease; people would die frozen in their apartments and all industry would grind to a halt.

As well as the cold, there is the isolation: to the north, the Arctic Ocean; to the east, Magadan, 2000ks away; drive south and, after some 5000ks, you will reach Vladivostok. There is no rail transport for passengers from Yakutsk, only a small airport, and the road, which, illogically, has been built on the eastern side of the Lena River - ten miles wide opposite the city - and there is no bridge. This means that trucks carrying goods can only reach the city during two short windows: when the river is navigable by ferries and when the ice is sufficiently thick to carry the weight of trucks. The city is cut off from all vehicular transport for long months when the river ice is too thin, when the ice is breaking up and when the river is in flood during the spring melt.

But enough about the extremes of Yakutsk. More important issues need addressing: I have to replace my tyres before I tackle the Kolymer Highway. Whilst I am carrying the spare front tyre I bought along the way, it's a cheap, Chinese-made one and I'm a little suspicious of it; my rear tyre will probably make it to Magadan but it won't bring me back.

I find a Yamaha dealership and there meet Alexei, a tall, fair-haired man in his early thirties who, it turns out, not only speaks a little English but is an avid enduro rider. Immediately he takes me under his wing. They have no tyres for sale, specialising in Skidoos for the long winter months, but he leads me in his car to a Suzuki dealership close by and explains to them that I need tyres and a service. The manager nods and gives instructions. Tyres are fetched - Super Enduro, strictly not for highway use and with wide-spaced, wicked-looking knobblies. Just the ticket. I decide to lash out and replace both front and rear; I'll keep the cheapie Chinese one as a backup.

The mechanic is more willing than able and seems unsure of what to do with my bike. This business, too, focuses on snowmobiles and outboard motors. With some help from other mechanics, a strap is tied around the frame, the bike is lifted using a fork-lift truck, the wheels are removed and sent to a tyre shop somewhere equally useless, I'm afraid to say. While we wait for the tyres, my bike is jet-washed and checked over: all seems OK; understandable wear and tear but, as they have no spares, little can be done.

After over *four hours* of hanging about, a van arrives back with my wheels but, after fitting them, we discover that the front has been punctured. Now I understand why the guys who delivered the wheels looked so sheepish. They'd battled all afternoon to fit two tyres on the rims, putting a hole in one tube. Realising that they were out of their depth, they gave up.

I tell them I'll repair it myself and take out my wallet to pay, annoyed because of the long wait and trying to work out how to explain that I am unhappy paying for shoddy workmanship. But the foreman closes his hand over my wallet and says, "Present from Russia."

I hug them all - it's the least I can do.

I fire up the bike and set off very slowly to negotiate six kilometres of snarling 5 o'clock traffic with a flat front tyre. Dangerously beaten up roads don't help, but I make it back to the hostel, get out my tyre levers and settle down on the side of the road, surrounded by a cloud of mosquitoes, to do the job. It then takes me, I am ashamed to admit, a further two hours to find and repair not one, but two holes in the front tube.

It went like this: Remove front wheel and take tube out, find hole and patch; find second hole (I've learned by now never to assume that there is only one) and patch that too. Replace tube and pump it up. All good until I notice the tyre has not seated properly in one place. Let out air and use tyre iron to ease tyre further onto rim. Puncture tube with tyre iron. Take tube out and patch third hole. While it's drying, insert spare tube. Try to pump up but discover I've pinched it. Mutter some bad words. Remove spare tube and patch. While curing, insert first tube again (with three patches now). Pinch tube again with tyre iron. Swear more loudly. Remove first tube and add fourth patch. Insert spare tube. Pinch spare tube with tyre iron. Swear some more while flapping mosquitoes. Remove spare tube and patch. Insert first tube yet again, very carefully this time. Pinch a hole in it again. Swear very loudly so that pedestrians look alarmed and pass me on the other side of the street. Remove tube and add fifth patch. Insert spare tube - *very* carefully.

Sorted.

My humiliation is complete. I had assumed that, of all people, I was an accomplished repairer of motorcycle punctures, a seasoned adventurer who could fix punctures in his sleep. But is seems that I am not. When push comes to shove I am, in fact, just plain useless and I now have to face the Road of Bones with a front tube with multiple patches and an acute awareness of my fallibility.

(In retrospect, however, it was good that I had perfected my puncture repair skills here, on the side of a tar road outside my hostel, because it prepared me for the real thing a few days later, as shall be revealed.)

Sweaty, filthy, still being eaten alive by mosquitoes, I strap my bike to the railings - and may I say here that, throughout this journey across Russia, I have felt happier about the safety of my bike and my person than at any time in the UK where, if you are stupid enough to leave your bike on the side of the road anywhere, even if chained to a lamp post, there is every likelihood that it won't be there in the morning.

I shower, collect my newly-washed clothes from the lady upstairs then walk to the local *magazin* to buy the makings of my supper. As I leave, the manager calls to me and invites me to take some fruit - anything I want: "Melon?" he says, encouraging me to help myself. "Pomegranate?"

I select an apple and he smiles his welcome.

My roommate, Michael, is a devout Russian Orthodox Christian; morning and evening he prays in front of a worn picture of a saint, crosses himself, then begins or ends his day. I wish I could talk to him but the language barrier is too high. He lives in Magadan, he tells me, and is flying there tomorrow.

Oh, the ease of flight!

Later that night I discover a large tick on a particularly intimate and sensitive part of my anatomy; he's a tenacious little beggar (the tick, that is). Hard tugging does not budge him and, after some time, I wonder whether I might be attempting to rip off a malign growth of my body's own making, a bloated skin tag of some sort, perhaps, so hard does the little fellow dig in with his fangs. Because I do not want to pull off a part of my own flesh, I carefully inspect the bleb more closely, using a torch and wearing glasses, and I see his little legs moving, like a suckling baby's kneading hands when tugging at the breast. Revolted, I make a more determined effort and manage to dislodge him, kicking and screaming, from my sensitive bits.

(I'm glad I had those tick-borne encephalitis shots now.)

*****

Through the good graces of a young lady called Lena, I have made contact with a shipping agent who assures me she can arrange to put my bike on a train from Yakutsk to Omsk. My relief is palpable. When planning this trip it was so easy to trace a vague finger across the map (as one does): Kyrgyzstan... Kazakhstan... enter Russia south of Omsk... turn right *tum te tum te tum* all the way to Magadan... turn round and *deedle deedle deedle* back to Omsk then *jumpy jumpy jump* home via the Russian deep south west. Just re-riding about 7,000ks of road. But having ridden 10,000ks already, eight to ten hours a day for a month with only two days' break, I am tired and do not relish retracing my steps (there really aren't any other viable roads out here) back to Omsk. Shipping the bike will mean I need to ride the Road of Bones twice - but this section is, when you come down to it, the main reason for the journey anyway - but I will only cross this country once instead of the one and a half times as originally planned.

My hope is that the Road of Bones is not a bike killer and my brave little mount will be able to cope with the 4,000ks of dirt that faces us tomorrow. We shall see. I hope, too, that my many-patched tubes will keep the air inside and that the bears will respect my personal space.

*****

Thunder rolls like stones in an empty barrel across the city as I make my way back from my meeting with Lena. In moments the streets are rivers and lakes. Obviously drainage wasn't a priority in the city's planning. Cars and buses wade through, pushing waves of dirty water before them while pedestrians attempt to find ways round. Over the rain-drenched city centre, the massive statue of Lenin stands, as he does still in many Russian towns and cities, his right arm held out, as always, as if he is still saying to any who will listen: *You see all of this wilderness, this endless tagia, this snow and ice? I give it all to you.*

I pick my way back to the hostel through the puddles and lakes and begin to pack. My bike is as well prepared as I have been able to manage. Fortunately I have a soft introduction to the route: Yakutsk to Khandyga - 418ks along flat marshland between the Lena and Aldan Rivers. The second day to Ust'Nera, 561ks, will be more testing because the road enters the Verhojansk Mountains which were covered with snow just before I left the UK. The condition of the road will determine whether I will be able to make Khandyga and Ust'Nera in one day so I might have to sleep wild. Again, we shall see. Day three: Ust'Nera to Susuman, 395ks - evidently very deserted with many abandoned, ghost towns along the way; finally, Day 4 - Susuman to Magadan, 622ks.

The Road of Bones awaits. I am packed and ready for an early morning start. Hopefully the late afternoon storm will have cleared the air of all its moisture by the morrow. No more rain, please.

Me? I'll cope.

Chapter Seventeen

Biggest cemetery in the world

"The devil knows how many people were murdered, but it was our era of greatness."

The Road of Bones runs for over two thousand kilometres through one of the most remote areas in the world, north eastern Siberia or, to give it its correct name, the Russian Far East, connecting the cities of Magadan and Yakutsk. On the way, it makes an enormous loop through the Suntar-Khayata Mountains in order to reach the hundreds of gold mines that once operated there. Locally, the road is known as "The Route" since it is the only route that can take a traveller from Yakutsk to Magadan on the coast.

Every kilometre of the road, which was begun in 1932 and only completed in 1953, was constructed by forced labour - at first by inmates of labour camps, but later by prisoners held in the gulags that were established throughout this region and other near-uninhabitable provinces of Stalin's Soviet empire. More than a hundred camps in this region provided labour for the road and the many gold mines found here, but those who worked in the mines faced worse conditions and died in greater numbers.

Many of the prisoners were Russian POWs, banished to the region after being labelled German collaborators, but the inmates were made up from a wide cross-section of Russian life: hardened criminals, Christians who refused to renounce their faith, petty crooks, dissident intellectuals, peasants who had objected to Stalin's collectivisation programme for their farms, party members purged because they had slipped out of favour, ethnic minorities suspected of disloyalty - basically anyone who had been sentenced, however arbitrarily, to three years or more. All were dispatched to the Gulag, which became a vast prison.

Many prisoners died during the long journey into the wilderness by train and ferry, and once set to work, thousands more died from overwork, exposure and starvation or were shot by guards for not working hard enough. The temperatures here are extreme: 40C in summer and minus 60C in winter - and prisoners laboured for 12-15 hours a day, surviving on a diet of little more than porridge and bread. Any worker who died was "buried" where he fell, to become part of the log foundation because, as the road is built on permafrost, digging new holes through the ice seemed impractical. Survivors' reports indicate that bodies were as common a sight as fallen logs. Because of the number of bodies buried just below the surface, the road is treated as a memorial to this day.

"It's the biggest cemetery in the world," a woman who lives in one of the dying towns along the route of the road commented. "At least twenty five people died on that road every day and nobody knows who most of them were. Bones are always breaking through the surface." She continued, "My grandfather was a guard in one of the camps, but he never liked to talk about it. He just said that they were grey, awful places where people were always hungry and cold."

Chapter Eighteen

Road of Bones

"Grey, boundless as loneliness, without light on the horizon - yet feels strength, faith, hope, movement, desire, love..."

Galina Zaraynova

I wake at 3... 4.30 and then again at 5.30, as if my brain is unconsciously counting down the hours. At six I get up and make a cup of tea then load up the bike while sharing a little more blood with the mosquitoes who have also decided to make an early start. I fire up the engine and, while it's warming, I check the tyres; the pressures are still holding.

Two men, smoking in the outside doorway, trade pleasantries, excited about Manchester - "Manchester *United!*" one cries, like a hundred others just like him. He lifts his jumper to show me his T-shirt, which sports a Magadan Boxing Club logo. We shake hands, he calling me "foreigner", expressing mutual appreciation of our home cities.

A short ride through the early-morning, rain-washed streets of Yakutsk to the riverbank. The old ferry is loading and I ride straight on but, like African taxis, we wait a frustrating hour for the ferry to fill. The sky is overcast but not threatening. Three gnarled truck drivers gather around the bike, staring. Then come the usual questions: *"Otkuda?"*

"Anglia," I reply.

They shake their heads, absorbing this. *Where you going?* one asks in Russian.

"Magadan."

They shake their heads again.

"*Adgin?*" holding up one finger and pointing to me.

"*Da,*" I confirm, admitting that I am, indeed, travelling alone.

"*Ochin delico.*" (It's very far.)

"*Da,*" I agree. "*Ochin delico,*" and I experience a quick spasm of emotion that is a strange mixture of excitement, fear and pride that I am attempting something that makes even Russians, when they hear of it, shake their heads and seem to retreat into themselves as they contemplate the sheer folly of it.

I detect some movement from the crew manning the winch; then, with a loud clanking, the anchor is raised followed by the loading ramp, which is briefly dipped under the water to wash away the gravel; we pull away from the bank and swing into the stream as the current catches the battered steel hull.

At last I am on my way.

An hour later, on the eastern side, I follow a good tar road heading north under a leaden sky then, shortly after the road curves to the east, the tar ends. The dirt road is, shall we say, acceptable: not great dirt that makes one happy to be a biker; nor, fortunately, is it bike-killing dirt - just slightly corrugated and bumpy, wet and puddled from last night's rain. The edges look smooth but are very soft and have me sliding about in a disturbing manner whenever I stray there when attempting to escape long muddy sections or bad corrugations.

For about eighty kilometres the road makes its way along a raised causeway across flat swampy land - not the usual taiga where trees predominate and thousands of small ponds and lakes gentle an otherwise uniform landscape; here it is mostly water and reeds and mud and the dead, drowned bowls of trees.

Mosquitoes cloud the air and descend upon you if you are unwise enough to pause, immediately attacking any exposed flesh.

A gentle enough introduction to the Kolymer Highway, I think to myself, feeling cold and in need of coffee. And then, as if it has been planned, a small village appears with cows wandering about the dirt streets and, yes, sweet, strong coffee.

This is how adventure biking ought to be...

I ride on through the day, the sky overcast, the air cool, the road roughly divided into four categories of equal length: corrugated and bad; slidey mud; slidey marbles and slidey sand. At first, feeling the bike slewing from side to side and thinking I have a flat tyre, I stop a number of times to check the pressures. But after a while I come to accept the somewhat alarming movements and trust my new ultra-enduro tyres, taking the sand, mud and marbles at speed, revelling in the slidey bits and having fun.

Small settlements of log-built houses pass by; ponds and lakes, silky still, reflect the sky; a herd of Camargue-like horses stomach-deep in green grass watch me as I pass. Then I come upon abandoned settlements with rotting wood and leaning walls, wrecks of cars, collapsed roofs and the emptiness of glassless windows that speak so sadly of lives ruined by this harsh, unforgiving land. I pause to explore a strange wood-and-mud construction surrounded by the broken walls of a house and rusted machinery; in an overgrown yard a large metal boiler, two metres high, stands over a smouldering fire. I look about me, conscious of trespass and remembering the warnings about feral men living off-grid in these eastern wilds. No one is about so I make my way through the discarded clutter already being reclaimed by the long grass and peer through a small window. It is clearly a huge animal barn, fifty metres long and fifteen wide, made entirely of logs, the walls and roof thickly plastered with a mixture of mud and straw.

Inside, a single cow is chained to a pole. As I make to leave, from an opening in the wall a white horse appears, looks at me quizzically then slowly walks away through the weeds. It is a surreal moment and I laugh at myself as my thoughts turn to fairy tales and princesses.

Then on again, dodging puddles. My fears of the Road of Bones at last begin to diminish. In my joy I reflect that I'm like a boy with his first bicycle; a dog with two tails; a man whose wife holds him close and with toothpasty breath whispers in his ear, "Hi there, pardner, what'cha bin doin'?"

Mid-afternoon clouds turn threatening and dark, roiling against the skyline of trees and I know a bad one is heading my way. I stop to don my cheap waterproofs and then the rain hits me like a bucket of warm water poured over my head. Instantly, the road becomes a river, every depression a deep pond; both my feet are wrenched repeatedly off the pegs by the force of water flung back from my front wheel.

And then, just as suddenly, it is over. I ride on until late afternoon along a rain-wet track until a wide river blocks my path. Moored to the sandy bank, loading ramp down, is another metal barge, this one attached to a rusty paddle-wheel tug, its riveted plates dented and worn. No one is about. I ride up the ramp and park against the railings. I am the only vehicle here. I know the wait will be long when I see a crewmember emerge from a metal door carrying a fishing rod and a tin full of worms and wet earth.

Leaving the ferry, I explore the sandy bank, twelve foot high and deeply undercut by the river during the spring floods. Under the dark sky and the endless presence of trees that I know continue uninterrupted for thousands of kilometres in every direction, the slow moving of water and the old paddle steamer waiting and still, I am transported elsewhere, to an older, unpeopled world separated by space and time from the one I am used to. And I can understand why Russians say that Moscow isn't Russia; that Siberia is another country, existing in its own isolated world. And I can understand too, more clearly now, why during Soviet times, this place was deemed so suitable for establishing penal work colonies. The extremities of space and climate make fences and walls redundant; you don't need them when there are thousands of miles of forest between you and freedom: mosquito-infested swamp in summer, frozen solid in winter - although, even in these remote places, prisoners were kept penned behind barbed wire with crude wooden guard towers constantly manned.

Khandyga, I learn later, was once a gulag camp, established in 1939. There are no memorials to the victims who died here.

Over the next three long hours, vehicles appear in desultory fashion, a few trucks but mostly UAZ 4X4s. While I sit on the metal deck, waiting, a UAZ makes its way through the sand, a disturbing clatter coming from underneath as it crests the ramp. Two men emerge, peer underneath then produce tools and whip out the rear side-shafts then unbolt the prop shaft and open the diff. It's clear that they've done this before. The diff is broken so they dig out some pieces of cardboard, cut them to shape and block the side-shaft holes by bolting them into place, then close up the diff and reattach the prop. They will continue to wherever they are going by using the front diff only.

Evening begins to fall across the land and the river seems to slow, moving darkly against the side of the barge. The whole world becomes silent, holding its breath. Still we wait. Drivers sleep in their cabs or eat the food they have brought with them. I have nothing. But the broken UAZ is parked close to me and the driver saunters over, checks out my bike. We talk as best we can. He and his family are on their way to somewhere about 400ks away but will be passing through Khandyga. There is only one hotel, he tells me. Have I booked? I shake my head and he looks concerned. He will take me there, he says, because it's difficult to find and we will be late.

"How far to Khandyga?" I ask him.

"Forty kilometres," he tells me, "but the ferry takes one hour forty-five minutes."

"What time does it leave?" I ask him.

"Eight o'clock." It's going to be a long day.

There are two women in the UAZ - his wife and daughter, he tells me. The older woman gets out, her face leathery and deeply wrinkled. Without speaking, she brings me black tea and then two boiled eggs, a container of rice and a hunk of bread and, using only her hands, encourages me to eat.

We continue to wait and darkness comes. The banks of the river merge with the trees. The mosquitoes have gone to sleep; a deep calmness settles over the land and the river surface turns to silk. At last the man who has been fishing pulls up his line, drags the chain across the ramp entrance and, with a clatter from the winch, the heavy metal ramp is raised, dipped into the water to wash off the soil, and then secured. The ancient paddle-wheel tugboat nudges us into the flow and we set off up river. I stand at the stern watching the huge paddles churn up the water, the empty riverbanks sliding by on either side and feel like Huckleberry Finn looking out on the wide, slow-flowing Mississippi long, long ago. The river is so deep that at times we pass just a stone's throw from the low, pebbly riverbanks and in the evening stillness arctic terns dip and weave just above the water, showing off.

It is very dark by the time the ramp is lowered into the sand up river on the opposite bank. Engines fire up and I follow my friends in their UAZ across soft sand then, blinded by dust, onto an atrocious road, stony and ridged with scree, that threatens to have me over. I fear for my tyres.

Finally the lights of Khandyga appear and I am led down rutted back streets puddled with rainwater. We stop in front of a rough wooden building; my friend leans out the window, pointing, and then drives away. I am grateful - I would have struggled to find this place on my own in the dark.

The owner, a plump, grey-haired woman, welcomes me and shows me my room and the kitchen where there is a stove and a kettle.

I'm tired and dirty. Today has been my introduction - just 400-odd kilometres along a reasonably good road. Tomorrow will be the test: 560ks into the mountains.

Content, I unpack my bike and ready myself for the morrow.

Chapter Nineteen

Willing little soldier

"Russia needs a strong hand. An iron hand. An overseer with a stick. Long live the mighty Stalin! Hurrah!"

Of course I was riding too fast, I don't deny it. Perhaps it was because I just wanted to reach Ust'Nera before I started growing mould.

There is a small rise in the road ahead of me and it is only as I crest it that I see the river. It isn't a particularly big river but it is flowing strongly, has a stony bottom and I have no idea at all how deep it's going to be.

I hit the brakes but, probably because they've been wet all day, nothing happens and in a moment I am calf-deep in a strong, icy flow amongst the rocks, and the engine dies.

Suddenly, except for the rushing of the water, all about me is silent. Mountains surround me, shrouded in mist and rain, and I feel very alone.

I give it a moment or two for the heat of the engine to dry the electrics and to allow me to gather my thoughts. I'm not in any real danger but I recognise I'm in a predicament where riding alone is not wise. I'm a very long way from anywhere, there've been no other vehicles on the road for a while now and I have no big son to leap off his bike, wade into the flow and steady the bike while I try to extricate myself. I tell myself that drowning the engine is simply not an option. Not out here. (Not anywhere, really.) Lifting a laden bike in the dry and on a firm surface is bad enough; lifting it, alone, when half under water and being resisted by a strong flow will be well nigh impossible. Well, it would be for me. Fast-flowing water is a scary thing and if I get my body trapped under the bike I could drown.

Having gathered my thoughts, and knowing that I just *have* to do this thing, I press the starter and she fires immediately. But there's a strange lethargy about the running that I assume is the result of wet electrics. Again she stalls. I fire her up again but she stalls almost immediately. There's a large rock trapping my front wheel and I can feel the bike trying to climb it even though I have the clutch in.

And with a sinking heart I realise that my clutch has gone. My willing little soldier is actually starting in gear without a clutch, and the rear wheel spinning in the gravel and trying to mount the rocks is causing the lethargy I noticed before.

Now what? Alone, half way across a river, water flowing calf-deep and no clutch. Each time I fire her up the engine dies within seconds, straining against the rocks. I decide there is only one thing I can do. I engage neutral, fire up, give the engine a handful of throttle, stamp the bike into gear and, keeping the revs up, she gains traction over the rocks and I wrestle her free and out of the water.

Now, the clutch. Fortunately it's only the adjuster that's worked itself loose and, after repositioning it, I am on my way again, very relieved that things haven't gone pear shaped as they so easily could have.

*****

There really has got to be an easier way to have fun than this. For ten hours today I have ridden along sodden roads through a rain-drenched, lonely mountain landscape. I was conned into believing that it was going to be a fine day by the small splodges of blue in an otherwise lead-grey sky when I loaded up at five in the morning.

The road east towards the Verhojansk Mountains across the flat, marshy plain was good and for the first hour all went well. But as I began to ascend the foothills, it started to rain and so it continued all day. Rivers turned orange and frothy; water cascaded down mountain slopes and into ditches and onto the road which became black and slick with mud; every depression and pothole became a puddle of unknown depth; the road seemed to become the chosen route for rain water to make its way downwards and rivulets formed wherever trucks' wheels had left indentations.

As I climbed, the mountains became obscured by mist, the riverbanks, in places, still encased in a thick rim of blue-white ice. And so I continued to ride through a beautifully remote, mountain landscape, fighting to keep the wheels facing down on a very slippery track. My clothes became wetter by the hour as the rain and spray kicked up by the wheels penetrated my defences and I began to wonder whether the sun would ever shine again.

Finally reaching Ust'Nera in a continuing downpour, I splashed my way through roads that had turned into rivers, looking for somewhere to spend the night. I plodded up two flights of creaking wooden stairs to the only hotel for 500ks in any direction, hoping the lady sitting behind the glass screen of her office wouldn't say *Nyet*.

She doesn't. I unload, dripping water and mud up the stairs and into the foyer where a damp-haired dog curled up on a chair looks meaningfully at me.

Later, my room festooned with all my belongings in the vain hope that, by tomorrow, they might have dried or, more realistically, become less wet, I look out my window onto a drowned land, a town of tattered buildings and broken things. Cold and wet, as I settle into my cosy room, I think about those who live in places like this, less fortunate than me, desperate people who do not have the luxury of a warm, dry room after a day in the wet. Perhaps for them, a bridge or a doorway or an abandoned building is all they have to call *home* until the weather lets up. I have a home waiting for me when this trip is over; it is my anchor and my refuge.

And living in this place during the long, dark months of winter, when the sun barely breaks the horizon and where the snow is chest deep... What if something goes wrong - the heating pipes burst or the gas supply is interrupted? The water pipes freeze and the food runs out? How does one survive in a place like this under such circumstances?

Will faraway Moscow care - or even know?

The town itself seems to be barely holding itself together; broken and discarded things are scattered everywhere; the roads are a mess. I assume that in this far-away corner of the Russian state, funds for repairs and regeneration are far from the minds of politicians whose Moscow base rubs shoulders with the European Union.

And as I look out over the rain-sodden streets, I see people carefully picking their way through the puddles and wonder what makes a person choose to live here. But then, I suppose, I'm reasoning like a westerner - I would imagine that many of the inhabitants of this place have no other choice; poverty and straightened circumstances, the unimaginable distance from anything other than what they have known all their lives is a barrier as high as a prison wall.

The whole town is flooded; rivers of brown, froth-covered water runs down the street outside my window. Just up the road from my hotel a man uses a backhoe to dig a trench across the road, blocking it - but it helps a little to drain the floodwater away. There is no restaurant so I sit in my room and eat pot noodles bought from the local *magazin*.

Outside, the rain continues to fall. Will it ever stop? I am half way across the Kolyma Highway (well, a quarter, if you consider that I need to ride this all over again, back to Yakutsk) and I do so pray that my little friend, standing forlorn and wet in the swampy street outside, will keep its heart beating for just another 3,000ks - and then it's onto a train and back into comparative civilization where, just perhaps, it will be warm and not raining.

Chapter Twenty

Dying communities

"We'd all like to have faith in something, but we can't. No one cares about anything any more, and the future is shit. That's not how it used to be... Oh! Poems, poems... Words, words..."

I wake to a strange light in the room. The sun is shining.

All is forgiven.

I pack up quickly, strap my panniers onto the bike while beating off mosquitoes and fire up the engine. The backhoe stands next to the trench it has dug across the road and I have to pick my way through deeply puddled back roads to make my way out of town. I am on my way and, although it's already clouding over, there are still hopeful patches of blue in the sky. The road shimmers ahead of me like hammered silver in the low sunlight reflecting off its wet surface.

For about an hour I ride in a state of relative bliss until, yet again, the sky closes down and rain begins to fall, intensifies to another deluge that lasts, without cessation, throughout the day. Once again I ride along mud-slick dirt roads, mostly in good condition; the rivers and streams are swollen now and deluge across the track, seeking lower ground, the clouds heavy and low, partially obscuring the mountains all about me.

For hours the road follows the meandering valley of the Indigirka River that boils and swirls below me, carrying with it tangled knots of trees that spin and cartwheel in the mud-yellow waters.

What strikes me about this 395km section of the Kolymer Highway between Ust'Nera and Susuman is its desolation; even more desolate than the first 1,000ks, if that's possible. Throughout the day there is nothing but the muddy road and swollen rivers under a leaden sky - and trees.

Possibly there are some people living here; I have no doubt that they do. But I don't see any and the only man-made structures I ride past are wooden pylons carrying dipping cables into the mist, broken wooden bridges across swollen rivers, the occasional settlement - one quite large, almost a small town - but, in every case, as I look more closely, I become aware of broken windows, doors ajar like the open mouths of dead people, the wrecks of cars and the usual detritus left behind when a family or community is forced by circumstances to abandon their homes, their shops and garages, their places of work, everything they used to call dear as if suddenly, one day, by mutual decision, every one just closed their doors and walked away.

I'm sure it wouldn't have been like that; I'm sure it was a gradual thing as happens in any dying community - first the post office, then the pub, then the local school closes and parents with young children move away and the old can't cope.

From the road, these communities look quite normal - run down, obviously, but then all human habitation in this desolate place seems run down, rotted and fallen, cars left to rust, abandoned machinery, leaning fences, broken and rusted things that have lost their value. It's a matter of priorities, I suppose: survival first; coping with life, second.

In a brief hiatus in the rain, I come across yet another ghost village and leave my bike to explore. When planning this journey it was my feeling that the most obvious place to get mugged was when exploring the mouldering buildings of an abandoned community just like this but now that I am here, I feel quite safe - just sad. I am all alone, walking down a muddy street with small wooden houses on both sides, some of them looking as if the occupants have just stepped out to visit a friend and that, if I were to peep inside, I would see a still-warm kettle on the stove and coals glowing in the hearth. But, other than the mosquitoes, there is no life here except for two large dogs that appear from somewhere, investigate me with intelligent eyes and, after a cursory bark, job done, they continue on their way to wherever. And for the next twenty minutes I walk about this village, its streets waterlogged and overgrown with tall grass, weeds taking over the front gardens that used to be so carefully tended, broken toys, a single boot, an old crash helmet, worn car tyres, bottles and rusting cars standing outside the houses as if waiting for the occupants to return with their keys. Walls bulge and tarpaper peels away from roofs in long strips. Vegetable patches in back yards are overgrown with weeds; a telegraph pole leans to one side, its wires hanging - there's no one here to speak over these wires any more. The wooden cottages usually rot first and some are already beginning to lean but some stand firm and whole except for broken windows. If you cast your eyes quickly over the street without looking closely, it could be any village on a Sunday afternoon when the occupants are resting or watching a game of football on the telly.

I feel ill at ease walking through the sad memories of others' destroyed lives, like a voyeur or one who pauses to stare at a traffic accident but I need to see this, to pay my respects, as it were, for this is the evidence of the dying of Russia's far-off rural communities.

Reluctantly, I leave the two stray dogs and the houses watching me with their vacant windows and press on into the rain that has started to fall again. I ride on alone except for the occasional truck that passes by, flinging a thick shower of mud over me from the road. Despite the wet and cold, things are going well and I am enjoying the smoothness of the track and the challenge of keeping my willing little steed's wheels facing down on a very slick surface.

But then something changes; I can feel it. The engine seems to be labouring more than usual, a slight reluctance. Then the movement of the bike along the road - is it more pronounced than usual? It's easy to feel a flat tyre on a hard surface - the bike's slewing is clearly pronounced; but when riding on a muddy track, the bike is sliding about anyway and any added movement could just be a more slippery piece of road.

I decide to stop and check - and, with a sinking heart, I can see that my rear tyre is flat. With the engine off the silence and desolation press in upon me and I feel very alone and vulnerable. Remembering the hassle I had sorting out the punctures in my front tyre in Yakutsk, far easier to repair than a rear tyre, makes me dread what I know I have to do. A rear tyre is heavier, more difficult to break the bead, to remove and replace, alone, with the added complication of the chain.

Knowing that there is no option but to *do* it (no friendly tyre shop just down the road; no biker mate to use his side stand to break the bead), flapping at the cloud of mosquitoes that halo my head in a feeding-frenzy of blood-lust, I unload the bike, retrieve my tyre irons, tools and pump, and lift the swing arm onto my special piece of wood that rather precariously holds the rear wheel off the ground. Removing the wheel is fairly straightforward. Making sure the bike doesn't fall over, I lie the wheel on a piece of cloth on the least muddy part of the road I can find. Breaking the bead is more difficult but with the help of a tyre iron, a large rock and my boot, I finally manage to separate the tyre from the rim. With the tube removed, I quickly find one small hole and patch it. I then commit the most basic of schoolboy errors: I insert my spare tube without checking it first for punctures then, *very* carefully, lever the tyre back onto the rim. I attach my pump and switch it on.

The tyre won't inflate.

Bugger, bugger, bugger!

Sitting in the mud, surrounded by biting mosquitoes, I do the whole thing again, finding an old pinch-hole in the spare tube that Gareth and I had obviously made two years before and not repaired.

Re-insert the patched tube - again without pinching it - and, with a knot in my stomach, switch on the pump.

It holds.

I now need to re-fit the wheel. So, sitting in the mud with the wheel gripped between my knees (and hoping the bike doesn't fall off my piece of stick) I hold both spacers in place, locate the brake disk between the shoes with an outstretched finger, roll the chain onto the sprocket with my thumb, line up the holes with my knees, locate the spindle in the hole (hoping the spacers don't drop out) and beat it into place with the ball of my hand. Not quite believing it, the spindle slides home and the job is done.

Chain adjusted, I load up, still flapping mosquitoes, and set off again, listening to the engine, my whole body tense with expectation that I would begin to feel again that anxious sway and wiggle of a deflating tyre. Two hundred and fifty kilometres to go.

And so, dirty, wet, knackered in mind and body, I reach Susuman in the late evening, in the pouring rain, and find a cheap hotel.

I seem to have skipped two time zones in the past week. I wondered why it was getting light so early.

Six hundred kilometres to Magadan. I don't think I can make it in one day. And if it's raining tomorrow, I'm staying here.

Chapter Twenty One

Come on, little bike

"I hate Gorbachev because he stole my Motherland. Yes, we stood in line for discoloured chicken and rotting potatoes, but it was our Motherland. I loved it. You lived in a third-world country with missiles, but for me, it was a great nation."

There is tiredness when the normal functions of the body begin to disconnect. I think I've reached that state. When riding the last few kilometres into Magadan (yes, I've made it), my eyes began to lose focus and I had consciously to will them to function; when I got off my bike at the Magadan stele at the entrance to the city, I found that my body wanted to lie down. My reactions had slowed and my limbs struggled to obey the reluctant commands of my brain.

The day has been a miserable one; a long twelve hours of endurance, no more...

It wasn't raining when I loaded up the bike at five am, readying myself for the long 600ks to Magadan. But, once again, the weather gods played a dirty trick on me, luring me onto the road with the enticement of good weather. Had it been pouring with rain when I woke, I would have delayed my departure for another day. But although the early-morning skies were heavily overcast when I woke, it wasn't raining so I decided to take a chance.

Wrong decision - but then, hindsight is always an admirable thing.

Within twenty minutes of my setting off, the rain began to fall, a long, cold sulk of a rain that lasted, without even the hint of cessation, all day, all six hundred kilometres, every long, cold, suffering minute of it. I hunkered down, trying to keep the water from dribbling down my neck, gritted my teeth and followed a muddy track of varying respectability, the mountains around me obscured by the mist, the depressing spectacle of abandoned houses and settlements partially hidden by trees and long grass.

It is difficult to look about one with enthusiasm when any movement of the head opens a gap at the neck for cold air and water to enter, to ooze and seep through the defences until you feel it begin to trickle down your chest, past your belt and into your trousers where it settles, cold and wet and miserable. And all the while water is creeping up your trouser legs from boots already sodden. So for most of the day I stared straight ahead at a muddy road, trying not to hit any rocks that might puncture a tyre. The very thought of going about the whole miserable task of repairing a puncture in the mud again, in the rain and cold, was inconceivable.

On the high passes, snow lay thick on the ground; many of the rivers were ice-bound - and still the freezing rain fell. My little bike, never a friend to water, began to hesitate and falter and, each time it happened, my gut clenched at the prospect of standing on the roadside in the freezing rain, many hundreds of kilometres from anywhere, hoping one of the few trucks on the road might stop and help. But after each stutter, each heart-stopping hesitation, she picked up again and continued, unhappy but strong.

After four hundred kilometres of this misery, a truck-stop cafe appeared out of the rain and I paused to eat my first meal of the day. But as I dismounted, I noticed that my front tyre looked soft. A closer inspection showed me that the valve core had ripped out and was hanging by a thin piece of rubber.

But - Oh, blessings indeed! - just to one side of the cafe was a shipping container with a pile of scrap truck tyres outside. I removed my front wheel in the rain and asked the man, who was teaching his two teenage sons the trade, whether he could repair it using my spare tube. We worked on it together in the dry comfort of his little container workshop and, in ten minutes, the job was done.

Despite my insistence, he wouldn't accept payment.

I rode on into the late afternoon, my little mud-covered bike stuttering and hesitating, threatening to cut out and leave me helpless on a rain-drenched, icy roadside. I talked to her as one would an exhausted pony, even patting her, encouraging her as if she were struggling to keep going just for me, "Come on, little bike, just keep going, just another two hundred kilometres. You can do it..." I must admit to a certain desperation creeping into my voice. The cold and the damp had got into my bones and I was merely existing, not living, and certainly not enjoying my experience. This trip had become an endurance test for me - physically, emotionally, mentally - and many were the times during the day I questioned the reason for my doing this. Surely there must be a better way to spend one's retirement: a week's B&B in a quaint village in France, perhaps, waking late and walking into town for coffee and croissants - "*Bonjour, gentil monsieur, bienvenue. S'il vous plaît, asseyez vousâ -*" and lazy countryside walks and supper with good wine at the local bistro.

But no - for me it was a matter of enduring, counting down the kilometres, first in hundreds, then tens and, finally, in ones until, out of the darkness, a rain-smudged Magadan appeared below me.

I found a hotel in the city centre; shivering and dripping mud across their clean foyer, I booked in, unloaded the bike and carried my sodden bags up to my room.

I've made it.

Now, I've just got to do it again.

Chapter Twenty Two

We live in the north, but we respect

"We sit atop the ruins of socialism like it's the aftermath of war. We're run down and defeated. Our language is the language of suffering."

Next morning I am still tired. My hands are swollen from holding the grips for so long in wet gloves; physically and mentally I am worn out. Perhaps that is why I suddenly find myself in tears - mainly loneliness, I think; the release of having made it and the fear of the return journey; the joy of knowing that I have achieved what I set out to do and the knowledge that, in a few days' time, when I set off to retrace my steps to Yakutsk, I will finally be on my way home.

In truth, I am not a true adventurer, one of those keen-eyed, chisel-faced individuals able to suffer untold privation alone with their thoughts; those who regard the world as their back garden and are at peace with their own company. I love my home, my kids and grandkids, the mucky presence of them, and whenever I travel there is always a cord firmly attached pulling me back. I think travelling with my son these past five years has caused me to forget the intense ache of loneliness the single traveller often feels. I know that if he were here with me now, sharing anecdotes about the horrific past four days, laughing at our discomfort now in the warmth of civilization, discussing the trip back and planning how to restore the bikes, I would be feeling very differently.

Then I receive a message from Aleksey, chairman of the local bike club: *Welcome to Magadan! Does your bike need any work?* and it's the kindness of strangers, more than anything else, that touches my soul.

Aleksey meets me at noon, leads me to a car wash where thick layers of hardened mud are stripped off the engine and frame; then to a parts shop for oil and, finally, to his workshop where he leaves me to service the bike and fit new brake pads. In the workshop his sleek Yamaha 1200 cruiser stands next to my tried little bike, which looks like the country cousin that no one wanted to invite to the wedding.

I consider asking Aleksey whether there might be a way to get the bike back to Yakutsk - in a truck, maybe, heading that way with some space in the back - but decide to man up and see the task through properly. I have a friend, Richard, in the UK who is an enthusiastic amateur weatherman and I message him: *Find me a four-day, rain-free window for the Magadan-Yakutsh region, please.*

I cannot face a repetition of a rain-plagued, 2,000-kilometre, Road of Bones.

Later he messages me that there will be high pressure over this region in a week's time. I've decided to wait. I need to rest and there's much here to explore.

*****

It is evening and there is a knock at my door. It is Alexander, my Facebook friend, landscape photographer and mountaineer, and his friend Sergei. Neither speaks any English and communication is difficult and slow. They invite me to supper tomorrow night. Sergei has gold teeth...

"Happiness doesn't concern the president," Sergei types. We sit in Alexander's lounge; on the walls, photographs of mountains and mountain climbers and old artefacts discovered in the wilderness. "We live in the north, but we respect," Sergei types again, with a serious, considered face, to answer an impossible question I have put to him using Google Translate: *What do you think of President Putin?*

It is an answer similar to others I have heard before - Putin does not really care for the sufferings of ordinary people. His interest is in the bigger picture, the nation state, the position of Russia in the world and the pride that will generate. But most Russians that I have spoken to seem to respect him, acknowledge the need in a country this large for a hard man to hold it all together, the man they hope will return Russia to that place and time when she and America stood toe-to-toe, equal rivals bestriding the world stage.

Alexander stands in the kitchen preparing our meal of salad, cold meat on black bread, dried fish, cheese and raw, smoked fish. And *borsh*, of course.

"Russian *borsh!*" he calls out, smiling, implying somehow that it is *borsh* that has stiffened the backbone of the nation through the ages - and probably kept millions from starvation.

I type another question for Sergei - an impossible one, I know, but I throw my bread upon the waters with an apologetic shrug: *What do you feel about Russia today?*

I imagine being asked to respond to a question like that about Britain, existential and wide ranging, by a foreigner whose language I do not speak.

But, again, Sergei takes my question seriously, thinks a moment, then types. The translation says: *There is a feeling that we were all friends without confrontations.*

Allowing for the vicissitudes of the translator ("tube", by the way, is always translated as "piano"), he has expressed, I believe, the heart-feeling of most Russians: the desire to be friends with the peoples of the world; a weariness of the suspicion, the petty jousting, the moral and ethical antagonism that has characterised E-W relations for so many long decades.

He takes back the phone and types again: *Russians love the world.*

Yes, I believe they do.

Good wine is served. Sergei doesn't partake and Alexander and I finish the bottle. Our evening together is relaxed and conversation easy despite the limitations of the translator. No vodka is drunk or offered; the stereotype I had in my mind about far eastern Russians as yokels only one degree removed from banjo-plucking retards is shown to be as ludicrous as the stupidity within myself for ever believing it.

Alexander is an artist - oils, photography and film documentaries of the Kolymer region. His work is exquisite. Sergei is a mechanic but, in his spare time, a mountaineer, a hard man despite his gentle face and balding pate. He and Alexander plan a 4X4 trip across Russia, filming, probably next year. How I would love to join them.

The evening ends with cognac and a twilight drive around the city. Magadan is no Yakutsk. Where there is an air of desperation about its chilly neighbour to the west, Magadan is sleek and cosmopolitan, the streets wide, its buildings gracious and stately. The Cathedral of the Holy Trinity holds centre stage with its gold-gleaming onion domes and bright white walls soaring 71 metres into the air (all buildings except the cathedral are limited to no more than five stories because of the permafrost). Outside the cathedral thin men with the look of stray dogs sprawl on the steps, hoping to tap into the renewed piety of those emerging from the church. In the bus station near the cathedral more thin men with haunted eyes shelter from the cold wind that blows down over the city.

I wonder as we pass whether they, too, will die of exposure or the numbing poison of bootleg alcohol when the winter comes.

A small city, Magadan lies cupped in a pretty hollow with snow-capped mountains on three sides and opening out into the Sea of Okhotsk on the eastern side. Its isolation doesn't seem to have held it back in any way; no frontier town, this.

On a high ridge on the western edge of the city stands The Mask of Sorrow, a memorial dedicated to the victims of political repression and totalitarian rule. It stands on the site of the original transit camp through which all prisoners sent to the Kolymer had to pass. And, for me, it is significant that in Putin's Russia one has a visual statement that cries out so vehemently the message that the new Russia is different from the old - despite the large and imposing statues of Lenin that still stand watch over town squares throughout this land. Perhaps the Lenin statues have no real significance any more - just that the cost and effort of removing and disposing of them makes it easier to leave them be, relics of a failed experiment to manipulate the lives of millions of people by suspicion and fear.

This monument recognises that in the past, especially in the Gulags that disposed of people's lives with such casual and shocking brutality, the state overrode its own moral authority, committed acts of such inhumanity that must never be forgotten or repeated.

The western side of the monument depicts a solemn, weeping face, some fifteen metres high, the tears themselves faces weeping, faces upon a face, tears upon tears, millions of lives like garbage tossed away. On the other side is a crucified Christ, lumpy with muscle, bunched and knotted; his hands, strangely large and compelling, his whole body twisted into a rictus of pain and resistance, head lifted as if in the anguished moment of his cry: *"Father forgive them..."* or, perhaps, more significantly, *"It is finished."*

At the foot of the cross a child crouches, wrapped in a foetal position of distress, a poignant symbol of the grief of all the world's children and the universality of suffering.

Chapter Twenty Three

If you don't, we will shoot you

"My grandmother was born in 1922. Her whole life, people had been shot and executed. Arrested. That was all she'd ever known. My grandmother's greatest fear was a new Stalin and another war. Her whole life, she'd been anticipating arrest and starvation..."

So - the Gulag. Where does one start?

Like the Nazi extermination camps, the Gulag was an abomination. One thinks of it as a *place* but it was, in fact, *many* places. In one's mind's eye, the Gulag takes the form of barbed wire and men worked to death - but, in essence, the Gulag was not a place but a *system* - of control, of fear and intimidation, of herding together opponents of a revolutionary social experiment to be used as unpaid labour for the construction of national infrastructure - like the Kolymer Highway.

But perhaps, to understand its genesis more clearly, we need to go further back in Russian history to the time when rich and oppressive landowners treated the peasants as slaves. In 1812, 90% of the Russian population consisted of serfs - men, women and children who were, in fact, slaves in all but name, the outright property of a landowner who could buy, sell, trade or punish them on a whim. So, the Revolution - understandable when one considers the poverty and suffering of the majority in Russian society and the wealth and privilege of the few, which led inevitably to the rise of Lenin and Stalin and Trotsky.

But although serfdom was abolished in 1861, the peasants were still not free. First they had to pay the landowners back the value of their land and were not allowed to move elsewhere until the debt had been paid; all villagers, too, were collectively liable for what was owed. When the revolution came, the peasants rose up and seized the lands which they believed now belonged to them but the Bolsheviks, ignorant of the countryside, seized their grain and, as a result, some ten to fourteen million people died of hunger in the four years after 1917.

This callous disregard for the welfare of their own people leads us to an understanding of what happened later. To keep the revolutionary movement pure, opponents of *any* kind who, if left to infect unseen, would bring the whole edifice down, needed to be purged.

Like in Apartheid South Africa, where the whole population needed to be divided into the two categories of Black and White, in Russia it was decided that the division would be between those who *worked* and those who *oppressed*. But who were the "workers"? Dividing an entire nation, multitudinous in its diversity, into two distinct groups will always prove difficult. Even with sheep and goats, there will always be some who are not sufficiently sheepish or a little too goatish. In South Africa, for example, were "coloureds" to be classed as black or white? And if you were white and shared, perhaps, a little black blood because a long-ago relative engaged in some cross-cultural nookie, how much of the tar-brush would be acceptable - 30% 10% 1%? And how would you know? And what about Indians, Chinese, Malaysians?

In revolutionary Russia it was decided that, because of past history, landowners were "bad" so workers must be "good", and, to make the good-bad dichotomy easy to understand, a worker must, by definition, be someone who owned almost nothing.

Enter the Kulaks - were they sheepish or goatish? Kulaks were middle-income peasants, perhaps employing one or two labourers and owning a few animals. But in this new world order, owning a piece of land, however small, and working it with a paid labourer and a couple of animals, was unacceptable. As a result, the Kulaks were labelled "counter-revolutionaries" who had to be eliminated to keep the spirit of communism pure - at whatever cost. So they were arrested, their farms confiscated and, like in Zimbabwe, the people starved.

And as atheism was one of the basic tenets of Communism ("Every religious idea, every idea of God," Lenin declared, "every flirting with the idea of God, is unutterable vileness"), all those who refused to deny their faith needed to be purged as well (which, of course, included all priests and clergy). And what of intellectuals? Well, they didn't actually produce anything so they, too, needed to be cleansed.

This added up to a *lot* of people. Stalin and his *apparatchiks*, in an orgy of suspicion and revolutionary fervour, worked tirelessly to identify and pull up the weeds. "To educate with executions," as one put it.

Alexander Solzhenitsyn writes of Stalin's paranoia in "The First Circle": *"Distrust of people was the dominating principle of Joseph Stalin; it was his only philosophy of life. He had not trusted his own mother. He did not trust his party members, especially those with the gift of eloquence. He did not trust his comrades in exile, nor did he trust the peasants to sow their grain and harvest the wheat unless he forced them to do it and watched over them. He did not trust the workers to work unless he laid down their production targets. He did not trust the intellectuals to help the cause rather than to harm it. He did not trust the soldiers and the generals to fight without penal battalions and field security squads. He had never trusted his relatives, his wives or his mistresses. He had not even trusted his children."*

Anyone living in Russia, farmer or member of the Politburo, always knew that descent into the inferno was only one careless word or deed away; *anything* you did that might be construed as anti-Communist - the merest suspicion was enough - would lead to arrest, torture and interrogation until you confessed (almost everyone did in the end) - and then came the inevitable questions: *With whom are you collaborating? Who have you been speaking to? Who are your friends?* And the torture would continue until you gave up some name - and then *they* would be arrested and tortured until they gave up some names... And, naturally, because your wife hadn't turned you in for your seditious activities/thoughts/comments against the state, she was guilty too and would be arrested and deported.

And then there were your children...

From the beginning of the October Revolution up to 1959, a total of eighteen million Russian citizens were arrested and sent to gulag detention camps; of these, it is believed that 1,053,829 were worked to death.

Oliver Bullough in "The Last Man in Russia" writes: "Trust between people is what makes us happy. Any totalitarian state is based on betrayal. It needs people to inform on each other, to avoid socialising, to interact only through the state and to avoid unsanctioned meetings. This was unspoken, of course. No official came out and said that the communist state survived only because of suspicion, distrust and slander, but it was true. The greatest enemy of the state was its own people. If they began to trust each other, it could not command their fear and obedience.

"No one trusted anyone; people were living in solitary confinement in the middle of crowds, and it was killing them. Every activity had to be sanctioned by the state. Any person could be an informant. No action could be guaranteed to be without consequence."

"If you always look over your shoulder, how can you still remain a human being?" wrote Alexander Solzhenitsyn in "The First Circle". Stalin and his cohorts had unlimited power and could threaten and torment people until they came to the realisation that resistance was not just futile but wrong.

Now then, what to do with all these arrested enemies of the state? First, one must inter them, separate them from all the good citizens who might be corrupted if allowed to mingle; then they must be punished as a warning to others who might be tempted to stray. And, once interred, why not use them as cheap labour, build the infrastructure, make Russia great again.

And so, the Gulag camps...

"With an iron fist, we will drive humanity to happiness" - sign over the entrance to the Slovki special prison, Solovetsky Islands.

Reminds me somehow of a similarly disingenuous sign in Poland - "*Arbeit Macht Frei*".

At any one time, more than two million people were imprisoned in what Solzhenitsyn referred to as "the world's largest killing machine", the system of labour camps that spread like a contagion throughout the Soviet Union between 1918 and the 1950s. Most prisoners were innocent of any crime, but were forced to work in mines and factories and building sites, developing the nation's infrastructure through the building of roads and railways, working on farms and as lumberjacks.

Life was hard. This description was written by a veteran of a Solovetsky Islands camp and related by Solzhenitsyn:

"At the end of the work day there were corpses left on the work site. The snow powdered their faces. One of them was hunched over beneath an overturned wheelbarrow, he had hidden his hands in his sleeves and frozen to death in that position. Someone had frozen with his head bent down between his knees. Two were frozen back to back leaning against each other. They were peasant lads and the best workers one could possibly imagine. They were sent to the canal in tens of thousands at a time, and the authorities tried to work things out so that no one got to the same subcamp as his father; they tried to break up families. And right off they gave them norms of shingle and boulders that you'd be unable to fulfil even in summer. No one was able to teach them anything, to warn them; and in their village simplicity they gave all their strength to their work and weakened very swiftly and they froze to death, embracing in pairs. At night the sledges went out and collected them. The drivers threw the corpses onto the sledges with a dull clunk. And in the summer the bones remained from corpses which had not been removed in time, and together with the shingle they got into the concrete mixer. And in this way they got into the concrete of the last lock at the city of Belomorsk and will be preserved there forever."

Solzhenitsyn continues: "There was a famous incantation repeated over and over again: 'In the new social structure there can be no place for the discipline of the stick on which serfdom was based, nor the discipline of starvation on which capitalism is based'. And there you are - the Gulag managed miraculously to combine the one with the other."

According to the Soviet way, strict production quotas were imposed on each camp - whether miles of road built, number of trees felled or cubic yards of rock dug out of a mountain. And if the quotas were not met (or could not be falsified), the camp leader would be punished.

Bullough writes: "The prisoners here were units to be worked to death. They died in their thousands, and were not remembered. Mochulsky was told to build an embankment for a bridge over the River Pechora. 'If you pull this off, you will get an award; if you don't, we will shoot you,' his supervisor told him bluntly. With such management techniques, it is hardly surprising that the bosses worked their labourers to death." *(The Last Man in Russia)*

But housing, feeding and clothing millions of prisoners was expensive and the new Soviet administration needed every rouble it could get. The camps needed to pay for themselves, to calculate input-in, work-out algorithms in a way that ignored the humanity of the machines that did the work. So, if someone got their calculations wrong and there wasn't enough food or clothing or housing for the prisoners, an official in Moscow would send out an instruction: *Reduce prisoner numbers.*

But this was not achieved by releasing or transferring a few prisoners, nor even shooting some. It became a matter of cost-analysis: Give the food to those who could do the work. In this way, the weak and the sick and the elderly died quickly and were no longer a drain on resources. It seems the Socialist slogan popularised by Karl Marx "From each according to his means, to each according to his needs" had taken on a more sinister meaning in the camps.

Solzhenitsyn continues: "Multitudes of 'goners', unable to walk by themselves, were dragged to work on sledges by other 'goners' who had not yet become quite so weak. Those who lagged behind were beaten with clubs and torn by dogs. Working in 50 degrees below zero Fahrenheit, they were forbidden to build fires and warm themselves."

And with the twisted logic of early Soviet thinking, ordinary criminals were regarded in the camps as of more worth than the politicals because they - the criminals - had merely committed a crime. For this, they needed to be punished - but politicals were worse, they were *traitors*, and, as such, they were of lower status and were in need of re-education, a realignment of the mind.

Now a mind "unrealigned" could be revealed in a multitude of ways. Again, the details below have been loosely gleaned from Solzhenitsyn's "The Gulag Archipelago":

You could, for example, be arrested for writing a poem. Tanya Khodkevich received a 10-year sentence for writing:

> "You can pray freely
> But just so God alone can hear..."

Furthermore, the religious education of children was classified as a political crime under article 58-10 of the Code: counterrevolutionary propaganda.

Failure to make a denunciation was regarded as a crime. First it was restricted to denunciation of political offences but this was soon extended. Simply failure to report the theft of state or collective farm property earned three years of camp or seven years of exile. This "theft" could be almost anything. For example, tens of thousands of peasants, many of them small children whose parents had sent them out at night to snip ears of corn from the fields because they were starving, were given ten years for what was regarded as an especially dangerous theft of socialist property: grain. And, if, say, a husband were arrested for something, it was inevitable that his wife would be arrested too for failing to denounce him. Children were encouraged to denounce their parents and many thousands did.

Up to 25 years could be imposed for over 205 articles, such as:

Anti-Soviet Agitation

Counter-Revolutionary Activity

Suspicion of Espionage *(suspicion?)*

Contacts leading to suspicion of Espionage *(what contact and what suspicion?)*

Counter-Revolutionary Thought *(thought?)*

Dissemination of Anti-Soviet Sentiments

Socially Harmful Element

Contacts with Dangerous Persons *(what kind of contact?)*

Member of a Family *(of a person convicted under one of the above).*

(The comments in the brackets in italics above are Solzhenitsyn's.)

And the judge had no discretion - the directive laid down the sentence to be imposed and these became increasingly harsher as the years progressed:

1937: ten years; twenty years; execution by shooting.

1943: twenty years hard labour; hanging.

1945: ten years for everyone plus five of disenfranchisement.

1949: twenty-five years for everyone.

"Given the fact that the cases were always fabricated," Solzhenitsyn writes, "violence and torture had to accompany them. As always, the interrogation began with the hypothesis that you were obviously guilty. Interrogator Mironenko, 1944, said: 'Interrogation and trial are merely judicial corroboration. They cannot alter your fate, which was *previously* decided. If it is necessary to shoot you, then you will be shot even if you are altogether innocent. If it is necessary to acquit you, then no matter how guilty you are you will be cleared and acquitted'."

Some other examples, noted by Solzhenitsyn, are informative of how out of control the paranoia had become:

An old man was asked to carry a bust of Stalin to where it would be displayed. It was too heavy for him so he took off his belt, put it around Stalin's neck and carried it this way through the village - 10 years.

A shepherd swore at a cow for not obeying: "You collective farm whore!" - 10 years.

A deaf and dumb carpenter hung his jacket and cap on a bust of Lenin - 10 years.

Children in a collective farm, playing, knocked a poster off a wall. The two eldest were sentenced under Article 58 (under the Decree of 1935, children from the age of 12 had full criminal responsibility for all crimes). Their parents were also sentenced.

A 16-year-old boy made a mistake in Russian in a slogan (it was not his native language) - 5 years.

A woman called Irina Tuchinskaya was arrested when leaving church and charged with "praying in church for the death of Stalin" - Terrorism, 25 years.

Even after serving their ten or twenty five years, prisoners were not free. Many were immediately re-arrested and given another "tenner" on the day of their release. And, most often, "release" meant little more than permanent exile somewhere into a far-off corner of the vast anonymous expanse of the Soviet Union where they would live out the rest of their lives under a cloud of suspicion.

"After Stalin died, people started smiling again; before that, they lived carefully. Without smiles." *Second Hand People* - Svetlana Alexivich.

Chapter Twenty Four

Am I going to get a new mother?

"I am so envious of the people who had an ideal to live up to! Today we are living without one. I want a great Russia. I don't remember it, but I know it existed."

I sit at a plastic table in the Lucky Ace hostel kitchen with three Russian men, labourers by the look of them, shaven-headed and large, their hands work-worn, their stomachs paunched. We eat our breakfast together (after the usual questions and shaking of heads) in a mood of good-natured camaraderie, watching the football on a small screen attached to the wall. We break bread together, literally, as a dry loaf is ripped apart and shared.

Outside, a group of children jump on the roof of a wrecked car then smash the windows with rocks before running away, laughing.

The football is over until the next game and I bide my time, rationing the hours, waiting for my promised rain-less, four-day window with increasing impatience. My body is healing of its aches that seem to become a part of life's ageing, tolerated because ever-present. The weather is good and I am fearful that it will change so I walk about the town and rest and cook my food with the workmen as they cook theirs: potatoes and carrots and chicken and onion. The television fills the kitchen with voices, keeps me company, and I watch it mindlessly, filling in the time before I go to bed and sleep and wake to one day fewer of waiting...

Day after day the sun continues to shine and I yearn to be on the road again. But I need spare tubes, especially for the front wheel. I am fearful of being caught half way across the Kolymer Highway with another ripped-out valve stem and no spare.

On the beach of the Sea of Okhotsk just outside Magadan are the rusted hulls of flat-bottomed barges and a broken pier where fishermen cast their lines, flotsam mixing with the discarded beer tins and empty vodka bottles and pale, fat women who expose their flesh to the sun. In the distance a few hardy souls fling themselves into water that must be freezing, the snow still visible on the surrounding hills.

It is only later I learn that this pier, beaten up and partially collapsing as the ice of successive winters has knocked it about, is the same structure onto which prisoners, sentenced to the Kolymer Gulag, were disembarked during the time of the purges. Having been herded into cattle wagons and transported by train across the USSR to Vladivostok, a journey that could take months, prisoners would then be loaded into cargo holds and shipped to Magadan. Once here, they were unloaded and taken to a transit camp before being dispersed across the region.

One afternoon I visit the Gulag Museum; a middle-aged woman glances up from her mobile phone, nods in reply to my greeting and watches me as my footsteps echo in the empty rooms. I am the only visitor.

In glass cases are the pathetic remains found in what is left of the camps in the surrounding mountains: prisoners' cloth caps; photographs of dark, crumbling stone walls, the remains of a roofless accommodation block, stark against the snow; graves and an exposed skull; a rosary made from knotted string; a pile of snow-hardened boots, twisted and gnarled and oft repaired, like the pitiful display of footwear collected from Auschwitz.

Somehow it is the pathetic personal belongings left behind that speak more eloquently than words of the lives lived and lost in this austere and terrible place.

Then there is a crude Soviet five-pointed star, constructed from rough planks and illuminated by electric bulbs to remind the prisoners that even here the rule of the red star was all powerful; barbed wire; crude iron bars to seal windows, and watchtowers knocked together from rough logs - as if anything other than distance and isolation would be needed to ensure that none could escape; crudely-made tools, wheelbarrows, spades worn to the nub; quilted clothing, threadbare and oft-sewed; the lid of a food tin, perforated by a nail to form a number and nailed to a wooden stake, used to identify a body that had been dignified with a grave burial...

*****

Early morning at the hostel: seven Russian guys watch the football around the communal kitchen table with me - England vs Columbia. They eat leftover supper for their breakfast and we take selfies and together celebrate England's win. It is a special time of togetherness and again I value the cheek-by-jowl existence of the cheap hostel compared to the polished isolation one so often finds in a more expensive hotel.

I discover that Alexander has posted an encouragingly kind message about me on Facebook and a nice-looking lady called Galina, who lives in Vladivostok, asks: "Is he married?" I "friend" her and we have a long translated conversation during the football game.

My daughter sees my new lady friend's question about my marital status and asks, "Am I going to get a new mother?"

(Six months later and widowed Galina, who has come, over time, to understand that I am not interested in a new relationship, has become a real, although virtual, friend with whom I keep in touch each week.)

At midday, I am concerned as I watch fire engines and police cars, sirens wailing, fly past the Lucky Ace in the direction of the coast. I fear a serious tragedy has occurred until a beaming labourer informs me that Russia has just won another game...

Aleksey has located two spare tubes for me. I am ready for the return journey. The sun still shines, I am well rested, the bike serviced and prepared for the journey (sort of). A different route, called the Tenkinskaya Trassa, has been suggested for the first 600km from Magadan to Susuman via Ust-Omchug - a small dirt road leading to the turnoff to the disused Old Summer Road, said to be very beautiful with many passes and fewer vehicles.

Small road... many passes... even fewer vehicles... I'm not sure of the wisdom of this but will go with it. As soon as my wheels begin rolling tomorrow, my long journey home (what an evocative word, *home*) will have begun.

The Road of Bones awaits once again and I am ready.

Chapter Twenty Five

Stray-dog-looking men

"That's how our children will remember us: 'Our parents sold out a great country for jeans, Marlboros, and chewing gum,' they'll say. What made us close our eyes and run to this mother-fucking capitalist paradise? We traded everything we had for cars and rags."

It is early morning and I am confronted in the kitchen by a very hung-over young man, his head shaved clean as a spoon, who has to be shushed by the lady of the hostel for disturbing the sleepers. He apologises like a reproved child but continues speaking loudly, digs a hole in a raw egg and offers it to me to suck - "Give Russian strong!" he assures me.

He wants to compare tattoos, flexes his biceps then adopts a boxer's stance before embracing me as drunken young men do. The other workmen straggle in, wish me a safe journey and I begin to load the bike.

There are no clouds in the sky.

It is the unknown that always engenders fear - the dark presence behind the bedroom door that threatens until the light is turned on. Once the dressing gown is revealed, the fear disappears.

So it has been for me with the Road of Bones. It was an unknown and I was fearful. But now that I've ridden it - albeit in atrocious conditions - it is no longer an unknown and the fear is gone.

And so, I set off from the Lucky Ace with a light heart, confident that my little friend has the fortitude to keep going until the end; my tyres are good, the tubes new (with four spares) and I am ready for anything.

I ride at a sedate pace towards Ust-Omchug along a narrow dirt road with the encroaching trees that threatened me so earlier in this journey. I am enjoying the isolation, the silence, the sense of solitude as snow-patched mountains pass by and the road weaves its way towards the west. I am on my way home.

I come across deep snow high above a long scree slope, pull off the road and switch off.

The silence is crisp and pure as I strip off my riding gear because of the heat and begin to climb. Sharp rocks slide and tumble as I struggle upwards, clinking like metal being struck on metal, sharp in the still air. Reaching the snow, I sit in its cold softness and look out over the tree-covered mountains; I take a handful of snow and put it in my mouth, suddenly aware: *This is Siberian snow, pure, untouched; it could be that my feet rest on rock that no person has ever stood on before...*

Much later, tired and dusty, I reach the small town of Ust-Omchug in the heat of the mid-afternoon. As I ride through its dusty streets, I am reminded of one of those places where, after the world as we know it has come to some violent and apocalyptic end, angry, flat-eyed men range about looking for people to hurt just because they can. Its very name, the sound of it - *Ust-Omchug* - hints of violence and deviance. The battered *khrushchyovka* apartment blocks, ranged like battlements, are difficult to distinguish from the buildings that stand abandoned on the lonely roads of the Kolyma.

Two men lounge on a wooden bench outside a structure made from a rusty shipping container. I pull up and kill the engine. The heat gathers about me like a presence. One, although young, is bald as a potato and has no teeth. The other speaks to me rapidly in Russian.

I ask about somewhere to sleep. They confer, shake their heads, then make a phone call and gesture for me to wait. A man in an old 4X4 arrives, sticks his arm out of the window to shake my hand; another phone call is made. *Follow me,* the driver of the 4X4 gestures and I thank the two young men who return to their bench.

I follow after the man through mouldering tenements along an atrocious road - *Sing Sing,* I think to myself, feeling as if I am entering that notorious prison where amoral men with tattoos smudged like bruises on their bony limbs grin while they commit atrocities on other men in the showers.

Mothers push babies in prams along dirt streets; children play in a brightly-painted playground; a truck trundles past, spraying water to lay the dust; old women sit on crude benches outside their tenement doors, watching life pass by; from a hundred identical windows comes the mutter of radios.

Wait here, the man gestures.

A group of young men in their twenties begin to gather, stray-dog-looking men with shaven heads and bad teeth, wet lips and stringy muscles on their arms like bicycle tyres, their trousers loose on their hips - the kind of men who make you wish you were somewhere else or, at the very least, had your back to a wall and only a little money in your wallet.

They greet me, smiling their ragged smiles and gathering about, examining the bike.

"*Vy Anglichanan?*" one asks in Russian. "*Na Suzuki?*"

"*Da -*" I nod. They look at each other blankly as if I have told them I come from outer space.

A lady arrives and greets me. Her name is Magda. *Come,* she gestures and I follow her into a building that authorities in any normal country would condemn, stringing yellow tape across the entrance to deter bored teenagers from killing themselves or lighting fires.

I leave my bike with everything on it in the care of the young men, not worrying for a moment that anything will be stolen or damaged.

The apartment on the fourth floor is Spartan but clean. Malthoid on the floor, peeling pink wallpaper; the toilet doesn't flush (but there's a bucket and a tap) and there's no hot water; the fridge is warm and smells of sour milk. But Magda fusses and *tutts* me in Russian and insists on hanging up my jacket.

Back at my bike and the lads are still there. They want to carry all my kit up to the room, which they do, grabbing the panniers and tank bag and toiling their way up the four flights of stairs, depositing them in my room and shaking my hand with their hard, bony fingers and then leaving.

"How much?" I ask Magda in Russian, my arm sweeping the apartment.

At first she seems to say 800 roubles but then she speaks rapidly and seems to want to hug me. I don't understand so she dials a number, hands me the phone and a man with a thick Russian accent tells me, "No charge - you are our friend." (I leave the R800 on the bed when I head off the next morning.)

Later, at the corner *magazin* I buy a potato, carrot, onion and some pasta for my supper. An old man with a hooked nose approaches me, some small change held in his hand. I don't understand what he says to me but his voice has the tone of someone asking for money. Then I realise that the lady at the till has turned him away because he doesn't have enough to pay for his purchases: a half-loaf of bread and a beer. I open my wallet and ask him how much he needs. He shows me a rouble coin and holds up five fingers - five roubles or roughly 5p. I give him ten roubles and he thanks me as if I have been excessively generous. I feel like a fraud. He goes back to the counter, completes his purchase and walks out with the bread and beer.

I walk about this ratty, *Apocalypse Now* town and see the children and the cats and the old women gossiping outside the entrances to their unspeakable tenements and the young men discussing what young men the world over discuss with sniggers and covert glances and I realise that, despite being alone, I am amongst people who are the salt of the earth and a sense of peace settles on my soul.

And then suddenly I remember that today Glynis and I would have been celebrating our wedding anniversary - 44 years.

*****

Later, on the steps outside my apartment, four stories down, three old women wearing shapeless dresses lean towards each other and talk. Their voices float up to me like the chirrupings of birds. They have gold teeth and wear scarves tied about their heads.

Outside of town, the river runs shallow and dimpling and clear as ice. A woman lies on the stony bank in her bra and pants, exposing her pale fat to the evening sun.

An old UAZ on the other side of the river engages low range, slithers down the gravel bank and drives across through the water. Further down the river an older man with red whiskers and no upper teeth approaches me; his open shirt reveals a livid scar from abdomen to his sternum. He seems to be asking for money and I demonstrate that I do not have my wallet with me but he negates this with his hands, asks me where I am from and when I tell him he clasps my hand and then hugs me to his bony chest in a tight embrace.

I walk across the river on a cable-stayed footbridge and through a rotting settlement on the other side where dogs bark at me. The sound of the river flowing over its shallow gravel banks is loud in the still evening air.

Three men in their early thirties sit on a river-washed log in front of a fire close to the water. Their voices tell me that they have been drinking. I approach them and we shake hands. One has rotten teeth and his grip crushes my hand. They are shirtless, their torsos lean as whippets. One, called Sergei, pale-skinned and unshaven, has a tattoo of a skull gripped in a fist on his arm and the Madonna and child across his stomach. They ask if I'm American and I tell them I'm British and they smile and exclaim. I sit with them on the smooth-skinned log, white-bleached from the sun; they offer me vodka in a crumpled plastic cup. I accept, stressing *malenkie* - small! They pour me cup full and break off a piece of stale bread.

We toast Russia and England and drink. They offer me more but I decline and they don't insist. Instead, they fill their own plastic cups and drink deeply, as one would water. It's going to be a drink-yourself-motherless night, I can see. I leave them to their drinking and walk on. Their parting salutations are genuine and effusive.

These are the young men who will die young, pencilled tallies on a statistician's sheet; lads with vodka in their veins and tar in their lungs and eyes filled with an empty desperation that this throw-away place in the wilds of eastern Siberia will be unable to satisfy.

When I return to my apartment block, two young ladies, a little worse for the wear from alcohol, blow me kisses. In my room, there are dead things in the sugar and my bed feels as if there are a number of knot-headed dwarves living inside the mattress.

*****

Late when the old women are sleeping, a knocking on my door quiet as a murmur and I open it and one of the young ladies who blew me kisses is there with soft red lips and slippers on her feet, her eyes asking me a question even as they glance sideways towards the wall and my blood roars through my veins; some buttons are loose near the top of her blouse and the flesh of her is sweet there, the shadows musty-sweet, the knobs of her shoulders showing smooth through the cloth of her blouse and her red-wet mouth says *Nine hundred* and with the blood roaring in my temples I shake my head, sadness like a rebuke lying cold on me and quickly she says *Five hundred* and I want to take her warm and alive in my arms and press her contours into mine, hungry for her woman smell, the blood-warmth of her flesh, oh!, the touch of her skin, oh!, but numb with the fatigue of negation and exhausted with the wrestling in my own deep soul, oh!, I smile so so sad for both me and for her and I close the door softly with hot blood still loud in my ears and lie myself down with the musty dwarves living inside my mattress.

Chapter Twenty Six

Feral dogs and a disturbed man

"The Soviet regime? It wasn't ideal, but it was better than what we have today. Worthier. No one was excessively rich or poor, there were no bums or abandoned children... Old people could live on their pensions, they didn't have to collect bottles and food scraps off the street. They wouldn't look at you with searching eyes, standing there with outstretched palms... We've yet to count how many people were killed by perestroika."

I leave Ust-Omchug early and am on the road in the cool of the morning, just as the sun lifts above the horizon and lies yellow on the road with even the stones casting long shadows. The dirt is basically good, the trees and the mountains a continuing presence and, with these as my only companions, I ride through an empty land, the taiga, Siberian boreal forest, all day. At times it feels as if I am riding through the far north of Alaska, the rivers and streams flowing clear and blue, the sky cloudless.

Then, in the distance, I see buildings strangely bright against the dark trees, concrete anomalies that jar the senses. It is the abandoned town of Kadykchan and I take the dirt road there; the rectangular concrete *Krushchyovka* apartment blocks stand lonely and loose with their dark windows empty now of the bright faces of children, sad mausoleums to all those who once lived here.

I park my bike on a main street and switch off the engine. The wind has got up and it moves through the trees with lonely murmurings. Mosquitoes whine about my ears and I need to flap constantly to keep them at bay. A car is parked on the roadside but on closer inspection it's an abandoned wreck. Paint flakes from bare walls and wires hang loose from poles already beginning to lean. Where there once was a shop, faded advertising posters flutter in the wind. A movement within this stillness of dead things tugs at the corner of my eye: it is a pack of dogs, five of them, large, hairy and of indeterminate breed. They approach me, huff a few times then make off as soon as I turn to face them, as if afraid I might fling a rock. And then there is a man. He has about him the creased look of a rough sleeper and he plods along the muddy road towards me following the outthrust keel of his grizzled beard; he passes within a metre of me without any acknowledgement, as if he hasn't seen me. And then he is gone.

It seems somehow right that the only life in this place are feral dogs and a man more at home within the disturbed workings of his own brain.

Then with the wind still gusting between these silent walls, the rain comes - not hard, but annoying - and I don my waterproofs and ride on through a wet and muted land.

*****

Sometimes during the long day, when a trillion images will enter one's retina, a particular scene will stand out from the passing blur and imprint itself onto the memory. For me, today, it was this: After Kadykchan and a few dark hours of mizzling rain, suddenly the sun flared bright above me like a child pleased with life and the rain-slick road ahead seemed to glow an ethereal yellow against the darkness of the trees and the sky...

Such are the insignificant things that bring pleasure to the long-distance traveller and lift a weary spirit.

And, after the rain, came the heat.

It is only when you stop your bike on the roadside and the silence envelops you like a living thing and the dust begins to settle that you come to understand something of the punishment laden bikes have to endure when travelling thousands of kilometres over rough, dirt roads; you feel the heat rise from the ground and hear the small clicks and ticks from the engine as the metal adjusts itself; you see up close the rocks embedded in the track and the corrugations that looked so benign from above and you realise that the tyres and the suspension and every nut and bolt holding this delicate machine together have to absorb that punishment, hour after hour, day after day.

I mention this because at some point in the afternoon my bike hesitated as if a cord or bungee or some piece of roadside debris had become snagged in the chain momentarily before ripping free. It was a sufficiently serious hesitation for me to pull over and investigate. Nothing seemed amiss. As the heat rested on me, and the weight of my riding jacket became oppressive and I realised just how tired and dirty I was, I concluded that, for that brief hesitation, my engine must have died before picking up again. And my vulnerability way out in the midst of nowhere became an issue again.

I fired up the engine and set off, listening with one ear to the heartbeat of my little bike, a pulse I have come to depend so much on.

The heat has become unpleasant; I ride with an open oven door in front of my face. My fear is back and it discomforts me. My rear tyre is being ripped apart by the sharp stones embedded in the road and the knobbles are worn to the nub. I'm not sure the tyre can make it the 1,000ks back to Yakutsk, but there's nothing I can do about that except slow down and try to miss the rocks.

In the intense heat of the early afternoon, a high-pitched sound begins to emerge from the front of the bike. I assume it's the front wheel bearings beginning to seize. I have spares, but not relishing the idea of attempting to replace them on the side of the road in the heat and dust, I stop, pour oil over the bearings and press on. I wonder, though, whether it might have been coming from the engine, the terrible heat nipping the piston in the barrel.

Just 1,000ks to some degree of safety, I tell myself, willing the bike on.

Late in the afternoon, hot and uncomfortable, I make it into Susuman, covered with dust that has worked its way into every pore. Just seven days before, I had ridden into this same town soaked and freezing, an inch of mud clinging to most surfaces of my bike. I'm not sure which I prefer - the heat or the cold.

Neither, perhaps.

Later, a Finnish biker whom I had met in Magadan on his large Africa Twin pulls up outside my hotel. The heat is of concern to him too. The clothes I have washed and hung over my bike are dry within half an hour.

Kneeling in the stones and gravel, I remove my front wheel and replace the bearings, using a handy rock as a hammer. My left front shock seals have blown and oil pours over the front brake disk and is flicked back by the wind over my jeans and the rest of the bike. We are looking rather sad at the moment, my little friend and I, but still strong.

Because of the heat and the stress it places on us, I plan to wake early and get away by 3am for the long 600km stretch to Khandyga. Edvard, the Finnish guy, will be following later so will catch up with me along the road if I break down.

My headlight has given up the ghost so I hope there will be sufficient light to travel by.

Oh, dear...

Chapter Twenty Seven

A rosy-cheeked child on a reindeer

The road without a border with the horizon, I wonder what a lonely pilgrim thinks about overcoming this uninhabited monotonous path?

(Message to me from Galina, Vladivostok, my social media friend.)

I had set my alarm for 3am so I could break the back of this 600km stretch to Khandaga before the heat could lay its heavy hand on us.

I awake with a start. The room is light - have I overslept? I look at my watch and it tells me *Ten*.

In the morning?

Then my brain begins to function and I realise that it's still night, still the day before, as it were, the same day as yesterday... or today. Whatever. I'd slept for three hours. But then, *What the hell*, I think to myself, I'm awake now, let's just *do* it. And, anyway, if I were to set off at 3am, as originally planned, I would still be riding in the intense heat of the day before I reached Khandaga. However, if I leave now, I'll be there by mid-morning, well before the heat begins to oppress.

I pack up quietly so as not to wake the other sleepers, load the bike while the mosquitoes are still resting, and set off into that strange half light of a northern summer where a book can be read outside at midnight without the need for light.

Mist hides the bowls of trees on either side of the road so that only the dark froth of their leaves and upper branches are visible. The road is a pale narrow ribbon through the sepia light and I ride through a silent daguerreotype world. The pale glimmer of my park light is little more than a yellow smudge on the road ahead but will, hopefully, illuminate me in case I meet a truck on a dark mountain bend. The sky is pale and low under the horizon, holding still the last flush of the sun that moves slowly from west to east on a flat trajectory rather than the dramatic, sudden dipping in the tropics. The air is still warm, trapping within its molecules the intense heat of the day and the dry smell of dust from the road.

Occasionally I ride into cold pockets of air that taste of the night and the swamps and muddy ponds hidden between dark trunks of trees that glint silver in the twilight as I pass. They remind me - the cold pockets of air - of my long childhood walk with my father and brother from Durban to Lourenco Marques in Mocambique when we would continue to walk into the night or wake early and begin in the before-dawn dark, finding these strange, cold air-pools gathering in road dips and along the banks of rivers, smelling of Africa.

I ride carefully, favouring my worn tyres, happy that the engine is being properly cooled; it really doesn't need the added burden of near 40-degree heat as well as the multitude of other stresses I have thrust upon the poor little beast during this journey. But now she purrs sweetly in the eerie half dark and I begin to relax, revelling in the strange sensation of riding all night.

In a way, it is like a childhood adventure - creeping out into the darkness, playing *tok-tokkie* on neighbours' dark doors, a midnight feast of a ride into the night.

And it is beautiful! Mist gentles the landscape, rising like a veil above the ponds and swampy places on either side of the road, the rivers reflecting the bloody colours of the sky; there is a softness about the landscape lost during the heat of the day, when colour is leached from the air and things are harsh and blunt. In this light, even the dirt of the road, the very stones, seem softer, more welcoming.

I am happy in my solitary ride through the night air and I make steady progress across this smothered land, the trees and the rivers and the mountains moving past like ghosts in the pale light.

It turns cold - suddenly, as if the last exhaling of warm breath from the day has lifted, begun its rising that will form the ballooning dark clouds of the next day and the afternoon rain. I begin to shiver but console myself with the thought that it's better me too cold than my engine too hot, and I hold my now zip-less jacket about me with my left hand to preserve some body heat and ride on.

Some time after 3am I begin to fall asleep. I wake to find myself, oddly, riding my bike somewhere along a dirt road amongst the rocks and mountains of a strange land. I tell myself that I have been sleeping - momentarily, in all probability - but asleep nonetheless. I shake my head and ride on. It happens again, this time as I approach a corner. I wake and find myself on the wrong side of the road, confused and disorientated. Stand on the pegs, raise my visor to let the cold air beat against my skin, sit and fall asleep again. Even in the act of forcing my eyes open, I feel the weight of the lids dragging down... and down... and with a jerk I wake again. I know I should stop, lie in the roadside dust with my jacket as a pillow and sleep, know that sleep-riding off a cliff or into the forest in this place is not to be contemplated. If I died here, deep off-road in the mountains amongst the shadows of trees, if I were to break a leg or my back, no one would ever find me. I would join the statistics of those who have disappeared without trace here in the Russian far east. But I don't. I stand up on the pegs, bash my hand against my helmet, slap my face *hard*, shout and sing - and keep on riding.

The drowsiness passes and I am still alive. But then the hallucinations begin. It's a strange experience. I see a rosy-cheeked woman leading a rosy-cheeked child on a reindeer. They are very real; they could have stepped out of a tourist brochure for Lapland. I tell myself that what I have just seen is impossible, that I am hallucinating, but then their dog chases me - and I'm not sure whether the dog itself is not a hallucination. Pale-barked logs on the roadside take on living forms, get up from their slumber and walk about, stare at me; I see animals moving amongst the trees and people who stand mutely and watch as I pass. They have about them a disturbing reality that flutters between wakefulness and dreams. And then, strangely, I find myself outside my body looking down at myself riding. I observe this person that is me change gear to take a corner, see the dusty clothes I am wearing, the load strapped to my bike from above, the pale plume of dust hanging behind my wheels. And during that time I have a profound understanding of myself such as I've never had before, looking down and seeing myself foreshortened, the flesh and blood of me, the *me-ness* of me, my weaknesses and my faults, all that has made me into me over the many years of my life. And I know I'm hallucinating; know that I'm not, in reality, hovering above myself looking down, looking into the very soul of me, but I'm still there, watching, observing this other person that I now know so well and with such bitter clarity. After a while, perhaps another brief sleep, I don't know - it was a disjointed time - I return to myself, back into my body, my mind, and ride on.

At about four in the morning the sun finally breaks free of the horizon; it is behind me so I catch only glimpses of it in my mirrors as it emerges from behind a mountain, an intense red ball, mist-occluded, radiating little light and no warmth, covering the world with rust.

I begin to count down the kilometres in hundreds: into the 5's... into the 4's... now the 3's...

The low sun begins to draw webs of mist off the surface of water, the lakes and ponds and wide, swift-flowing rivers, mist that hangs trapped in the branches of trees. Stones in the road cast long shadows and the sepia landscape begins to take on colour.

My rear tyre is wearing fast now - I can notice the difference each time I stop - a little less left on the knobblies, more bits ripped off the edges, star-shaped cuts where a rock has penetrated but not quite punctured the tube. But now I am into the tens - 90... 80... 70... All is well with the world.

I'm going to make it. After this, just one more day - a short one at that, just 450ks and then the wide Lena River and Yakutsk and the train and Omsk and a hop, skip and jump to Europe. 60... 50...

Nearly there.

By now both front fork seals have burst and a fine spray of oil covers everything, even smudging the glass of my instruments. My boots are bright with oil, my jeans yellow to the calf where dust has clung to the wet.

40... 30... 20... Oh, the relief! Bed, some food...

The engine dies.

Without warning, without hesitation or stumbling, it's gone. My speed quickly drops, a Doppler-effect of despair as I fumble with a petrol tap, flip it onto reserve in the vain hope that my fuel is low, waiting for the hiccough, the stutter as fuel runs through... but there's nothing.

My wheels come to a stop on the side of the road, in the dust, amongst the stones and the trees, the silence pressing down on me, the heat beginning to rise from the road.

Chapter Twenty Eight

Unwritten laws for extreme travellers

"The world shattered into dozens of colourful little pieces. We were so terribly eager for the grey Soviet everyday to turn into an American film."

The engine is dead. So near...

I flip the right-hand fuel tap onto reserve in case there's a blockage on the left, give it a moment to flow through and press the starter. Nothing. Stand next to the bike feeling helpless. I've passed no vehicles on this road for - what? - seven hours. Nothing in my Rotopax fuel container - I used that in the early morning hours.

An engine noise fills the silence with hope; a plume of dust approaches and I flag down the car. "How far to Khandyga?" I ask in Russian.

"Eighteen kilometres."

"No *benzin*," I tell him, pointing to the tank. I hold up my spare fuel container and ask if he could drive to Khandyga, buy me some fuel and bring it back. He nods.

I give him the container and a thousand roubles and he drives away leaving me to the lonely company of the road and the trees. Of course I might never see him, my fuel container or my money again but I trust him as I have trusted all Russians so far on this trip. When you're helpless on the side of a road, trust is pretty much all you've got left.

While waiting, I oil my chain, check the bike over and then, on a whim, open the fuel cap. Odd - there's at least four litres still in there. I press the starter and she fires up. *Damn!* I decide to ride on and meet my Samaritan coming back. I strap on my panniers and set off, slowly, but within 200 metres, the engine dies again. Now what? This time she won't start again.

I unload again, piling my stuff in the dirt. The sun is higher now and already the heat is unpleasant. I know it's electrical and begin to look for obvious faults: a bare wire or loose connection, perhaps. Tracing an intermittent fault in a wiring loom is well beyond my pay grade.

Nothing obvious. Try the starter again. Nothing. Select neutral, press the starter and she fires, putters away happily. *Yes!* Select first gear - the engine dies. Neutral, she fires up. Engage a gear and the engine dies.

Ah! I *know* what the fault is - the side-stand cut-off switch, an annoying and unnecessary safety device that Gareth and I disconnected when we were preparing the bikes for Central Asia. All I have to do is trace the wires to where we joined them, reconnect - problem solved.

But for the life of me I can't find the wires. I lie under the bike, in the dirt, in the stifling heat, flapping at impudent flies, and feel about; remove the front sprocket guard, follow wires with oily fingers. Nothing.

I hear another engine: It's Edvard on his Africa Twin. Travelling faster than me, he's caught up. I'm hoping he's some hot-shot auto electrician who will say: *Side-stand cut-off switch? No problem - here...* and Bob's your Uncle, sorted. But he isn't.

"Is your air filter blocked?" he suggests instead. "Lots of dust," and I realise he knows less than I do, which is saying something.

I continue to lie in the dirt and fiddle about, looking for those two loose or poorly joined wires, grit in my eyes, while Edvard stands about, waiting. I remove the seat and the side covers, fiddle about inside bundles of dusty wires like a child examining a toy he has dismantled and can't put back together. My usual approach to electrical trouble-shooting is to peer vaguely at the rat's nest of wires and hope that something obviously wrong will leap out at me. Where's Gareth with his multi-meter when need him?

Nothing. Engine fires up in neutral; kick into and gear and it dies.

An engine noise and my Samaritan returns with the fuel. Although unnecessary, I empty it into the tank - perhaps unconsciously hoping that this might change something. It doesn't.

I need to get to Khandyga, find a place to stay, clear my head and approach the problem logically, systematically, tracing each wire until I find it.

"Can you tow me?" I ask Edvard hopefully, assuming this to be the logical solution, something Gareth and I would do, have done a few times before. In fact, I wonder why he hasn't already offered.

"No," he says, straight-faced and somewhat to my surprise. "I don't tow."

"Why?" I ask him, expecting him to break into a smile and say, *Gotcha!*

"I towed someone once," he says, "and I fell over. I won't do it again."

I am confused. Big, tough biker. I've always believed in the age-old maxim that it's not how many times you fall down that makes a man, it's the number of times you get up again.

I look at him in his biker gear, still wondering whether he's joking, whether he's going to laugh and move his bike in front of mine, ready for the tow, but he doesn't. I am confused: I know that if he were broken down, I would tow his heavy Africa Twin with my little DR even if we had to wait until the day cooled before we attempted it; that if, in the attempt, I dropped my bike a few times we'd have a chortle together - *Oops, bummer!* - pick it up and press on again.

My Samaritan - whose name, I discover, is Egan, has hung about. *Will you tow me?* I ask using sign language. He nods and we tie a strap to his bumper, wrap it twice around my handlebars, the end to be gripped in my hand for quick release in case I fall and am being dragged, and off we go, slowly, all eighteen long, painful kilometres, my right hand and shoulder muscles spasming with the strain of countering for an hour the rope's sideways pull.

Edvard, to give him credit, rides behind me all the way but then, as we reach the outskirts of Khandyga, he disappears.

And here I have to pause in my tale to say this, although some of you might take issue with me here: I believe that, by disappearing in my hour of need, he broke the unwritten laws of all extreme travellers: *Never leave a fellow traveller without food, water, spares, broken down or whatever until you know he or she is OK; give whatever aid you can before moving on; always ask whether it's OK to leave.*

Just saying...

Anyway, Egan tows me to a wooden house that doubles as a guesthouse and I unload, shower then brave the heat to strip the bike and, methodically, look until I find those wires. And it's not long before I discover a badly chafed wire behind the headlight, insulation worn away, bare wire exposed. Hopeful, I tape it up and press the starter, get on the bike and select first gear. The engine keeps running! Found it!

An indescribable feeling of joy and accomplishment comes over me and I behave like a silly person for a while, shouting and punching the air. Now, find some fuel and I'll be ready for tomorrow and the final section of the Road of Bones. My GPS tells me there is fuel two and a bit kilometres away so I mount up and, filled with a sense of purpose and elation, I ride through town and into the outskirts following stony, pot-holed tracks until, just before I reach the fuel station, with despair knotting my stomach, the engine dies again.

Same problem. I've achieved nothing.

Crestfallen and depressed, I begin the exhausting task of pushing my bike in the intense heat along a yielding, rocky track two kilometres back to the guesthouse. At times during that push I wonder what it's doing to my heart but all seems OK so I press on, resting when my body can't take any more.

Back at the guesthouse, I collapse onto my bed, bathed in sweat. What to do? I decide to see if there is an Internet signal on my phone, stand up and the room begins to lie on its side and my knees give way. I brace myself against the wall, head hanging, and wait for the world to come back but my lady host has seen me and guides me back to my bed. I hear her on the phone and, shortly afterwards, a nurse with Mongolian features appears. She takes my pulse and makes questioning noises so I get my phone out and type on the translator: *I'm just tired. 3 hours sleep, rode bike 12 hours and no food since yesterday.*

She gives instructions; the Russian man sharing my room makes me sugary coffee and my lady host prepares *borsh* and fusses about me like a mother.

Afterwards I feel a little better but know I will have a restless and unhappy night if I don't sort out my bike so, resisting their protestations that I should remain lying down, I go onto an Internet forum and write the following notes in my journal:

- Wire attached to clutch lever
- Connector under the seat
- A wire across the front of the engine, just as it passes the horn, there is a green connector.

I know it's not the first because there are no wires connected to the clutch lever. But I brave the late afternoon heat, remove the seat and check for wires. Nothing. One left. I'm doubtful because I don't remember any wire across the front of the engine but I crouch down and peer into the shadow near the horn - and immediately I see it: a green connector and I know this is it. I quickly remove the wires, reconnect them and fire up the engine, select a gear and she continues running, sweet as a nut!

Oh, the intensity of joy! I'm not sure that there can be *any* feeling quite like the one you get when, tired, hot, dirty and alone in a foreign land with a broken-down vehicle you manage to find and sort the problem so that your journey can continue... a lifting of the spirit, the removal of a heavy burden, a setting free of the soul!

My room mate who had made me sweet coffee and I walk to the local *magazin* and buy beer to celebrate; he also buys a tin of disgusting-smelling fish that he insists I share; I buy fruit - it's too hot to eat anything else.

Job done. One more sleep, one more long push to safety and an easy life.

PS After returning to the UK at the end of my journey, Edvard made contact with me via social media. I asked him (rather bluntly, I'm afraid) why he had abandoned me in my hour of need. He explained that shortly after he had found a guesthouse somewhere else in the town he collapsed from heat-stroke and had spent the rest of the afternoon recovering.

I'll take his word for it.

Chapter Twenty Nine

I am a man

"Today, it's embarrassing to be Russian. Our parents lived in the country of victors, we live in the country that lost the Cold War. We have nothing to be proud of."

I wake early, eager not to miss the ferry across the Aldan River that leaves at 7. Because of the ferry, I have no option but to ride through the heat of the day. The thirty kilometres of jumbled rocks that passes for a road to the ferry crossing is not an auspicious start and I wonder whether my tyres will make it.

At the river, the ferry is waiting, tethered to the sand by a single cable, and I plough through soft sand and onto the ramp. A very loud and hung-over deckhand entertains me on the hour-long trip down river, communicating in slurred Russian and not deterred by my repeated assurances that I do not understand.

At last we nudge the far bank, drop the heavy ramp and I accelerate through the soft sand onto another atrocious road that attempts, for the next 120ks, to beat my poor little bike to death. This is the type of road hated by all bikers, constructed with a layer of fine white sand, almost powder, over a bed of sharp rocks. Over time, the sand is pushed and ridged onto the sides and middle, exposing the rocks, some loose, some embedded - and over this surface one is forced to ride. There is no other way.

In places like Kazakhstan, an abusive road is treated with contempt by the drivers of trucks - they simply leave it and make their own way across the smooth sameness of the steppe; firm sand and a sparse covering of tufty grass makes this easy and while the bad road is left to its own devices (much to the annoyance of the government who spent vast sums to build it, I am sure) smooth, firm, sandy tracks weave their silky way across the steppe like the branching threads of streams.

But here, in the taiga, an impenetrable barrier of trees confines all roads and one has no option but to ride over them. Usually, on most dirt roads one can find a smooth section - on the edges or in the middle - but on this road (dare I grace it with that term? - *abusive track)*, attempt to seek the deceptively smoother edges and you are immediately bogged in deep, fine sand. In between these tracks are high ridges of scree so one is forced into the ruts left by the passing of decades of heavy trucks.

Fearing for my tyres, I ride slowly, attempting to miss the biggest and sharpest rocks. And as I grimace and curse and endure, I wonder yet again how any machine can remain intact after being subjected to a beating this prolonged, this extreme, without breaking apart. That it didn't is testimony to the design and construction of this dated but magnificent machine.

Of course, on a long trip like this, it is impossible not to anthropomorphise one's bike, especially when travelling alone; the bike becomes one's daily companion, a mechanical presence with temperament and moods akin to all sentient beings (except that it doesn't sulk or bear a grudge) and subjecting my little friend to this relentless abuse became akin in my mind to repeatedly beating a child and not explaining why.

Trucks that blunder their way past me fill the air with a cloud of white dust so thick that all visibility except for a few metres in front of the wheel is obliterated. Slow down and you risk being killed by a truck coming from behind; in that obscuring cloud of dust, no driver would see you until he felt the crushing of your bones under his wheels. With all visibility in front gone, I ride blind for an uncomfortable length of time, hoping I am keeping to my side or that the road hasn't curved away; in the disorientating, opaque swirl of white I grip the bars, terrified that I might have strayed into the path of an oncoming truck. There is nothing I can do but pray and verbally abuse the truck drivers and press on blind until the dust begins to settle and, ever so slowly, reveal the darker outlines of things - until the next truck bellows past and smothers me with more dust.

It is two long hours before the road begins to improve and I ride in the heat through a land bleached of colour, an atmosphere paled by dust and the smoke from forest fires that plague the taiga each summer. By now I am filthy with a layer of dust covering my clothes, sand in my teeth and my eyes, oil from the blown forks spewing onto my jeans and boots which absorb a thick layer of sand only to be coated with oil again. The heat is enervating and by midday I can feel my body weakening. Just 200ks to go.

At last a truck-stop cafe. I can begin to smell civilization. Outside is parked a UAZ 4X4, the occupants standing about in the sun. I park my bike and wearily swing my leg over, remove my helmet and gloves. The occupants of the UAZ stare at me; one lifts a camera. I make my slow way up some wooden stairs hearing my boots thud on the wood - and suddenly, very powerfully, into my mind comes the profound conviction: *I am a man...* For that moment - and the experience takes on almost existential significance for me and, in a way, has defined this entire journey - as my dust-encrusted boots thump up those wooden stairs, helmet and gloves in my hands, I am Clint Eastwood dismounting from his sweat-soaked horse, stepping with dusty, spurred boots up the creaking steps of a dark-cool saloon where he orders whisky, double and I'll keep the bottle, carries both to a table, sits, lights a cheroot, tosses down the first and pours another, leans back on his chair and tips his hat down over his eyes because he's not afraid of anyone and even in his not seeing he is at ease in this room full of resentful and trigger-happy men who glance at him warily and know it. And walking up those stairs with the occupants of the UAZ watching me, taking photographs, I can feel the testosterone pulse through my veins and smell it rise from my skin and I could have taken on the whole world and won; the sweat and dust and oil defines me and I *know* that I am a man; know that I have taken all the shit that this journey has thrown at me and I've not given up; I've seen it through.

And throughout the rest of the day, now that the land becomes more peopled as I near Yakutsk, whenever I stop, men approach me, wanting to talk, to take photographs.

It is the state of me and my bike - our obvious physical distress, the haggard, oil-splattered state of us - that speak of hard times and trials beyond that which normal people encounter in their daily lives and that, for some reason, draw men to us and I am humbled and uplifted by the experience.

*****

For the next 200ks the road surface changes from stone to sand, a smoother ride but the sand is gouged and pitted with deep ruts and dips and again I find the bike taking a beating. I know I should slow down but I don't. The end is too near and its call is hard to resist. Finally, 30ks from the banks of the Lena River, the good tar returns. Nothing can stop us now.

A ferry is about to disembark. I ride up the metal ramp, park my bike between two large 6WD Kamaz trucks, kill the engine and drag myself wearily off the bike.

A group of men watch me. I approach them, and ask, "Yakutsk?" It's a stupid question but I don't want to make a mistake when so close to home.

"Da," they nod, taking in the state of me with their eyes.

It is done.

I strip off my gear and stand at the bow, willing the water to rush by and wondering how many times over the past two weeks and 4,000kms I have thought about this moment, the time when I would have completed my solo, double crossing of the Road of Bones and am now safe, carried along peacefully by a battered, rust-covered ferry - a vehicle I am not riding, not responsible for, in the hands of someone else - while I relax and watch the water move across her battered plates and feel in my bones the throb of her engines.

Chapter Thirty

My car just every day swearing

"I'm learning how to be a free person. I don't want to die the way I am now, all Soviet. I'm dredging the Sovietness out of myself by the bucketful..."

And so, another phase of my journey begins. Tomorrow I will place my small creature into the hands of people who will knock up a crate of some kind and load her into a dark train carriage bound for Omsk, due to arrive there, so I am told, in a month's time.

A *month!* Something to do with floods, I am told, but communication is difficult. So I have booked a flight 800ks south to the town of Neryungri where, an eternity ago, I spent a night on my way north. It took me two long days to reach Yakutsk from there; the flight will take two hours. I will then board a train that will continue south to Tynda and then west for four days, brushing the northern shore of Lake Baikal at Severobaykalsk on the way to Novosibirsk. It's everyone's dream, I think, to ride the trans-Siberian railway and I have the privilege of exploring a section of it.

So, for a month I will enter the world of the back-packer, become one with the earnest 20-somethings out to discover the world. And the responsibility for getting me wherever I decide to go will be someone else's, not mine. I won't have to worry about a stuttering engine or worn tyres or the heat or punctures or oil spraying over me from blown fork seals. It's a different lifestyle, one I haven't experienced before.

I celebrate my new-found freedom with pizza and a glass of rather earthy red. And while I sip my wine, I think to myself: this is what Russia is all about - *earthy.*

The Russian far east is not Moscow nor is it St Petersburg. They are different countries, worlds apart. The Far East is Asian; the west, European. Here, the harshness of the climate, the brief blooming of summer, the limitations imposed by impossible distances leave little time for refinement. Buildings are utilitarian and erected quickly, rough-shod - quick-quick, before the ice shuts you down. You need heating or you die so the state provides piped hot water for all buildings and there is no choice about the temperature. The massive, lagged pipes carrying the hot water are often laid deep in channels covered with rough-cast concrete slabs; from these, steel hoops often protrude, a trap for the unwary, the old or the partially sighted.

In fact, being disabled in the Russian far east must be interesting, to say the least: pavements wiggle about like creatures in pain and will have holes calf-deep or large blocks of concrete or reinforcing rods or the stumps of trees sticking out of them in the same way that the roads have pot-holes and reinforcing rods and manhole covers that jut out of the surface or collapse into it leaving exposed cliffs and holes that will write off any car that hits them. In fact, I can't remember seeing a manhole laid flush with a road surface anywhere in Russia (well, perhaps I exaggerate a little here).

But there is no namby-pamby compensation culture here - *Oooh, I tripped over loose brick in the pavement and sprained my ankle. Give me £5,000,000.* I can imagine the response of Russian authority to someone trying to make a claim for a broken leg as a result of falling down a hole in the pavement - *You should look where you're going next time, comrade.*

(I don't think people are referred to as "comrade" here any more. My bad.)

Flex your muscles, toss back a vodka, touch two fingers against your jugular, shout *Rus-si-a!* and laugh. *This is Russia - if you don't like it, piss off.*

Later I post on social media a light-hearted comment about Russians playing tricks on the disabled, attaching some photographs of wheelchair ramps with wooden slats missing, massive holes and bits of concrete and reinforcing rod sticking out of pavements and manhole covers missing. Expecting a few guffaws, I receive a number of sad and angry responses - not directed at me for pointing out the crumbling infrastructure but at those in charge, those who produce the shoddy work.

Here are a few (with the usual Google Translate inaccuracies):

This is our everything.

And hurt and ashamed.

There really is something to criticise. Let those who do these devices for the disabled themselves would try to drive them on a wheelchair.

It's sad everything. If you do so, you do normal... (ie If you're going to do a job, damn well do it properly as normal people do.)

In small provincial cities there are no ramps at all. On a wheelchair with a child, it's impossible to drive.

And as a car driver, I just curse every day, driving through the cut or sunken wells on the road. My Japanese car just every day swearing about her wanting to go home to Japan. Why in Japan and Europe can you make well-being with the dear and we have no way?

Here in Russia, the main rub for disabled people is simply going downstairs. As they also live in all that frightful Soviet apartment houses we call Kruschevky. It not only looks awful but there is not any ramps by default. That's why you can't usually see wheelchair guys out of the streets. They prefer to stay at home. (By "ramps", read "lifts". There are no lifts at all in any of the old Soviet apartment blocks.)

I have familiar girl disabled, she lives with mom. She hasn't been on the streets for years. Street for her open window.

Unintentionally, I have struck a nerve. I understand now more clearly why so many Russians feel that whilst Putin is a strong leader in his quest to return Russia to the high table of international leaders, he seems to have lost touch with - or doesn't care about - the problems faced by ordinary Russian citizens.

Chapter Thirty One

A lady's fiefdom

"Our parents want to feel like they led important, not worthless lives, believing in the things that are worth believing in. But what do they have instead? From all sides, they hear that their lives were total shit, that they never had anything but their terrible missiles and tanks."

My last day in Yakutsk and the heat is execrable, trapped between the buildings and radiating from the roads where tar melts and is sticky under foot. The only compensation is that women walk the streets in short shorts and skirts and expose the curl of their navels in a delightful way. But in the late afternoon heavy clouds build and rain falls warm as a bath. The roads steam, water pools in potholes and depressions, and pedestrians huddle in doorways.

Then it is gone. The air is muggy and still.

Now for the airport and my flight south. As usual I am early. Stupid early, as is my wont. Despite being African by birth, I live in a perpetual fear of being late. A bewhiskered taxi driver gets me to the airport without killing me, although he tries. The terminal is small but modern, chic almost - until I visit the toilet. No paper. I have learned to check first. But I find a dispenser on the wall by the hand basins. I need to predict what toilet paper I think I might need and unroll it before entering a cubicle. There are no seats on the toilets.

Come on, Russia, you can do better than this. Put the toilet roll dispenser *inside* the cubicles; join the real world. What's the worst that can happen, huh? I steal a few extra sheets to put in my pocket for later? And, while you're at it, go on, add some perforations in the paper - it's not technologically difficult, trust me. I'm sure if you Google it, there'll be a video that'll point you in the right direction.

Just saying...

We are summoned to the aircraft, a small turbo-prop. A prisoner, shackled between two burly guards, is loaded onto the plane before we are allowed on. A large Alsatian sees him off, only relaxing once he has entered the plane. Job done.

We take off and cross the wide, blue Lena River with its islands and sand banks and filigreed channels. The aircraft is old and worn: threadbare seats, patched vinyl, and the seat frames sloppily touched up by hand with black paint in the manner of a child with a paintbrush clenched in its fist. In the seat next to me a mother holds a fat little baby girl who could have been featured in a film about Inuit whale hunters of old. Throughout the flight, the child stares at me with her black, almond-shaped eyes.

Outside the windows, the taiga fades into the smoke of forest fires that rise like grey columns into the air then settle. The whole landscape is pocked with small lakes like a war-ravished land when the bomb craters subside and fill.

Later the shaven-headed, shackled man, policemen handcuffed to both wrists, is led down the narrow corridor to the toilet. The image of any man, shackled, saddens me; one's freedom is such a precious thing.

We land and the pilot is applauded in the Russian way, extolling him for delivering us to our destination without killing or maiming a single passenger.

I make my way to the station. It is large and airy and heavily Soviet. On benches along the walls men loll and attempt to sleep; women feed babies, their belongings contained in rag-bag suitcases and plastic bags; a small shop sells the basics - tea, milk, pot noodles, water, some comfort food - all you need for a long trans-Siberian journey. In one corner are shelves of books - take one to read on the train and drop it off at the next station when you depart. I leave my bag and scan the shelves for a book in English but there are none. While I am looking, a smartly uniformed policeman cautions me politely not to leave my luggage unattended. I want to tell him that I have come to trust that no one will steal from me, but I don't have the words. Anyway, as in all countries, unattended luggage is anathema in public spaces in this sad age of men who carry murder in their hearts.

I sit on a bench and wait. Pretty blue curtains hang in the windows; the bruised concrete floor is clean; crayon drawings by primary school children on the theme of the railways are displayed on one wall - warnings about the dangers of playing on the lines, anti littering, save and protect our world.

Only later do I realise that I've been caught out by the common mistake of foreigners new to the system: not remembering that the entire rail network, spread across the time zones that cut this land into longitudinal slices, works on Moscow time. Consequently, I have arrived at the station ten hours early only to discover that, according to Moscow time, it is a mere sixteen hours before my train will leave. This makes my habit of getting there early somewhat ridiculous. But I am offered, for a small fee, a rest room - these are attached to all main stations throughout Russia and are a godsend. I pay, am showed to my room by a stern-faced lady whose domain I am entering for the duration (and whose ire, trust me, one does not want to raise), make myself at home, brew a cuppa and sleep well knowing that, when my train is due, this lady will knock on my door and rouse me with the same clunky efficiency with which the entire system is run.

And I am fast asleep when the knock comes. My lady cracks a smile and nods, pointing to her watch. It is time. I dress and pack quickly, afraid, as I always am, that the train will leave without me.

Outside it is still dark and the humming, animal presence of the two huge diesel-electric engines fills the station with a sense of purpose. The coaches, too, are massive, their lit windows revealing another world inside that soon will absorb me, carry me across the curve of the globe in an intimate cocoon, a microcosm of life that I will share for four days with a group of strangers who will become not-strangers until we separate again. The faded romance of the trans-Siberian rail journey...

I am an outsider. I don't know the rules of the game. Clutching my ticket, I mingle with other passengers - those about to embark as well as those already part of the train-world out for a quick smoke and a stretching of the legs or joining the queue at the station shop for a cup of tea. I notice that outside each coach door, a smartly-uniformed woman, middle-aged and pleasant of face, stands, as if on guard. This, I learn, is her domain - like the stern-faced lady in charge of the station rest room. Here, her word is law. These are the women (and they are always women) who, throughout Russia, have been placed in charge of some small section of life, of society, a small cog in the functioning of the larger machine. Without them the entire system would collapse. You will find them sitting at a desk when the lift door opens on each floor of a hotel; that floor belongs to her and she rules it with a rod of iron. She observes and takes note of everything: who enters your room, your behaviour, your comings and goings. A woman will be in charge of a toilet - *this* is her fiefdom and her power stems from Putin himself; each room in a museum is under the control of a woman who sits all day on a chair and observes the movements of every visitor. Step out of line and you will be reprimanded. Don't mess with these women. Disobey an instruction the police will be called; ignore the police and, if you're lucky, you'll be locked up; challenge the government and there's always Novochock...

The system works well, I have found. Although somewhat authoritarian, it leads to a well-regulated society where yobbishness is seldom witnessed. Once in the UK I observed two bobbies surrounded by a gang of yobs thrusting their mobile phones within inches of the bobbies' faces, filming them, taunting them, while they stood, attempting to act as if the louts weren't there. There was nothing they could do; pointing your camera in someone's face is not a crime. Their hands were tied. This would never happen in Russia - and rightly so. I felt ashamed that our society had come to this.

Enough. If I'm not careful, I start typing, "In *my* day, they'd have got a clip about the ear," and then I'll sound like my father.

But still, in *my* day...

And so it is with these ladies and the fiefdom of their coaches. I approach one, show her my ticket while adopting a facial expression that says: *I'm totally out of my depth here - please help!* and am directed with a smile to my coach further down the platform. There my lady guard scrutinises my ticket, nods and asks for my passport. This, too, is scrutinised, *every* page, then she asks me for something else. I understand that, like the receptionists at every hotel, the ticket sellers at every bus and train station, showing my passport to prove that I am *me* is not sufficient: I have to produce the twin portion of my immigration card, filled in at the border and, if lost, will lead to the imposition of a "Very big fine" - as threatened by a stern-faced border control officer when I entered the country. This too is inspected and I am given the nod.

I haul myself up the metal stairs and into the carriage. In front of me is the conductress' cubicle with narrow bed and table; to the left a large, industrial samovar with water-level gauge like you would find on a steam engine. Down the length of the carriage are bunks in sections of six: two to the right parallel with the passageway, the bottom bunk turning into a table with two padded seats if the owner opts to sit instead of sleep; above this, and close to the ceiling, an upper bunk. To the left, four bunks, two upper and two lower, at right angles to the passage with a small table under the window. I have the upper bunk, it seems. The lower is occupied by Zhonny, dark-haired and thin with crudely-drawn tattoos on his fingers and arms that bleed into his skin as if the ink has got wet in the rain, and a knotted scar, three inches long, across his scalp. But he smiles at me and there is no meanness in his face.

With a slight bump the train begins to move. Our lady conductress beckons me and I follow her to a large pile of rolled-up ticking mattresses and folded sheets held behind wooden slats next to the samovar. I take my mattress and sheet, lower my bunk and store them there.

Initial information and pleasantries are shared with difficulty between Zhonny and me, using the translator. Outside the window, lights pass by with the rhythmical *click-clack* of the wheels and the swaying of the carriage - and then it is dark.

"Chai?" he offers and I nod. He leaves and returns shortly with two glasses of hot water held in filigreed, pewter holders (these, I learn later, are available on request from the conductress who will also loan cutlery if a passenger, like me, hasn't brought any). Zhonny digs in a coat pocket and produces two tea bags and a biscuit, presents them to me with a flourish and says in English, "Welcome!"

Outside the window, darkened trees pass by...

Later Zhonny says in a conspiratorial whisper, pointing to that soft spot under the jawbone that warns of serious drinking to come and says, "Drink - you?"

I shake my head. *"Ne manoga,"* I tell him - just a little. *"Peeva -"* only beer.

"Wodka," he whispers then, looking about with lowered eyelids and gesturing with his eyes towards his bag under the table, he whispers, "Wodka - no police."

Whether he means actual police or our lady conductress, I'm not sure, but I have come to realise that, throughout Russia and also here, on the trains, the consumption of alcohol in public is strictly prohibited, as is smoking, and, because of the severe penalties imposed on those who breach the rules, the obeying of these laws is almost universal.

Later he suggests hopefully, "Sleep?" and only then do I realise that he can't sleep with me occupying the seat that forms part of his bed so I nod and unroll my ticking mattress, spread the sheet and climb onto the high bunk with some difficulty. I realise that we two need to cooperate like Siamese twins: if he wants to sleep, I have to lie on my bunk (there is insufficient headroom to sit) or be offered a seat by the occupants of the other two lower bunks of our sextet; he can't sleep if I want to sit - but, as it's his bunk, I must defer to him. I'm beginning to understand the dynamics.

If I bend my chin into my neck, I can just make out a dark landscape flashing by through a narrow gap between my bunk and the top of the window; this could become claustrophobic, I think, knowing I have to live like this for the next four days. A prison train? This is not the romantic vision of the Orient Express I had in my mind - but then, I am travelling cattle-class, one of the people, and that's how it should be.

Outside the sky is heavy with cloud. A narrow dirt track winds through the dark trees and I wonder where it's going.

Around me people snore. A large woman sits across the isle from me; she is of a certain age, dyed blond hair cut short, painted eyebrows, lipstick painted beyond the natural lines of the mouth, overweight. Next to her sits a thin man with a gammy leg, not related that I can discern. They have the privilege of a permanent table. Squashed in my narrow, upper bunk, too short to straighten my legs, I am the puppy sucking on the hind teat, it seems.

A small settlement of wooden houses slides by. Smoke rises from the chimneys and mixes with the mist.

And then it's just the trees...

Later, some small lakes and a massive cutting through rock. The trees, as they are throughout the taiga, are thin and spindly, seldom exceeding nine inches in diameter, stunted by their fight against each other for light, the short summer and the struggle against the dark and intense cold of winter.

Large swathes of forest have been thinned by fire, the dead trees stark and blackened, those clinging to life seared by the flames but putting out thin straggles of pale green new growth. It looks like the aftermath of a war.

The flies have joined us for this journey and they plague me with their persistence.

It was along tracks like these that the prisoners during the purges were carried to serve their years of exile and murderous work. Lying in my narrow upper bunk, I wonder what thoughts went through their heads as they clack-clacked for weeks through the unfeeling anonymity of this forest, heading east away from all that they knew and all whom they loved?

A river runs past, brown with run-off from the night's storm, flowing strong and high. It's beautiful now; it must be even more beautiful when the snow lies heavy.

I wake to the sweet smell of vodka rising from the bunk below. Zhonny is awake and making ready for the day. The next stop is his. The thin man with the gammy leg catches my eye and makes smoking gestures with his fingers. He's desperate for a nicotine top-up but, unlike Zhonny, can't indulge without being caught.

A small town approaches; the rotting remains of a factory slide by. The train stops and the smokers alight and drag at their cigarettes with intense suckings. Police wearing anti-stab vests and guns on their hips stride about the platform. There are no little shops here, no *babushkas* with baskets of hot food held up to the windows as I had imagined. Travel is a learning experience; I'll know what to do next time - but, for now, it seems like it's a bottle of water and some pot noodles for the next three days.

I've gone hungry before.

Outside the window a dog licks at something between the tracks.

Later the train stops at a town and the engines disconnect. The smokers scramble off to puff. I find the station cafe and eat quickly in case the train decides to leave before I get back. I assume we have reached Tynda and will now begin heading west.

Suddenly, out the window I see the coaches begin to move. I bolt my food, rush out only to realise that it's the new engines coupling up. I picture all my belongings and documents disappearing down the tracks to be lost forever.

My new travelling companion is Ola, a twenty-something, Asian-looking Russian. She doesn't say much. I sleep a lot and still the trees slide past the upper slit of window that is available to me. It has rained and the trees are wet. There are puddles in the tracks that lead into the trees. The rivers flow black and strong.

Late afternoon and most of the passengers are sleeping. One tends to sleep a lot on the trans-Siberian express; you either sleep or look out the window at the passing trees. In the rain, the smooth surface of the lakes is dented like the rising of trout.

Evening comes and the passengers rouse themselves. Smoked sausage, opened tins of fish, black bread, pot noodles heated with water from the samovar fill the carriage with warm smells. Tea is brewed and sunflower seeds cracked and nibbled like so many mice for afters.

And still the trees blur past in a damp, mosquito-filled world, separated from us by the rain-flecked glass of the windows.

A slight man, dark-skinned like those who live way down near the south west borders, takes the place of Ola and sits opposite me. We do not speak but, after an hour, he takes a carved wooden thing, like a rosary, from his pocket and hands it to me. Our eyes meet: it is a gift. I can see that it has been hand carved and worn smooth from much touching. I ask him, using the translator, what it is - a rosary? - but he can't respond. I show it to a group sitting opposite and they smile and say, *"Chotsky."*

A man takes it and, with a practiced gesture, flips it through his fingers in a rhythmical, tactile way and I realise it's an aid to keep the hands busy, like the Japanese *netsuke*, a non-religious rosary, if you like, and this one has been often used, rubbed to the smoothness of silk against his skin. The man's name is Mkrtchyan, as far as I can make out; he's Armenian and has been working in Magadan as a driver of heavy machinery. He's going home.

And, so, the night sidles in and the trees darken and become shadows sewn together and the hills are now one with the night sky and I climb into my upper bunk and sleep to the rocking of the carriage.

And in my sleep, the train hurries west and the trees continue to slip darkly by.

*****

Much later I awake and the trees are still there. It is as if we are travelling on a loop: trees, trees, trees, trees, trees, small muddy track, trees, trees, trees, trees, fire-blackened trees, trees, trees, trees, trees, trees, lake, trees, trees, trees, trees, trees, rotting house with smoke oozing from chimney, trees, trees, trees...

The Russian taiga stretches for 5,800ks from the far east coast to west of the Ural Mountains - about 15% of the earth's land surface, some 764 million hectares or 12 million square kilometres, the largest expanse of untouched boreal forest in the world. With a population density of 2.7 per sq kilometre, it is also one of the most remote regions on earth.

For years, when I pictured myself crossing Russia on the trans-Siberia railway, it was always with my face pressed to the window, drinking in every moment of this exotic and wondrous landscape. Reality is always different from one's dreams, though. Here, now, I could sit up and look out at the blur of trees for a few minutes each hour, acknowledge that what I am seeing is exactly the same as the last time I looked (and the time before that, actually) and then go back to sleep knowing that, when I wake and look out the window again, the looping endless blur of trees will still be there, just the same as before. The bogs and rivers and lakes continue to astonish me with their beauty, reflecting the changing moods of the sky and the mountains. The small, muddy tracks that disappear into nowhere, somewhere, with a purpose all of their own, tug at my spirit with a deep siren call.

Already I am forgetting the pain and the worry and the mosquitoes and the discomfort that such roads carry with them, a payment they take as their due for the excitement they offer in return.

And so, another day on the train begins...

Chapter Thirty Two

Nibbling sunflower seeds

"If it weren't for Stalin, we'd be licking the Germans' asses."

At a small station, passengers buy dried fish from ladies wearing faded dresses and bright headscarves who stand alongside the tracks and, for the next few hours, the coach is filled with the raw, smoky stench of dried fish that is picked from the head and the bones and gnawed like biltong.

The train *clack-clacks* its way west, through bright sunshine now. In the perceptual concept of figure-ground, here it is pretty much all ground; and for ground to be ground, there needs to be a figure. And so, gradually, as the time zones slide by outside the window, the *ground* of the trees becomes little more than a blur; one's eyes seek out figures to lend perspective to an otherwise monotonous landscape - a small, startlingly blue lake; a mountain in the distance; a blurred glimpse of the BAM Road that roughly follows the rail line; the remains of a wooden bridge, partially destroyed by spring floods; wires outside the window that rise and fall, rise and fall...

One's focus inevitably turns inward: the little child that runs up and down the corridor, laughing; the young man, Sasha, who eats dry bread spread with condensed milk washed down with black tea because he hasn't much money; a hung-over man, shirtless, who grunts in his sleep, his exposed belly hanging over his trousers like a bag of lard; the woman who has, for two days, filled in the answers to a 560-page crossword puzzle book called *Super Giant;* her teenage grandson who sits silent, absorbed in his phone; my Armenian friend who insists I take a banana from him; the pleasant lady in charge of our carriage, always smartly dressed, who keeps the carriage ship-shape and makes sure, like a mother hen, that after each station pause the smokers and others under her charge are all back where they belong.

In the heat of the afternoon the line brushes the northern tip of Lake Baikal. The train stops and we all get out. Our lady conductor instructs Sasha, the young man of the dry bread, to take me to see the lake. We have an hour to kill so I take him to the station cafe and buy him lunch, then we walk in the heat a short 300 metres to the lake shore; the stony beach is leached of all colour, pale and shimmering with heat. In front of us walks the hung over man from our coach. Sasha points to him and reaches for my phone. "Alcohol is evil," he types. "There should be less."

He is an earnest young man, four years married with a baby daughter, travelling to Moscow for work. We make our way back to the train. He asks me about salaries in the UK and the cost of a one-bedroom apartment and expresses sadness that conditions are so poor for ordinary people in Russia and that the other world, the one I take for granted, is denied him.

Later I wake. The train has stopped again. In my microcosm, things continue in the loop: the fat lady cracks sunflower seeds between her teeth and opens her *Super Giant* crossword book; Sasha sleeps, wrapped in his rough blanket; the Armenian goes out onto the weedy platform for a smoke; the hung over man is awake and taciturn, eating dry bread. Our lady conductress, still smartly uniformed as if she's just come on duty, chivvies the smokers back into the carriage. The train begins to move.

I have lost track of time. I had thought we would reach Novosibirsk this morning but my fellow passengers laugh and tell me: *Another day.*

Nobody has washed. There is only one small basin about the size of a child's potty for each carriage. The system is clunky, over-engineered and remarkably efficient. One gets the impression that it has worked in just this way for decades and will continue unchanged for decades to come. If it ain't broke... The requirements for each self-sufficient carriage are minimal: water for the basin and loo; hot water in the samovar; ticking mattresses and two small sheets given to each passenger on arrival, blankets on an upper shelf; one lady conductress to keep things clean and orderly. That's it. The trains arrive and leave exactly on time - the system *works*. It has to work. I get the impression that Russia would grind to a halt if the railways imploded. Moving goods by truck across this hemisphere of a country is impractical and expensive. Ditto air. That leaves the railway.

Sasha asks me wistfully how much it would cost to spend a week in the UK.

"Very expensive," I tell him and he looks sad.

"The rouble is worthless," he says to me and the others in our group, using the translator, and they nod. Then he types: "What do you think of our cream?"

My face evidently reveals my confusion. He takes my phone, looks at it and laughs, makes a change: "What do you think of our president?"

How does one answer a question like this? I take back my phone and type, "Very strong."

Sasha looks doubtful so I give him the *so-so* rocking hand gesture. He reaches for the phone and types: "In the foreign policy he is strong. But the Russians do not think about the Russians."

*****

I have lost track of time, both the day and the hour. Because the rail network works on Moscow time and I am unaware of which time zone we are currently passing through, I have no idea where I am. When I rub my aching back from sitting too long and sleeping in a too-short bed, Sasha laughs at me and uses his fingers to make a joke about my losing an entire day of my journey somewhere along the tracks.

In another world somewhere, Donald Trump is visiting the UK. I wonder how many European leaders he's managed to insult this time. From my upper bunk I watch the crossword woman mindlessly reaching for a sunflower seed, inserting it into her mouth, cracking it with her front teeth like a mouse, extracting the husk and nibbling on the seed while her hand reaches into the bag for another. I have a feeling that this repetitive action has some of the beneficial functions of running worry beads through one's fingers or stroking the smooth surface of a *chotsky*.

We pass a logging operation with a wide swathe of taiga clear felled. Sasha says, "*Buzz buzz -* " making cutting motions with his hands, points east and mutters contemptuously, "China."

I suppose there are enough trees here even to satisfy China's voracious appetite for natural resources. (But no - now that I am home, I check on the 'Net and it seems that illegal logging has been taken over by organised crime gangs in Russia and Putin himself admits that this has increased by 70% in the last five years. The WWF believes that, if logging were to continue at its present rate, the largest forest on our planet, the Russian taiga, could be destroyed in 20 to 30 years.)

By now, some of my fellow passengers seem to have gone into a state of suspended animation. Sasha and I talk, using the translator. His yearning to travel to Europe, to broaden his horizons, is palpable and it makes me so sad. I realise just how good we have it in the west, our freedom of movement, our relative financial security. I tell him that if ever he and his wife can save the money for the flight to the UK, they can stay with me; it will cost him nothing but the flight.

He is taken aback. "No roubles," he types then mimes sleeping, eating and driving.

"Nothing left over?" I type.

He thinks a while then types, "I will accept your invitation."

I hope he does but know it will never happen.

*****

It is evening. Tomorrow at 6am I will leave the train. Sasha and the others in my compartment have another three days until they reach Moscow. Six days in each other's company, in a shared space of 3X2 metres. But the five of us have become a small family (the hung over man keeps to himself, sleeping mostly and occupying the lower bunk so I am forced to share either Sasha's or the crossword woman's whose name, I discover, is Olga).

As the air yellows with the setting of the sun and the wild grasses flare and glisten, we sit, knees almost touching, and eat sunflower seeds in companionable silence (yes, like a reluctant smoker, I too have been drawn in). A meal has been eaten and shared; the long evening awaits. The carriage jolts and rocks and creaks; outside the window the landscape flashes by. Soon, one of us will get up, make his way past recumbent forms to the samovar, and make tea. The little boy runs up and down the corridor as he has done for the last three days, grinning at us as he passes; the young couple still play cards; middle-aged women gossip and laugh together and a group of men who have about them the look of soldiers out of uniform talk and laugh and eat smoked sausage cut into pieces on a sheet of greasy paper. If they weren't on the train, they'd be smoking and sharing a bottle of vodka.

A young lass has taken the place of the taciturn man; she sits opposite me and takes out a book. I can read the title in Russian and say, "Mmmm, Dostoyevsky. *The Brothers Karamazov -*" and she smiles and nods. It would make a good chat-up line. She asks if I've read it. *No, it is very long - but I will one day,* I assure her, lying through my teeth.

Over the last three days I have been drawn into the very lives of these people and I feel rested and at peace. It has been for me an opening up of Russian life in a way impossible on a motorcycle where chance meetings are necessarily brief.

Early the next morning the train reaches the historic city of Tomsk. I say my goodbyes and step out into the next stage of my journey.

Chapter Thirty Three

It was long ago and it was not true

"In our village, all of the best families were subject to dekulakization; if they had two cows and two horses, that was already enough to make them kulaks. They'd ship them off to Siberia and abandon them in the barren taiga forest. Women smothered their children to spare them the suffering. Oh, so much woe... so many tears. More tears than there is water on this earth."

I sit in the gardens of the Church of the Resurrection in Tomsk, eating fruit bought at a roadside stall. An old woman wearing a head scarf waters the flowers. She is thin as a fork, her face wrinkled and worn; she could have emerged from the pages of Gogol or Chekhov. A long-bearded, black-cassocked priest with a heavy gold pectoral cross hanging from his neck stands at an open door and surveys his domain.

Suddenly, crisp in the still air, small, tinkling bells begin to sound and I picture a young priest, tonsured, cords held lightly his hands, beginning the gentle polyrhythmic prelude to the bigger bells high up in the tower, a sound unique to Russian orthodoxy and as distinctive to this place as the early-morning cry of the muezzin in countries where Muslims reside. In my listening stillness I am transported to an older Russia, the black-clothed priest and the thin, old woman and the slow tolling of the medium bells now, just two, a rhythmical counterpoint, one slightly higher in tone than the other; and then, above the light, almost whimsical tinkling of the small bells called *zazvonny* in Russian, comes the slow, low tolling of the *blagovestnik*, the large bass bell, always blessed with a name and consecrated as one would a child in baptism.

The large bass bell is not housed in the bell tower but in a free standing structure that could be the gatehouse to a medieval castle. A priest, with total disregard to the damage he must be doing to his ears, stands next to the huge bell and swings the clapper with a rope. A newly married couple stand and smile self-consciously for photographs...

*****

Tomsk is a university city, rich in history and rightly famous for the many log-built apartment buildings still standing with their intricately carved wooden lace window surrounds. Whilst some of these are slowly sinking into the ground and others lean ominously, many have been carefully preserved. The city is clean and neat and pretty, the old, gas-powered, square buses with their crash gearboxes and rusty sides and the equally old trams - that seem to have been made out of discarded rail lines and sheets of corrugated iron - that trundle and shriek along worn tracks give one the impression that one has somehow time-shifted into the 1930s.

I walk into the city along tree-lined streets and watch old women and shopkeepers sweep their front doorsteps and the pavement like housewives used to do in the old days, actions that speak so clearly of a pride in themselves and their neighbourhood. Lenin Street (what else?) leads me into the centre and, naturally, a large statue of the great dictator dominates the town square. I take a photograph and later post it onto social media with a question asking why these statues of Lenin still dominate so many town centres throughout Russia a century after the Communist social experiment ended in failure. My Russian friend Sasha replies: "It's a strategic stock. We should just modify it in order to achieve some formal resemblance with current dictator."

Well, at least under Putin he is able to say things like that; in the bad old days, he'd have been given 25 years.

Then to the Museum of Oppression. On the wall outside, an acknowledgement: *"During the years of Soviet regime millions became victims of totalitarian governmental arbitrariness, were exposed to repressions because of political and religious beliefs, for social, national or other reasons. Everything that took place in Tomsk and Tomsk region during these years also was happening everywhere in USSR with a difference in scale of repressions, names of executors and victims."*

The museum occupies the actual building used by the NKVD here in Tomsk, the dark, dank, below ground interrogation rooms where the screams of the tortured were muffled by deep soil and concrete from those who walked the pavement above. A nondescript door opens from the street and I step carefully down worn stairs and feel the despair of vanished hopes deep down here brush cold against my skin. In front of me a whitewashed wall lined with heavy wooden doors, battered and thick with grey paint, metal peep-holes and small, square wooden latches for the delivery of food and water - bolt upon bolt, lock over lock; and, just in case any prisoner incarcerated behind these austere walls would even contemplate such a ridiculous thing as escape, the inside of each door, the part looked on by the prisoners, is metal-clad, even the bolt heads recessed. The food hatches are framed with welded angle iron, heavy enough for tank treads. Thick planks chained to the wall serve as a bed.

Abandon all hope, ye who enter here...

A map on a wall shows the distribution of Gulag camps throughout the whole of the Soviet Union; the red dots spread like a rash across the entire map and not, as many have thought, restricted to the Kola Peninsular and the Russian far east.

A young man, early thirties (ponytail, jeans and fedora) is employed as a translator and guide. His name is Cyrill. He sweeps his hand to take in the interrogation and punishment cells: "Lewis Caroll level of the absurd," he declares. "And some people say that Stalin didn't know. Yes, even today -" he says with contempt, "- that they were enemies of the state - you know, justifying it - even now, *today,* some people, Russians, believe that."

"Yes," I tell him, "I met some bikers a few years ago and they told me that Stalin never executed as many as Western historians claim and, anyway, those he executed were traitors."

"Yes!" Cyrill whoops. *"Justifying* it!" His moral outrage is obvious. "To industrialise a country you don't need a genocide," he continues, referring to the fact that Lenin used the free labour of political prisoners in the camps to develop Russia's infrastructure. "My grandfather," he tells me, claiming his right to the expression of his opinions, "was born in the Solovetsky camp; my grandmother spent her childhood and teenage years in Kolyma."

I ask him about whether Russians even want to recognise their past - "Like the Germans," I say, "who have memorials and museums dedicated to the victims of the holocaust. They even have laws making it illegal to deny that it happened or to glorify Nazism."

"The problem goes beyond monuments," Cyrill says. "It's about human *mentality.* In Germany, the Nazis are recognised as criminals. That didn't happen in Russia. The excuses: their execution was justified - they were traitors..." He pauses, thinking, then says, his face intense with emotion: "Until we are taught that there was a crime, we won't believe that crimes were committed."

We sit silent a while, considering this. Then he adds, "There's a Russian proverb: 'It was long ago and it was not true'."

"Yes," I tell him, "I read a book - I can't remember the author - it was called 'It was a long time ago and it didn't happen anyway'." (David Slatter)

He nods then adds, as if he is gnawing at a personal bone, "The Germans don't say 'We were killing Jews ... *but they were Jews!'* - you know? Trying to *justify* it. *Russians -"* He says this last word as if despairing for his nation. "Khrushchev was supposed to have closed the Gulag, but all he did was re-brand it. The camps were still there. Russians said, 'We were killing political enemies - *but they were political enemies'* - justifying it, you know? There has been no real apology or national guilt like the Germans."

We sit opposite one another, each inside our own thoughts. Then he tells me, "At first it was not forced..." (He means the settlement of those empty, far-off, hostile regions of the Soviet empire.) "...they called it 'Spatial Resettlement', the population and development of Siberia. Money and land were given as an incentive. Stolypin - Prime Minister at the time of Nicholas 11 - realised that people, workers, were needed to get at the natural resources in Siberia: wood, fur, coal, gold, diamonds - and the roads to get it out. Stalin had the same goals but the difference was he *forced* people; and there was no payment. It was free labour. And then there were the ethnic resettlements between '41 and '49 - Latvia, Lithuania, Estonia... also Ukraine, Belarus, Georgia, Armenia, Azerbaijan - millions sent to Siberia."

"A great manipulator of people," I say.

"Human cattle -" Cyrill clarifies, shaking his head.

The conversation lightens. I ask him if he's married and he says he's divorced but that's OK because now he knows what he's looking for in a woman. I think I've touched a nerve for he adds with some passion, "Slim Russian women are an aberration - it's an Americanisation of women. If you look back to the eighteenth century Russian women were solid and fat; they fed five children with one breast and left the other for their husbands. It's OK - now I know what I want in a woman. Young women in Russia *have* to be individuals, but by all being individuals they all become the same - with their mobile phones and their fancy clothes and their hair..."

Chapter Thirty Four
Skulls from the riverbank

The plan was to sail up the Ob River into a more remote section of northern Siberia but, on enquiry, I was told that no boats travel this section. If I want to use the river, I need to take a bus to a small town called Kargasok, 220ks north east of Kolpashevo, where I can get a boat to Nizhenevartovsk. The bus, however, only travels as far as Kolpashevo. How I will get from there to Kargasok I'm not sure - hitch, perhaps. We will see.

The bus, a small 24-seater, takes us steadily north for hours across the usual featureless taiga until we reach the town. And I learn that something happened here in this unassuming collection of houses deep in the taiga alongside the mighty Ob River, somewhere indistinguishable in the vast sameness of Siberia except for a small point on a map. It's something that should - *would* in most normal countries - be remembered with memorials, highlighted in the history books, but it's not. Probably what happened here happened also in so many other nondescript towns hidden in the taiga that those in the know have deemed it not worth the bother of remembering.

Anyway, so they say, it was a long time ago and it didn't happen anyway...

Scratch beneath the surface of any Siberian town and unhappy secrets will be revealed. During the purges, unspeakable things were done to human beings that remain hidden under the soil and deep in the memories of the inhabitants who would rather they remain buried. But in Kolpashevo, literally, the soil was stripped away allowing the bodies and the memories to rise to the surface.

Here is the story, which I have abridged (with acknowledgement to Sergey Parkhomenko, journalist and broadcaster, who reported it):

The River Ob makes a turn at Kolpashevo, and every year it eats away a few feet of a sand cliff there. On April 30, 1979, the Ob's waters eroded another six-foot section of bank. Hanging from the newly exposed wall were the arms, legs and heads of people who had been buried there. A cemetery at least several yards wide had been exposed. The bodies had been packed in and layered tightly. Some of the skulls from the uppermost layer rolled out from the sandbank, and little boys picked them up and began playing with them.

News of the burial spread quickly and people started gathering at the sandbank. The police and neighbourhood watch volunteers quickly cordoned off the whole thing. Shortly afterwards, they built a thick fence around the crumbling sandbank, warning people away.

The next day, the Communist Party called a meeting in the town, explaining that those buried were traitors and deserters from the war. But the explanation wasn't entirely convincing. If this were so, why was everyone dressed in civilian clothes? Why had women and children been executed as well? And from where, for that matter, did so many deserters come in a town of just 20,000 people?

Meanwhile, the river continued to eat away at the bank and it became clear that the burial site was enormous; thousands were buried there. People could remember that there used to be a prison on these grounds in the late 1930s. It was general knowledge that there were executions there, but nobody could imagine just how many people were shot. The perimeter fence and barbed wire had long ago been dismantled, and the prison itself was closed down. But what the town's people didn't know was that Kolpashevo's prison operated a fully-fledged assembly line of death. There was a special wooden trough, down which a person would descend to the edge of a ditch. There, he'd be killed by rifle fire, the shooter sitting in a special booth. If necessary, he'd be finished off with a second shot from a pistol, before being added to the next layer of bodies, laid head-to-toe with the last corpse. Then they'd sprinkle him lightly with lime. When the pit was full, they filled in the hole with sand and moved the trough over a few feet to the side, and began again.

But now the crimes of the past were being revealed as bodies fell into the water and drifted past the town while people watched from the shore.

In Tomsk, the authorities decided to get rid of the burial site and remove the bodies. The task, it turned out, wasn't so easy. Using heavy equipment so near a collapsing sandbank wasn't wise and there was no time to dig up all the bodies by hand. The Soviet leadership was in a hurry.

Then from Tomsk came new orders: two powerful tugboats were sent up the Ob, right up to the riverbank, where they were tied with ropes to the shore, facing away from the bank. Then they set their engines on full throttle. The wash from the ships' propellers quickly eroded the soft riverbank and bodies started falling into the water, where most of them were cut to pieces by the propellers. But some of the bodies escaped and floated away downstream. So motorboats were stationed there where men hooked the bodies as they floated by. A barge loaded with scrap metal from a nearby factory was moored near the boats and the men were told to tie pieces of scrap metal to the bodies with wire and sink them in the deepest part of the river.

The last team, also composed of local men from the town, worked a bit further downstream where they collected any bodies that had got past the boats and buried them on shore in unmarked graves or sank them by tying the bodies to stones. This cleanup lasted almost until the end of the summer.

At the end of the report of his discoveries, Parkhomenjko writes: "If someone out there doesn't understand yet, let me say plainly that I consider these events to be remarkable. This isn't a story about the Stalinist repressions, of the Great Terror, or the NKVD, or the state's system of destruction. This is a story about the Soviet man. It's about our compatriots and our countrymen, and our brothers and our sisters. It is a story about life in Siberia. It's about the moral code of the Builder of Communism."

*****

The River Ob slides past in front of me, keeping its secrets; I sit on its banks and allow my mind to travel back in time to when these purges were taking place, on the inhumanity of man to men, of social experiments gone wrong and the impact it has on the lives of ordinary men and women seeking little more than the opportunity to live and love and bring up their children and survive - until the great boot of the state stamps on their faces.

For me, now, on the banks of this river, I feel as if I'm near the edge of the world and well outside my comfort zone. There are no boats running upriver from Kalpashevo to Kargasok; no buses. So I'm gong to hitch. I just hope that the good lady who advised me knows what she is talking about and there are boats continuing downstream from Kargasok to the larger town of Nizhnevartovsk.

I study my map - I'm on the last centimetre before the rest of the landmass of Russia disappears somewhere north into the Arctic Ocean. Kargasok lies on the 59th line of latitude; Nizhnevartovsk on the 61st.

I'm pretty sure cars or trucks will be travelling that road tomorrow and, knowing the Russians now as I do, I have no doubt someone will stop and give me a lift. If not - well, I'll cross that bridge when I come to it.

Chapter Thirty Five

Sunday mornin' coming down

The ferry is large and industrial, its wide, bare-metal deck designed for trucks and earth-moving machinery. Here the Ob splits into a number of wide fingers leaving tree-lined islands in the middle of the stream. A yellow patrol boat flying the Russian flag makes its slow way upstream. It is early and the air is cool, the sky clear save for a thin straggle of cloud on the horizon. Nowhere, except for the ferry and patrol boat, are any signs of human habitation, just the dirt track leading to the water's edge and the wide river making its slow way north through tree-lined banks. It makes me think, somehow, of the Mekong Delta or somewhere on a remote stretch of the Amazon. Far to the left, the riverbanks are high, about ten foot, soft sand and easily eroded. In my mind's eye, standing on the ferry deck and watching this silent, desolate place slide soundlessly by, I can see the body parts emerge like strange tubers from the collapsing bank and, further back in time, the barbed wire and the crude wooden guard towers, hear the rifle cracks as another and yet another man, woman or child is silenced with a bullet through their brains. I see it and I hear it in the silence of the moment, in the hollow lappings of small waves against the metal hull of the ferry.

*****

Later, I stand on the edge of a dirt road, waiting for a car or truck to appear. I am a teenager again, in Natal, South Africa, standing on the roadside with my thumb out. It was the 60s then and we all did it; before we were old enough to own a car, anywhere too far to ride on a bicycle was achieved with an outstretched thumb and an appealing facial expression. Those were the days before seatbelts and long before the word *paedophile* became part of everyday vocabulary.

Yet, despite my early start, the ferry took over two hours to travel up-river to the western side and the morning is almost gone.

My expectation was that drivers would be queuing up to give me a lift, given the innate helpfulness I have experienced from all Russians so far. But the hours pass and no car stops or even pauses to give me the once-over. I play *Hit the Tin Can with a Stone*, and *Lie Down and Play Dead in the Road;* I walk up and down and raise some dust; I build small castles from stones and try to knock them down - those games all of you who have stood for hours on the side of an empty road waiting for a car to stop will have played. The memories of hitching, softened by the lens of time, don't seem so rosy any more.

I listen to the silence and the clicking of insects and smell the dust and oil-spill on the tar, straining my ears to pick up the approaching sound of an engine.

Mid-day comes and goes. It dawns upon me that I have never, not once, seen anyone raising a hopeful thumb throughout Russia and Central Asia. The concept seems to have no meaning here - strange, as hitching a ride is usually the last resort of the poor who need to get from one place to another but who do not have the money for a bus.

Finally, as I was wondering whether I would be standing on the roadside in the darkness, a tatty UAZ, driven by a small, be-whiskered man, pulls over and opens his window.

"Kargasok?" I enquire with hope etched on my face.

He nods, *"Da -"* and opens the door.

We drive in silence - he has no English; the UAZ rattles and clatters, its engine filling the cab with noise and fumes. The road is atrocious dirt, the kind of road one would expect when nudging 60 degrees north in Siberia. Dust seeps through gaps in the doors and even the trees on the roadside are furred grey with it. Two hours in, almost as if at that very point the sun produces insufficient heat and light to sustain adequate growth, the trees thin and become stunted. The land flattens even more, small lakes multiply, and rivers meander lazily in coiling loops as if they have lost their way.

At last, after three hours, in the late afternoon, habitation begins to appear... and then there are shops and, hallelujah, a small hotel with a shared room where a very large, shirtless man sleeps. I pay for two nights. The river, muddy and swept by a cold wind, is just a few hundred metres away and as I walk along its bank, a hydrofoil appears in the distance, grows larger, slows and docks almost in front of me against a rough wooden jetty.

My cup runs over and I am filled with a strange sense of elation. Time to celebrate with a beer, methinks...

*****

In faraway places, when the roads give up because building or maintaining them becomes untenable, it is the rivers that stand in as wilderness highways. So it is here. In Kargasok (which means "Bear Cape", so I am told) the roads end - unless you have one of those tracked ATVs or strange hybrids that have more tyre than vehicle and can, when push comes to shove, float. From here until the roads begin again two hundred or so kilometres west, the water allows boats to travel during the brief period of warmth and when the ice is thick enough to support trucks during the cold. In between, when the ice is breaking up or too thin to hold a vehicle's weight, no one travels. This vast area becomes cut off except for those who have the means to fly.

Most of the small wooden houses here have a boat in the back yard; most, too, have a large vegetable patch out back (mostly potatoes) and the front brightly coloured with flowers, as if those who live here seek out a brief, bright flowering to compensate for the long, cold, dark winter days and nights.

When I get back to my hotel room, my roommate has surfaced. It is clear immediately that he has a problem with drink; one eye is bloodshot and partially closed and the sour, stale smell of alcohol oozes from his clothes and skin. There is a small fridge in the room and I count ten beers stored there. Later, when my large Russian roommate disappears, none are left.

In the wee hours, long after I have gone to bed, I am woken by the sound of a man retching. The sour smell of alcohol mixed with bile fills the room...

*****

Morning comes and I leave my hung over friend and make my way down to the river. The Ob flows darkly against the moored hydrofoil, the water stained brown, like beer, and lines of froth mark the shoreline.

In front of me, an old man casts a lure and hooks small fish, six to nine inches long, just off the edge where the water deepens. He sees me watching, talks to me in Russian then shows me his catch held in a bag slung around his waist. The fish have big heads and thrash about. He tells me their name but I forget. Later I discover that they are baby sturgeon.

The next morning I am early, as usual, packed and ready to go. The hydrofoil, tethered to the bank, noses without apparent life into the river flow. The lady at the guesthouse told me to be here at eight for the boat's departure at ten. I find myself sitting on the riverbank at seven thirty and wait two and a half hours.

No one comes.

To fill the time, I walk up and down the shoreline, beach combing. This place is a treasure trove for archaeologists. I throw stones at things, play games, watch a man fishing. Time passes slowly and a cold wind begins to blow riffles on the dark surface of the water.

Eventually a woman emerges from the hydrofoil in slippers and dressing gown and tells me grumpily that the boat leaves at six tomorrow evening.

I drag my jacket over my shoulders, pick up my bag and make my way back to the guesthouse. The wind strengthens and lifts small eddies of sand about my feet and into the road. It's Sunday morning and no one is about. Into my mind come the words of the saddest song ever written:

"Then I crossed the empty street and caught the Sunday smell of someone fryin' chicken. And it took me back to somethin' that I'd lost somehow, somewhere along the way. And there's nothin' - short of dyin' - half as lonesome as the sound, on the sleepin' city sidewalks, Sunday mornin' coming down."

Kristofferson captured long ago the sense of loneliness I am feeling now and, although my life, fortunately, isn't complicated by the burden of drugs and alcohol as recounted in the song, the emptiness of the Sunday morning streets in far north Siberia is very real.

Later, killing time, I take a wind-swept walk along the riverbank amongst the clutter of flotsam that has accumulated here over the years and, as I walk, I meet too the discarded flotsam of human life - the wrecked and rusted boats and the hollow, wrecked people who loll on the sand and shout at me drunkenly and ask for money and expose their pink gums and rotten teeth.

And I reflect, as I walk, how hard it must be here for the discarded, for those who can't cope and those who do cope for a brief time but with the lying assistance of the bottle. I suppose the winter here kills them quickly too, more quickly, perhaps, than those it kills further south.

Chapter Thirty Six

An old biker still riding

"Be here by seven," the crewman tells me in Russian, holding up stubby fingers to confirm his words. He stands on the rusty deck of a large vehicle ferry that has been pushed against the riverbank, its heavy ramp wedged deep into the sand.

I have given up on the hydrofoil. With the help of a man in an office whom I asked for help, I have discovered this ferry two kilometres out of town. It will travel slowly - but that's the way I like it. Its rusty, battered appearance suits the image I have in my mind of far north Siberian river travel.

I wake early and walk the two kilometres through empty streets inhabited only by a herd of brown-skinned horses and some cows that crop unkempt grass tufts on the side of the road. Nothing on the ferry stirs so I sit on the stony beach and wait. Clouds of midges conspire to make my life miserable.

I notice that on the ferry are twenty or so motorcycles that weren't there yesterday. As time passes and the sun lifts itself off the horizon, a few of the bikers emerge from what looks like a railway carriage without wheels on one side of the deck and that must be used for accommodation. I approach one of the bikers and he tells me that they're on a joint expedition to a small town 1,500ks further north and above the Arctic Circle.

They are friendly. I explain that I, too, am a biker and I tell them of my journey and why I'm now bike-less. *Deja-vu*, I think to myself, remembering Gareth and my meeting up with the Black Bears Club eight years before and their welcome.

I catch the word *"Anglia"* - a group of bikers is looking at me with smiles on their faces. One makes a *You got shafted, mate!* gesture with a crooked right arm and they laugh. I assume they are referring to the Football World Cup so, before thinking, I flip them the bird and, as I'm doing it, I realise that this, perhaps, is not the wisest thing I've done of late. The biker who made the gesture is massive and tattooed, his stomach bulging over his trousers like a sack of piglets, his neck and shoulders seemingly fused. He walks up to me, slowly, and I think *Now what?* - but then puts his arms around my back and crushes the breath out of me. The watching bikers applaud. I am relieved - sometimes you're not quite sure of the response you'll get when using the old middle-finger salute but, when delivered with a smile amongst fellow bikers, it's usually taken in the spirit that it's given.

If I'd had my bike, I could have joined them. I have no doubt it would have been a "'sperience", as the husky-voiced Malvina murmured to Gareth and me on the first evening after joining the Black Bears on their camping trip to the White Sea coast. There, too, we were bear-hugged by massive, tattooed Russian bikers who welcomed us into their fraternity like the brothers that we were.

Finally, at ten in the morning, the ferry engine rumbles to life, a crewmember casts us off into the fast-flowing, dark waters of the Ob and we begin our 24-hr journey downstream towards the northwest. It is so good to be on the move again after a three-day hiatus at a road-end in Siberia. My cabin, which I share with three middle-aged women, is painted bright green onto which has been pasted bright green wallpaper decorated with pictures of apples and oranges, whole and sliced. It's a little tight - 2.5m X 2.2m in size and designed to sleep four. In fact, the whole ferry functions in this utilitarian way: it's little more than a massive, unpainted, floating platform with a flat bit at the back and a slopey bit at the front for ramming up against the riverbank. An old railway carriage has been secured to the metal deck for sleeping; a shipping container houses a simple *magazin* with some wooden tables and benches for customers; inside, a large pot of *borsh* steams away on a gas stove. That's it - transport up and down river for people and vehicles, sleeping and eating with the minimum of fuss; old-world pragmatism like the trans-Siberian railway.

I place my camera, wallet and glasses on the small table between our bunks; a bit later one of the ladies taps me on the shoulder where I am lying and tucks my belongings under my pillow, whispers something behind her hand and gestures down the corridor to where the bikers have gathered. I want to tell her that I would trust those bikers with my life but I can't; the barrier of discordant language is too high. I thank her instead.

Later I walk down the narrow corridor and meet the bear-like biker who gave me the shafted gesture before; as we pass, he hugs me again. It seems that man-hugs amongst bikers are acceptable here.

The river slips by. We travel fast downstream. I find a sheltered spot behind a truck and lie down on the sun-baked deck. Close to me, a number of bikers sit on aluminium panniers detached from their bikes; they pass the extended tube from a hookah from one to another and pour vodka into plastic cups. For the moment I am alone, isolated, but at peace with the world.

Then it comes, as I expected it to: *"Hey, Englishman!"*

I sit up. The group clustered around the hookah beckon me over. One makes room for me on a pannier, a cup of vodka is thrust into one hand, sunflower seeds into the other. Introductions are made. They are from various bike clubs throughout Russia, coming together for what they have called the "Arctic Circle Expedition". They are happy, excited; a few work on their bikes as the riverbanks slide by.

Like the Black Bears so many years ago, they, too, have their "fixer", the hard man who, if necessary, will sort out any problems they come across along the way. His name is Max, an ex-soldier of numerous campaigns, mostly Chechnia, Dagestan and the other Balkan republics who fought so hard for independence but failed in the end, although they exacted a heavy toll.

Max is massive, his chest muscles like firm breasts. He shows me scars on his hands, his head (he has a metal plate inserted, one of the others tells me) and he points to his knee - another ragged scar.

"Motorcycle?" I ask, pointing to his knee.

He shakes his head. "War."

Despite our struggles with language, they make me welcome, tell me that I could join them on their journey north if I had my bike. And I am sad that I can't. What an adventure it would have been!

It's time for a ceremony; all line up at the railing and the sergeant-at-arms dips water from the river in a small bucket tied to a piece of rope. Each member of the group drinks from this - like the shared drinking of sacrificial blood in some obscure pagan ceremony, a bikers' rite of passage. I stand to one side, watching, but they insist that I join the line, drink river water from the bucket and ritually seal my inclusion into the brotherhood. Then vodka is produced - we all must drink. I am told, after swallowing my large mouthful, that it is home made and very strong. Almost immediately it hits my stomach and the whole world begins to melt. I remember the warnings: never drink homemade spirits in Russia, you don't know what horrors have been used to produce it - but it's too late now. The concoction flows warm through my veins and loosens the edge of my vision.

A small boat pulls up alongside, keeping pace, one man in the front holding onto the side of the ferry for balance. Smoked fish are offered; money is passed down to waiting hands and a bag of sturgeon passed up. We all gather about a pannier table and bits of smoky flesh are pulled off the bones and eaten. I am offered a skull to gnaw but I decline - like offering the choicest cut, a goat's eyeball, to the honoured guest. The biker who has offered it smiles, takes a bite, crunches the skull between his molars then flexes his biceps.

The day passes slowly; with it, the low, sandy banks of the river slide by, lined, as always, with the wall of taiga forest blurring darkly to the horizon. The river is broad and calm, flowing deep and dark towards the Arctic Ocean. The wind dies until only a light breeze disturbs the club flags that have been zip-tied onto stanchions and poles on the sides of the ferry. Like the riverbank, the hours slip silently by. Conversation has slowed; vodka is sipped instead of gulped; the hookah pipe is passed from hand to mouth; sunflower seeds are nibbled, the husks eddying as hot gusts of wind tug them about the deck. I sit with the bikers and we talk - one speaks passable English and he translates for the others. They ask me how much money I spend each day and I tell them about $30; they exclaim that I am a rich man, tell me they spend about 1200 roubles a day ($12) - the difference, one says amidst laughter, is the price of a Russian woman.

"What is your name?" one asks. He has braided hair, a darkly tanned torso with the body of a naked woman tattooed across his back. I am confused because they already know my name. The translator attempts to explain: Not my birth name, what is my *name* - my biker's name, a name given by my mates to reflect some attribute of my character, something I have done. (Like "Killer", I think, the name given to the Black Bears' *fixer* who beat the drug dealers to a bloody pulp on the White Sea shore eight years before and who showed us the blood on his hands saying with a wry smile, "Not mine - theirs!")

They seem delighted when I tell them I don't have a name and begin making suggestions; eventually *McCloud* is settled on.

"Why McCloud?" I ask, not then being aware of Dennis Weaver in his eponymous role in the 1970s detective series.

"It means you are still living," our translator tells me - then he ponders a while, realising this explanation is less than flattering. He tries again, "Still living - in a *good* way. Like McCloud - an old biker still riding..."

"Thank you," I say and then feel liquid being poured over my head. I look round and, surrounded by their laughter, I am baptised with vodka into their fellowship by the leader of the tour and they shake my hand all round. *I am McCloud, still living -* and it is one of the most special moments of my life.

At intervals throughout the afternoon, battered motorboats set off from isolated - very isolated - settlements along the banks of the river, keep pace with the ferry while transactions are concluded: money passed across while dried and smoked fish, sometimes bottles of home-brewed alcohol, are passed up. Then the bikers all gather, the fish is cut up with sharp knives and handed around, nibbled with white teeth and chased with vodka drunk from plastic cups.

Next to me, a biker called Oleg asks me what it is about Russia that has brought me back so many times. I try to express the vastness of it with my arms spread wide but he captures my meaning with just one word: "Majestic -" he says, looking out into the endless sweep of taiga against a sky heavy with cloud, the fecund smell of the river in the still air all about us, the throb of the engine rising through the rusty metal deck and the wide, slow river making its way north between islands thick with birch trees.

Much later I sit on the deck to eat my supper of *borsh* and dry bread bought from the *magazin*. A biker moves an aluminium pannier in front of me that I can use as a table. When I have finished, I walk down the ferry deck and a young girl in her late teens gets out of a car and hands me a peaked cap; on it, in ballpoint, she has drawn a heart and written on the peak, "With love from Russia".

The three ladies who are sharing my cabin are heading in the same direction as I am once we disembark and we agree to travel together. They will show me the way and organise the bus fares. Everything is falling into place.

What a blessing that I unknowingly opted to take the slow ferry instead of the hydrofoil. I feel as if I am, once again, mixing with the proletariat, everyday Russians who reveal to me the heart of this wonderful land. In life, one surely can't get much better than this.

Later one of the bikers tells me he wants to teach me some Russian. He gets me to repeat after him a Russian phrase and there is a flutter of amusement. I realise that I have been caught in the classic trick played on most foreigners in a place where they don't understand the language: asked to repeat, in all innocence, a filthy word in polite society. But he gets his comeuppance: a large lady tells him off like a naughty child, pointing to a little girl who was close enough to have heard us. Sheepishly he apologises and leaves the group. The large lady shakes her head, catches my eye and points with two fingers under her neck.

The sun sinks low over the trees, setting the dark sky alight; the wind rises again, blowing spray across the deck. I join a group of bikers clustered around a pannier, watch as they continue to cut strips of raw, un-smoked fish off the bone with sharp knives, lifting their heads and feeding the fishy strips into their mouths like spaghetti and chasing it with vodka.

"Russian whiskey!" one says to me, catching my eye and raising his plastic cup. I decline both the fish and the rocket fuel, despite their urgings, and they laugh good-naturedly at me, confirming, I am sure, in their minds the weakness of British men and the superiority of the Russian spirit. No matter - I'd prefer to be regarded as weak and live a little longer.

A damp coldness descends on the decks; the riverbank is a pale line of sand now against the dark trees and sky. The bikers have congregated in the shelter of the eating area; their voices are loud in the confines of the room with its few small tables and wooden benches. The lady in charge reprimands them and they respond like chastened schoolboys. I don't understand what she is saying but its meaning is clear: *This is a place for paying customers only so settle down, buy something or get out!* But she's taken a liking to me and her face softens and a smile forms on her otherwise severe face when I come in and she gives me biscuits for free with my coffee and refuses my offer of payment. She either likes the look of me or she feels sorry for me - I presume the latter.

*****

The morning dawns bright and clear and soon the bikers are up, seemingly unaffected by the alcohol consumed the night before. They fire up the hookah as the low sun warms the metal of the deck and throws long, dark shadows over the river. Water is boiled and coffee brewed. A steaming cup is put into my hand; one lifts his cup to me and says in broken English, "Good coffee... river..." Trying to express his feelings with the few words he knows, he points to the blue sky above us and adds, "Friends -" and I can only agree.

Just then a fast hydrofoil passes us - the one that had been moored to the riverbank for days at Kargasok, perhaps - and I realise that, but for chance, I might have been on that very different machine where people sit in plush seats like passengers in a bus - and I would have missed all this.

The landscape surrounding us is unchanged. Very little changes here - except the weather and that, I feel, is enough to make up for all the rest. I look out at the river twinkling past, bright in the early morning sunlight, and try to imagine it frozen over, the dark trees white with snow, the river an ice road, plumes of smoke rising vertically from the chimneys of small, log-built houses tucked away between the trees, the occupants huddled inside. What do they do all day throughout the dark winter? How difficult is it for young people way out here to find a mate? How do widows cope when their husbands die? What do they do when someone falls seriously ill or has an accident? How long does it take before the lame dogs of society die out here?

And again I am aware that I am little more than a voyeur passing through a majestic land and its people and, in all reality, I know very little about them and the lives they live.

But more than I did before, I suppose, and that makes all the difference.

Chapter Thirty Seven

Red square

I believe I've said this before - I hate cities. I hate them with a passion in keeping with my loathing of paedophiles and motorbike tyres that puncture on dirt roads in the rain.

I arrive in Moscow an hour before midnight having got a flight south from Surgut after my three middle-aged ladies had shepherded me onto a taxi, bus and train from where the ferry docked at Sirezhevoy. The bikers left me there to continue north.

I stand in the rain outside the train station in the middle of one of the biggest cities in the world and wonder how I can find a hostel or somewhere cheap to stay. I'm beyond tired. While my psyche is still attuned to a slow ferry on the deep-flowing Ob River somewhere in the Siberian wilderness, my body exists within the mind-numbing impersonality of Moscow.

I approach a woman waiting at a pedestrian crossing and ask for help; she recoils as if I have just exposed myself. There is a look of disgust and contempt on her face that transcends the barrier of language and which I find upsetting. Only later, when I see myself in a mirror, do I realise just how much like a tramp I look - my clothes creased and dirty, my pannier-suitcase looking like a homeless man's holdall, my white beard scraggy and unkempt. There is a look about me - and a smell, probably - that rough sleepers get after a few months living under a bridge.

A taxi driver, that most despised of breed and most prone to preying on unsuspecting travellers, rips me off. His stupidly fast, aggressive, rude driving reinforces the stereotype we've all seen on compilation videos of drivers behind the wheel trying to manipulate the statistics on the average life expectancy of Russian men. He stops, lets down his window and points out an inner-city hostel just twenty metres from where he picked me up.

Relieved still to be alive, I open a metal door and am subjected to what comes close to a strip search by an unsmiling guard. Then up four flights of bare staircase only to be confronted by one of those unsmiling, overweight, middle-aged women whom, I am sure, have been pensioned off from their normal jobs as guards in a penal settlement for violent and unrehabilitated criminals. She is brusque, rude, demanding - her usual manner, I assume, in her past job when she supervised the interrogation of prisoners in thick-walled rooms deep below street level where their screams can be heard only by those who like to hear them.

Yes, there is a room. Documents...

She scrutinises everything I've got, lays out the visa validation certificates on her desk that I've collected at random stops throughout Russia, and arranges them in date order.

Where is the certificate from jab to prod? she demands, stabbing a finger at the blank dates where, in her opinion, a certificate is missing.

I tell her that, as I am travelling and haven't stopped at any one place for longer than three days, as required by the law, no validation certificate for the time between those dates is necessary. People begin to gather behind me, weary travellers who are unhappy about the delay. Our argument continues, she stabbing at the missing gap in my documentation and me insisting that I don't need it.

She wins. They always do, these types - until, that is, someone kills them.

She kicks me out. I'm back standing in the street in the rain. Just next to me, radiating light and warmth and silly prices is the Radisson, a hotel as snooty as its name suggests. It's after midnight and I grit my teeth and pay. Up in my room, the coffee machine won't work. A man replaces it with another. There are only two of those silly plastic thingies of milk in the room. I phone for more and a disembodied voice tells me that I am only allowed two.

I give up.

Big cities - 1: Me - 0

This is not how motorcycle travel ought to be. I want my bike back.

*****

"If you're lazy or a bum in Russia - two years -" and he passes a horizontal V with his fingers across his face.

Sasha is the young biker Gareth and I met on the roadside eight years ago. We've kept in touch and I always knew that I'd meet him again one day.

Things are changing and the young want more, Sasha tells me. The old, the "Soviets" - those who grew up under a state system that provided guaranteed jobs and security, are lost now and don't know how to cope. "Still many jobs - state jobs - that cater for them, low pay and unnecessary, really," he adds.

Sasha and his wife Dasha, their children Julia and Martin, are of the new generation, the Russia of tomorrow. Well educated, articulate, sophisticated even in their small, two-bedroom apartment on the 5th floor of a modern-ish apartment block (it's got a lift) on the outskirts of Moscow where they live with Dasha's mother, Svetlana, all five of them in a two-bed apartment: kitchen, small bathroom and toilet, entrance hall. No living room - this is, by default, the tiny kitchen about whose small table the family congregates. Under the table, the microwave; washing machine in the entrance hall. Television is watched in the main bedroom where the bed converts into a couch. The rooms are sparsely furnished; they have to be - there is no space for anything more. Two beds. I sleep on a blow-up mattress on the floor of Sasha and Dasha's bedroom where they share their bed with their son; Julia sleeps in the second bedroom with her grandmother. In the bedroom Sasha has his worktable, cluttered with electrical components, a microscope for re-wiring mobile phones, tools and electrical testing and soldering apparatus. When I express misgivings about invading their privacy, Sasha tells me, "It's OK - Russians live like this all the time from long ago."

I am impressed with this young family. If this is the New Russia, things look good for the country. Whatever they have they will share with a gentle and understated giving. When I mention how long it might be convenient for me to stay - Monday? (I didn't mention *In your already overcrowded apartment, sleeping at the foot of your bed!*) Sasha replies, "Monday? This Monday or next Monday? No problem. I had a friend who stayed with us for a few months -"

Yes, things are different in Russia - better, I think. There's a down-to-earth openness here, no hidden agendas: just fit in, become one of the family, exist, live, endure, rub along.

(I have managed to check on the whereabouts of my bike: it's still in Yakutsk. Hasn't moved a single foot since I left it there nearly three weeks ago. "WTF?" - I think is the appropriate expression used by the youth of today.)

The next day we go for a picnic. Sasha puts an ice-cold beer in my hand. In the heat of the car beads of condensation gather on its surface. One pint - they do things big in Russia. I crack it and drink, not knowing whether I'm supposed to save it until later. But it's cold and needs to be drunk.

Outside the rain hammers down, the air muggy and damp. In the back seat, Dasha, the two kids and Svetlana. We wait in the car for the rain to stop so we can have our planned picnic after a long walk in Moscow's Tsaritsyno Park - 34 acres of well-managed woods in the heart of the city, founded by Catherine the Great in 1776.

Eventually the rain slows and we make our way to the banks of a lake and get a fire going. Other families have clustered under covered benches and have started their own fires and the damp smoke rises and settles in the heavy air. It starts to rain again and we huddle under a large tree and coax a reluctant flame from the charcoal and cook pale sausages on skewers. The children play in the rain; Svetlana cuts up the inevitable tomatoes and cucumbers; a friend of Dasha's joins us and adds his sausages to the fire. We eat standing up; later, in the rain, we pack up and drive to the friend's apartment - modern and spacious but with only one living/bedroom and a tiny balcony where, eight stories up, we look out over a wide expanse of maples.

He has a good, well-paid job in Moscow yet lives in this small space. It's comfortable, well appointed, tasteful - and *small*. But, despite the fact that the people I have met and lived with briefly in Russia have limited incomes and, perhaps, even more limited horizons compared to the freedom of movement and expression we have in the west, they seem to be happy. By comparison, we live wasteful lives, full of redundancies; and they navigate with stoicism between the small annoyances of life here in Russia - like having to carry some form of ID with them at all times or risk arrest; the awareness, too, that for those at the top, for the rich, the oligarchs, the people in positions of power, life is lived according to different rules; that the health system is poor and unless you have the money to pay into a private health scheme, you are in trouble if you become severely ill; that elections are usually corrupt in some way...

They shrug and grimace and say things like, "That's Russia -" and they know that things are changing for the better - slowly - and they wait for it to get better still.

Sasha and Dasha - what is it about this young couple that moves me so? Five of them living in such harmony in a two-bed apartment with no living space but the bedrooms and the kitchen, intelligent, gentle souls who have welcomed me into their cramped world with such ease.

This is the Russia I have come to love, the people I have come to respect and admire. I pray that, in the future, our governments can be friends too, just like the Russians I have met on this trip who so want to be friends with us in the west.

Sasha grew up hard. He tells me about his childhood in the *obshejitiye* - the ghettoes of the early nineties. The word is directly translated as "common place to live" - apartment blocks with rooms off a corridor with one shared toilet and cooking room per floor. People could only survive through the winter if they had something left over from the vegetable patch, Sasha tells me, otherwise they starved. There was much violence and anarchy after the dissolution of the Soviet Union. Many people found themselves undocumented and, without the necessary piece of paper, you couldn't get an apartment or a room. And even those who had a room, many died of cold and starvation, only being discovered when they started to smell. After leaving school, Sasha attended a basic college and then put himself through university once he'd started work. Dasha, when they met, was a flute player in a military band and one night, after supper, she takes out her flute and plays to us, a beautiful classical piece - I can't remember which - her short top rising above her bare midriff as she sways from side to side, eyes closed, a contemplative smile on her lips.

*****

Just twenty metres or so in front of me are the mummified remains of one Vladimir Ilyich Ulyanov, better known to the world as Lenin, dreamer of a dream that would change the world. It was a social experiment that ultimately failed, but the consequences still affect our world in altered national borders and mutual suspicion that, even today, hangs over us the ugly spectre of nuclear war. His embalmed body, like the statues that dominate city centres in most towns and cities throughout Russia and even the now independent 'Stans, endures. The cobbles under my feet are large and uneven and I try to close my mind to the thousands of tourists that throng Red Square and allow my mind to hold the image of these very cobbles under the marching, phalanxed boots of soldiers, rifle-straight, the tracks of tanks, missile launchers carrying their threatening burdens - a warning, always a warning - to the west: *Don't muck with us; we're armed and disciplined and ready...*

Standing on these cobbles I picture in my mind's eye the roll-call of Soviet leaders who have stood on the raised plinth, as geometrically squared as the platoons of marching soldiers below, like modern-day Caesars, the Hitlers and Mussolinis and Kim Jong Uns of this world, observing and being observed. And yet, too, in contrast to the brutal red walls of the Kremlin, just in front of me, the soft, multicoloured domes of St Basil's Cathedral, gaily painted like a child's toy or a Christmas bauble, icon of Russia, a symbol, perhaps, that, despite all the communist leaders could do to eradicate it, the church has outlasted them all, has proved itself stronger than totalitarianism, that love has outlasted hatred and fear and suspicion, the soft, bright curves symbolic of a different way.

And later, on rented bicycles, we ride twenty kilometres through Moscow's streets and along the bank of the wide Moskva River to a peaceful stretch of water and watch, as the sun sinks and lights from high-rise buildings in the city centre begin to twinkle and reflect off its surface, fat women and pale, skinny men in the water; and then we strip off and swim too, the water warm as a mouth, the air holding still the heat of the day. And Dema, a friend of Sasha's, long-haired and spare, Harley rider and maker of custom jewellery, opens a bottle of Ruby Port and we drink from plastic cups as darkness settles over the city.

"When I was a boy," Dema tells us, "we used to swim across the river just here and steal carrots and tomatoes and radishes from the farmer's field over there -" He smiles and his teeth are yellow and stained.

Chapter Thirty Eight

Not one step backwards

"Please try to understand this. It's not an easy thing to hear, but please listen. There is no morality in war. You kill children. You kill women. You kill old men. You don't seek them out, but they die. That's what happens in war" - from "Duty: A father, his son, and the man who won the war" by Paul Tibbets

South of Moscow, the taiga gives way to grass-covered steppe. I have experienced this before on previous trips but the sudden change is no less surprising for that.

Using the car share app BlaBlaCar, Sasha has organised for me to travel south with two taciturn Russian men from Moscow to Volgograd. They do not speak to me, which is fine because the strain of attempting to communicate in a poorly-understood foreign language is wearing me down. There is no ill feeling in the silence - it's a commercial arrangement and social chit-chat is not expected. The young man in the front passenger seat sleeps, the radio plays mindless Russian music and the gently undulating steppe passes in a yellow blur across my window. Flocks of crows darken the air with their wings, bright fields of sunflowers turn their faces heavenwards and, when we pass through small towns, the sweet smell of wood smoke and *sashlik* cooking creeps its way into the car.

My mind travels to my crated bike making its slow way west; I pray that she is making progress now and is not stuck, forgotten by some bureaucratic oversight, on a grass-grown siding somewhere on the BAM rail line amongst the trees.

We reach Volgograd and I am greeted by Veteslav, tall and spare, greying hair and heavy black moustache with some gold-capped teeth. I met him on social media through a friend of a friend in Magadan and he - rashly, perhaps - offered to show me around Volgograd if I ever visited there. With a month to travel around Russia before my bike arrives, I took him up on his offer. He is gracious, softly spoken and generous, depositing me at the hotel room he has booked for me (and refusing to accept any payment). His English is minimal but we make our way around the roadblocks of language and understand one another well. He leaves me with the promise that he will pick me up at nine the following morning.

In my room I idly peruse a pamphlet detailing the entertainment on offer in the city; alongside the museums and art galleries are directions to "brothel".

Mmmm. Not today, thank you.

*****

Eight years ago I was driving an ancient UAZ 4X4, a bunch of Russian bikers in the back, dodging washed-up logs and flotsam on the White Sea coast north of Archangel. Suddenly from behind me a disembodied voice, thick with emotion, cried out against the rattle of the van, *"We won the war -"*

This emotional outburst, apropos of nothing, has stayed with me over the years because it voices the deeply felt bitterness of so many Russians to the slur on their country's sacrifice during the Second World War. We, as Brits, feel it too whenever we watch American-produced films that imply, overtly or implicitly, that the war was won by the Yanks. British involvement, initially alone, throughout the six long years of war allows us too the right to claim the moral victory. But our feelings of resentment pale to insignificance when set against the Russians'.

Historians and public consciousness have often sidelined the Russian sacrifice during WW2 - and sacrifice it surely was. In terms of casualties alone the figures are shocking and informative, and make understandable that biker's cry that the eventual victory belonged to the Russians.

All these figures are approximate, especially where Russian casualties are concerned (no one can be sure just how many Russians died or were wounded during the war and estimates vary considerably) but the scale of the difference makes precise accounting moot:

United Kingdom: 451,000 dead (0.94% of the population) of which 67,100 were civilians

America: 418,000 dead (0.32% of the population) of which 1,700 were civilians

Russia: *23,000,000 dead* (13.8% of the population) of which 13,204,000 were civilians. *Twenty three million...* (Richard Overy in his book *Russia's War* writes that 19,000 Russian lives were lost *every day* for the duration of the war.)

So now we come to Stalingrad, a single battle that is as iconic to Russians as both Dunkirk and D-Day together are to the British. If any battle could be singled out as the one that changed the course of the war, this was it. After Stalingrad, German generals knew, with a grim certainty, that their war was lost; victory in this battle assured all Russians that, no matter how long it took, the hated invaders would be pushed back, that the rape of the Motherland would be avenged. But the cost was frightening and, especially to us in the west, difficult to grasp. It is this seemingly profligate sacrifice of men that offers a significant insight into the Russian psyche, as I will try to explain. It is my belief that if an outsider can come to some understanding of what happened at Stalingrad, he will make some small progress towards understanding what one writer has called "the mysterious Russian soul". (It was the poet Tyuchev who claimed that "Russia cannot be understood with the mind.")

To Hitler, the taking of Stalingrad was personal. After all, this was the city that bore the name of his hated rival; furthermore, destroying this city would open the way to the oil fields of the Caucasus, so vital to Germany's survival. To Stalin, too, the battle was a line drawn in the sand: No more retreat - not a single metre further. These two leaders seem to have weighed the lives of their men against their own personal egos, flinging millions of men into what Anthony Beevor in his book *Stalingrad* calls "a personal duel by mass proxy".

After initial successes, the German invasion stalled in front of the city. They had, in the words of Richard Overy, "collided with Russian tenacity". Winter was coming; Hitler insisted the city be taken regardless of the cost, but the Russian defenders proved heroically stubborn. And then, contrary to expectation, General Zhukov ordered a surprise counter attack that encircled 290,000 German soldiers of the 6th Army, trapping them in a prolonged battle for survival - mainly against the bitter Russian winter. For the Russian people, there was an intense desire to exact revenge for the brutal German atrocities against civilians, the scorched earth policy adopted by the Nazis in Russia since the beginning of Operation Barbarossa, and an almost suicidal determination not to be beaten.

More Russian soldiers and civilians were lost during this *single* battle - 1,100,000 - than the combined losses of both the United Kingdom and America during the *entire* six years of the war.

That Russian leaders are careless of the lives of their citizens is a given. In this country, the preservation of the Motherland will always take precedence over the sacrifice of any number of her citizens. (This, too, was the understanding during Stalin's purges: the success of the grand Communist experiment was of greater significance than the millions killed in keeping the vision pure and intimidating the population to such an extent that opposition became unthinkable.) Officers took the view that saving the lives of their men was not a priority - significant only was that the objective was achieved, the battle won. "Russia has plenty of people," one soldier commented bitterly. "She has enough of them to waste."

This callousness was all too evident during the battle. Stalin's Order No 227 became known as "Not one step backwards": *"Panic-mongers and cowards must be destroyed on the spot. The retreat mentality must be decisively eliminated. Army commanders who have allowed the voluntary abandonment of positions must be removed and sent for immediate trial by military tribunal."*

Anyone who surrendered was to be regarded as a traitor to the Motherland. Blocking units of well-armed Komosol volunteers or NKVD detachments were placed behind Russian lines - not to fight the advancing enemy, but to shoot any soldier who tried to run away. Penal companies - *shtrafroty* - were established to punish any infringement of discipline. Members of penal companies (known as *smertniks*, "dead men", because they were not expected to survive) were required to perform semi-suicidal tasks such as mine clearance during an attack (this usually meant that men from the *shtrafroty* were ordered to walk ahead of Russian vehicles and troops to detonate the mines with their own bodies). Altogether, in this way, some 422,700 Red Army soldiers would, according to Stalin, "atone with their blood for the crimes they have committed before the Motherland". During the battle, around 13,500 of their own soldiers were executed for behaviour deemed unfit as a Soviet citizen. This included all crimes including retreating without orders, self-inflicted wounds, desertion, corruption and anti-Soviet activities. (Vasily Grossman, a journalist who repoted on the battle, writes of a surgeon amputating the arm of a young soldier who had shot himself in the hand in a desperate attempt to escape the batttle, because he, the surgeon, knew that the young man would be executed the moment an officer saw the tell-tale wound in his left hand.) Russian soldiers were also shot or arrested if they, themselves, did not immediately shoot at any soldier, even if it were a friend, seen trying to desert, surrender or run away.

But Stalin went further than this, issuing his *Stavka* Order whereby even the family members of soldiers who surrendered were to be arrested, sent to detention camps and "deprived of all state allowances and assistance".

Furthermore, Stalin initially refused to permit the civilian inhabitants of Stalingrad to be evacuated to safety across the Volga. His thinking was that soldiers and local men would fight more desperately knowing that their women and children were still in the city.

And it went further: Any one who fell into enemy hands - regardless of the circumstances: a soldier so badly wounded that he was unable to fight - a soldier concussed and taken prisoner whilst unconscious, for example - would, on his return, be regarded as a traitor and either executed or sent to a labour camp (which was pretty much the same thing, only it took longer).

Solzhenitsyn writes with a deep-felt bitterness in *The Gulag Archipelago*: "All soldiers who had been captured by the allied forces, whether because they were wounded or simply overwhelmed by superior firepower, all returning captives were given *tenners* or longer and deported because, first, they should have fought to the death and their very surrender to the enemy was a betrayal of the Motherland but, second, because their time living amongst the enemy might have influenced them, altered their attitude to the Communist ideal, tainted them ideologically and thereby made them a possible threat to the purity of the ideal and they needed to be removed so they could not taint the ideas of others. That was because they had seen something of European life and could talk about it.

"There was something called Article 58-1b; in wartime, it provided only for execution by shooting. For not wanting to die from a German bullet, the prisoner had to die from a Soviet bullet for having been a prisoner of war. Some get theirs from the enemy; we get it from our own."

This is one, seemingly heartless, side of the coin when attempting to understand the Russian psyche. The other is more positive. Set against this brutal coercion must be laid a profound and visceral patriotism: *The Motherland calls*. The willingness of the ordinary Russian soldier or civilian to die, to give up all for the beloved Motherland, lies deep within the very bones of all Russians - something that was underestimated by both the German leadership and the ordinary soldiers on the front line who never ceased to be astonished at the heroism, the selfless bravery of the average Russian soldier, their refusal to give up no matter what overwhelming odds faced them. These were a people for whom loyalty and self sacrifice were woven into the fabric of their beings; a people for whom, after enduring decades of privation, suffering had become a natural part of life - tough and fatalistic and able to endure.

For months the Luftwaffe, almost unopposed, bombed Stalingrad until it was little more than a tangle of concrete and bent steel covered with snow, but the destruction seemed to do little more than provide hiding places amongst the rubble and in the sewers beneath for Russians who fought back with stoic heroism. In most of the city, not a house was left standing, just a wasteland of rubble, of burned-out shells of buildings which soldiers defended from room to room.

It is told that in make-shift hospital wards in bombed-out cellars, Russian medical workers gave so much of their own blood for transfusions - sometimes twice in an evening - that they frequently collapsed.

This, then, is the spirit of Stalingrad, that pivotal battle between two opposing worldviews that, because of the bravery and the sacrifice of the Russian soldiers and civilians who held the city for 164 days, turned the tide of WW2.

*****

On the way to the Stalingrad Battle Memorial Museum we pass a large building with a domed roof. "Street of Peace," Veteslav informs me, pointing. "Observatory. Gift from Germany."

I find this deeply moving, considering what happened here between 23 August 1942 and 2 February 1943.

Outside the museum stands the stark and ghostly remains of a six-story building, the old mill, built of red brick and left exactly as it was after the battle as a memorial. All the window openings, glassless, of course, are still raw, the frames and window surrounds blown away and left ragged, like wounds in a face. Some sections of wall have been completely shot out and are held together with metal rods.

Across the street is Pavolv's House. Veteslav points to it and says, "A few soldiers with Pavlov. The Germans couldn't take it." Slogans have been painted on the sides of tanks and tracked vehicles and Katyusha rocket launchers lined up outside the museum. I ask Veteslav to translate: "'To Berlin'," he reads, and, "'For our land'." Down below, next to an old army truck, is the touching statue of six children, hands clasped, dancing around a pool of water from whose depths a crocodile emerges. This is a reproduction of the original, a photograph of which was published during the battle showing the statue, covered in ash as Stalingrad burned, still untouched by the bombs at that moment (it was destroyed later), 23 August 1942, when some 40,000 Soviet citizens died from German bombing of the city. The photograph was a poignant reminder of the destruction of innocence but also of the heroic nature of the citizens and soldiers who defended their city.

On the weed-covered grass around the base of the building lie the remains of gun barrels, breech blocks, tank tracks, even the rusted metal prow of a boat used by the Germans to cross the Volga River while it was still unfrozen. These discarded bits, the unlovely detritus of war, mean more to me than the carefully restored examples of the guns and tanks on display, freshly painted in Russian green and German field grey.

The scarred remains of the mill chimney stands to the west of the building, its upper section shot away, the rest pocked with shell and bullet holes.

To one side, the remains of a Soviet T34 tank, its turret missing, the ring gear cracked, bullet holes through the heavy treads, its V12 engine seemingly untouched and exposed alongside a massive radiator, scored through with bullet holes, the two-inch thick metal of its sides ripped apart like paper - but what is most poignant are the wilting red carnations that have been laid on the shattered front plate, their petals like dark splatters of blood.

I find, by chance, that I am wearing my "No More Slaves" T-shirt and feel that, here, it's particularly appropriate.

We enter the museum. At the entrance, a concession stand selling, amongst other tat, busts of bloody Stalin! Would one expect to be offered busts of Hitler in the concession stands at the entrance to German holocaust museums, I wonder?

Inside are displayed the rusted and bent remains of arms and ammunition and torn pieces of shrapnel, the crushed and concertinaed skin of aircraft and broken aircraft engines. Against one wall is a darkened model of the shattered and burning remains of the city with images of the fighting projected onto the wall behind: an emaciated horse standing, head hanging, amongst the carnage; a soiled child being carried by a Russian soldier; bits of the walls of buildings and massive I-beams bent and shot-riddled; broken personal effects: a child's doll; a remarkably unbroken porcelain figurine of a lady sitting on a chez lounge with a little dog appealing to be petted; icons, blackened by fire - reflections of a more peaceful time.

On the roof of what was once a water tower, a diorama one hundred metres long and forty feet high depict the actual events as recorded from documents and first-hand accounts of those who were there on 26 January, 1943; in the foreground, dust-covered artefacts meld seamlessly with the painted background; the Volga River in the distance, the bombed city to one side, the second water tower with its concrete roof smashed in, a Soviet flag still flying; behind us, a battle takes place through a churned-up landscape covered with snow.

And later, in the heat of the afternoon, I stand in a large domed room - the Hall of Military Glory - where a flame of remembrance flickers and flares from the palm of a golden hand that holds a torch twenty feet high, the walls covered with thousands upon thousands of the names of dead soldiers, all in serried ranks as if they themselves are still standing to attention; close to me, two young soldiers in full dress uniform, so young that they look like children, stand still as dolls while haunting stringed music fills the void with sound and the tourists gawp and click-click with their cameras and phones, posing alongside the solemn young boys and I want to shout at them: *This is not a fucking tourist attraction...* and my throat constricts with the need to weep and strangely into my mind come Eliot's words:

That is all we could see. But how many eagles! and how many trumpets!
(And Easter Day, we didn't get to the country,
So we took young Cyril to church. And they rang a bell
And he said right out loud, *crumpets*.)
Don't throw away that sausage,

It'll come in handy. He's artful. Please, will you
Give us a light?
Light
Light
Et les soldats faisaient la haie? ILS LA FAISAIENT.

- and while I stand, watching, a uniformed officer marches up to each motionless, uniformed boy in turn, gently removes his cap and, with a cloth, wipes the sweat off his head and his face and his neck with the tenderness of a lover, as a mother would to a sick child, gently, lovingly, and the young men stand motionless as stoics and I can no longer hold in my weeping at the pathos of it, the loving man-touch of an officer to a uniformed boy, and part of me wants to call out to the Russian military and the Russian government, *Why? If you love your young men so deeply, why do you subject them to training so severe and unregulated that many of them would rather kill themselves than go through with it to the end?* and I want to cry out through my tears to the whole world, *Why, if you love your young men so much do you send them with such alacrity to fight and leak their hot blood into the soil of far-off lands, why the need to posture and to crow about who has the bigger guns and missiles that can destroy the whole world?* and I want to shout out to parents who allow a soldier at the entrance to the memorial to drape their children with bits of uniform and place guns in their hands and too-large helmets on their heads and photograph them, armed and uniformed and smiling, in front of an army jeep - *Why, parents, why do you want to put fucking guns into the hands of your children? Why do you want to glorify war that is at best an acknowledgement of the failure of good people to talk and come to a resolution of sorts that does not involve the slaughter of our little ones?* And I want to cry out like Owen: "*If you could hear, at every jolt, the blood come gargling from the froth-corrupted lungs, obscene as cancer, bitter as the cud of vile, incurable sores on innocent tongues, my friend, you would not tell with such high zest to children ardent for some desperate glory the old lie: Dulce et Decorum est pro patria mori*" - because, hear me, each one of the names on that wall is more than just a name: every one is a brother, a father, husband, lover and the tearing of his soft body to allow his spirit free will impact on countless lives in countless shocking ways for ever; and even those men who live through the holocaust with their flesh unripped, unpierced, are changed inside forever in terrible ways that we mostly cannot see except in the emptiness of their eyes and the cold statistics of suicide and the dulling effects of drugs to chase the memories away, ghosts that haunt and maim them on the inside as badly as the hot, twisted metal has torn others on the outside so that many of them can no longer function in our seemingly normal society.

And outside, amongst the statues and bas-reliefs of men overcoming impossible odds is a thirty-foot high stone statue of the Pieta, of Mary holding the dead body of her son, newly lifted down from the cross, his face covered with a stone cloth, her face soft and contemplative as she looks upon her murdered boy and tries to understand why and I weep afresh at the love of God revealed through the voluntary death of Christ who, unlike the soldiers torn apart as they tore others apart for little other reason than that they wore a uniform of a different colour, did not trade blows or insults but yielded Himself to the agony of the cross and the nails and the whips and cried out *Father forgive them for they do not know what they are doing.*

Oh, God, I whisper through my tears, *When will this hatred and killing end? When will leaders stop this profligacy with the lives of their young men?*

*****

Later, back in my hotel room, still emotional, I post on social media that the Hall of Military Glory ought, perhaps, to be renamed *The Hall of Sorrow*. Galina, my friend from Vladivostok, posts: "My grandmother (she from Ukraine) had four brothers. All four died in this war. One of them was Stalingrad. Only one of them was married, the others young guys. The last, the youngest, went to the front when Soviet troops were already marching west through their village and died in the first battle." Later, she adds, "The youngest died under the town of Belaya Tserkov, near Kiev. He never fired, his friend told him..."

Another called Alexander posts a gentle rebuke: "We have this tradition from the depth of centuries. The people have always praised, glorified their brave warriors who died on the battlefields. Our ancestors are called Slavs. Even the names are such. You were met by Veteslav. My father's name is Stanislav. A warrior carrying an oath swears to give his life if required for his glorious Fatherland - the Motherland. Therefore, we know how to call our rooms."

Chapter Thirty Nine

No touch! Only husband.

The road from Volgograd to Astrakhan is worn and neglected and the bus makes its way south across a dry, featureless plain where the earth shows through spiky tufts of grass. The sky is cloudless and big and the heat bakes all colour from the land so that everything seems pale and over-exposed. The man sitting next to me on the bus lifts his arms to rest them on the seat in front of him and his body odour makes my eyes sting. This is more Kazakhstan than Russia, the small communities through which we pass reeking of poverty and desperation. Every so often, dusty car tracks disappear into the steppe, going who knows where across a scrubby, uncomfortable land so unlike the watery taiga in the north. Occasionally the bus stops at some ratty, straggled settlement and the passengers alight into the heat to charge their veins with nicotine.

It isn't a pleasant journey; one to be endured rather than enjoyed. Bus journeys are usually made by the poor and needy out of necessity rather than choice. I generalise, of course. I could have stayed in Moscow, waited there for my bike, visited the museums and art galleries, sampled the nightlife. But I choose to travel, my spirit restless. Daily now, I check my phone, hoping for the text that will inform me that my bike has arrived in Omsk and is waiting, like a faithful dog, for my return.

And throughout the long eight-hour bus journey to Astrakhan, passengers sleep, smoke during brief stops and stare at their phones, the faded yellow curtains drawn closely over the windows to cut off the glare. I look down the long tunnel of seats at the bright rectangle of the driver's window and know that I should be riding this road and not sitting in the back of a bloody bus. One thing has happened though: travelling with these people, strangers though they might be, I don't feel so lonely any more.

Houses with walls made of discarded, wooden railway sleepers and corrugated asbestos roofs, Wild West accumulations of low buildings alongside of which a rail line passes - and this lumpy, narrow road, ruler-straight, across the steppe.

And then it turns to semi-desert, hot and dry and spiked with dying, twiggy plants that click and rattle in the wind - and a small part of me is glad that I am sitting in a bus and not out in that terrible heat on an air-cooled bike, my body wilting under heavy riding gear.

Then, suddenly, while I wasn't watching, the land turns green and wet; there are wide swathes of reeds and rivers small and large: we have reached the wetlands of the Vloga delta, all 27,000 sq km of it, 160ks across, the largest river delta in Europe.

*****

At the hostel, a thin, dark-haired man with skin burned mahogany from the sun cleans freshly-caught fish, cuts up an onion, arranges them in a cast-iron pot, covers them with sour cream and pushes it into the oven. He caught them in the river, he tells me with a shy smile. Most of his upper teeth are missing.

In the morning, wearing only a pair of shorts, I find him preparing his rod and line. "Can I come with you?" I ask him and he nods.

Outside it's been raining - a welcome relief. We walk through rain-wet streets and call in at a *magazin* on the way; he buys a 6-pack and a packet of cigarettes; I buy a carton of OJ and a pear.

Not criticizing - just observing.

The Volga River is wide and muddy here, the far bank thick with low underbrush; in the shallows, water lilies blossom between deep-green lily pads.

He baits his hooks with mielie pips cut from the cob with a knife, one per hook, casts, then prepares a second rod, sharpening the hooks with a file. He crouches on the ground with his knees around his chin like people unused to chairs do, feet flat on the ground - a crouching impossible for most westerners - and baits the second hook with worms kept in a mud-filled tin.

He catches nothing and I, impatient as always, wish him well and walk down the embankment past buildings that hold still a certain old-world elegance, pastel shades of pink and beige, faded and peeling, cast-iron broekie-lace balconies overhanging the street. I drink coffee at a boutique coffee house opposite the Kremlin. At a table opposite me a young couple talk in whispers, their faces close, then they lean forward and kiss and I know that drinking coffee alone is a sad thing and I wonder what I'm doing here.

Four more days until my bike is supposed to arrive...

*****

"Englishmen can't have tea without milk!" a large man tells me back at the hostel, laughing. His small wife gives me three small fish fried in batter.

"Russia is a functioning society without welfare," he tells me, speaking fluent English. "There is low unemployment here because people *have* to work. There is no safety net," - implying that this is a good thing and I see it in a new light. "We lost faith in Communism," he says, "and didn't acquire anything in return. Our life is based solely on human relationships. And they are strong."

*****

In the middle of the Volga River, just upstream from the new bridge, is a wooded island about two kilometres long where many who live in Astrakhan come on hot, still weekends to sunbathe and swim. I cross the thrumming bridge in the heat and walk along the riverbank, the sand fine and white, fat people exposing to the sun their wobbly bits and young people displaying their curvy bits. The sand is hot under my feet; I wade in deep, the river bottom firm and not muddy, the water cool on my skin, and I reflect that now I can claim to have swum in both the Moscow and Volga Rivers and Lake Baikal, and that makes me feel good.

Later I walk through the thick undergrowth across the island following dusty tracks and I could be somewhere in the Highveld of South Africa. A man passes me riding a bicycle, stops and greets me. He tells me he used to be a boxer, pressing on his broken nose with a finger to illustrate the point. He asks me if I want something to drink and I nod, thinking water, but as he begins to dig in his rucksack, he jabs in a practiced way into the jugular under his jaw and I apologise and say, *"Nyet, pashalsta -"*

He looks surprised.

And much later as the sun sinks like a red ball over the still waters of the Volga, and swallows dip and weave over the waters and the heat of the day rises damp and close from the ground, the fisherman and I eat sunflower seeds as he casts and reels in, casts and reels in, and he tells me, his mouth full of seeds and husks, about the two years he spent illegally working in the US and learning to speak English.

*****

Outside the rocking train carriage window the semi-desert steppe passes in hues of yellow and brown for the fifteen hours it takes to reach the Chechen capital of Grozney. A landscape nudging towards true desert, hundreds of kilometres of it, flat and gently undulating, the skin of pale sand showing through. And outside the train window the kilometres flash by with the rising and falling of electric wires strung from wooden poles under a big, big sky.

There is something fascinating about the remote south-western republic of Chechnya (as well as Dagestan, North Ossetia and Ingushetia). What are they, exactly, and what is their relationship with Russia? The connections are tenuous at best but they seem to have settled into a state of mutual tolerance based on suspicion and distrust after the two costly wars with Chechnya that lasted twenty years and has been referred to by some as Russia's Vietnam. Staunchly Muslim, these states are pretty much left to their own devices, *de facto* independent yet still part of Russia. The wars had killed over 100,000 people, mainly civilians, and Russia had shelled the capital, Grozney, into a wasteland of apocalyptic proportions. Concessions were made, Grozney rebuilt, life goes on. Yet the dark-skinned men I see from the train window have still a look about them that speaks of violence; personally, I wouldn't like to meet an angry Chechnyan in a dark alley or, as a young Russian soldier, come face to face with a band of them carrying Kalashnikovs in some remote mountain valley. The women are conservatively dressed, as most Muslim women are, their hair covered with colourful scarves.

At a train stop, a uniformed man with a thin, aquiline face warns an American traveller wearing shorts that in future he should cover his legs properly. The language they speak is no longer Russian and filled with guttural fricatives.

Later, Grozney, and the young man shaving my head in the Chechnyan style (bald head and big beard) touches my face lightly with his cool hands. A gaunt man wearing camouflage enters and speaks to him in the manner of one asking for help; outside on the hot pavement are a woman in traditional dress and a young boy. My barber puts his hand in his pocket and takes out a hundred-rouble note - the usual cost of a haircut - and gives it to the man who thanks him in a grateful but dignified manner and joins his wife and son on the street.

My hair now cut, I stand and reach into my pocket for my wallet. The young man waves me away: "Visitor -" he says.

I argue with him and only succeed by leaving the money on his counter.

And, on the street, I think to myself: Here is a young man attempting to earn a living. I was his only customer. After giving the ex-soldier a hundred roubles, most people would think to themselves, No problem, I'll make it up by charging this rich foreigner here double, he can afford it. Instead, he wanted to bless me by not charging for my haircut.

Once again I am humbled by the actions of seemingly insignificant people whose generosity marks them out in the great scheme of things as significant. Come now, rich people of this world - how much is enough?

Later I purchase air tickets to Moscow and then Omsk, ready to wing my way north and east where, hopefully, I will meet up with my little bike *click-clacking* her way towards me. Let it be soon; our reuniting will be that of old friends.

When the lady wearing a *hijab* at the airport desk gives me my tickets, I thank her and put out my hand. She recoils and says, *"No touch!* Only husband!"

I apologise and tell her, "I was trying to be polite."

She smiles her understanding. We part and I reflect on the seemingly unbridgeable chasm that separates us in this world.

Chapter Forty.

Looking for mushrooms

The flights from Grozney to Omsk are routine and I meet my good friend Rimma at her office in the language school. Later, in their apartment, Sasha smiles at me in what could be taken as sympathy for my abysmal lack of understanding of how things work in Russia, and says, "One week." Behind the smile I can detect a touch of sadness in his face. "One *week*, Lau-rence," he repeats. "This is Russia."

It seems I have been hasty, allowing my desire to be back in the saddle cloud my judgement, turning expectation into wish-fulfilment and, from there, certainty: *They said the 8th, maybe it will even be earlier,* my mind argued. *But definitely the 8th.*

Frustration rises within me like a wave but I beat it down. How does it help? There is nothing I can do but wait. Here, they don't track parcels or, seemingly, even goods carriages on the railways so no one seems to know where my bike is. For all I know, it might be sitting somewhere, forgotten, shunted into a weed-grown siding in the forest. And maybe, one day, some faceless official will discover a piece of paper behind a desk and send an instruction to some other faceless bureaucrat to issue instructions to a train driver heading west to couple it up and deliver it to Omsk where a man, when he feels like it, will pick up a telephone and say, "Your bike has arrived..."

There is no competition on the railways here, no pressure to do better. It is what it is - a slow, ponderous, state-run leviathan whose existence or performance cannot be questioned or challenged.

A new lesson learned: In Russia, train carriages from remote areas move only when filled. Hence the three-week wait before my bike even left

Yakutsk. Here, now, waiting, Sasha manages to persuade a very reluctant official (who insists it is illegal for him to reveal the whereabouts of the carriage) to tell him that my bike had, as of yesterday, just left some small town 2,500ks away to the north and will arrive, *in sha'a llah*, in Novosibirsk on Tuesday - five days' time. Then a day (or two) before it arrives in Omsk.

It's a relief to know and to picture my little bike finally making her way towards me.

Be still, my beating heart. All will be well.

*****

It is Saturday and after weeks of unbearable heat, the rains have come; the air is cool and damp under a heavy sky as Sasha, his mother and I walk through wet underbrush in a birch forest forty kilometres out of town looking for mushrooms. We each carry a plastic bucket and a sharp knife; I follow, crouched low under the tangled branches and observe. Not knowing a mushroom from a toadstool, I don't presume to touch anything that might kill me. A deep red one catches my eye, small and smooth-skinned. Tempted, I cut it cleanly, low down, the rich, earthy smell of damp soil, thick with a layer of rotting leaves, rises up at me. I show it to Ludmila but she makes a dismissive gesture and says something to me in Russian that I interpret as: *You eat that, mate, and you're a dead man.*

I carefully wipe all the toxic spores off the knife blade before continuing. Ludmila speaks aloud almost constantly, as some old people do, her voice low and seemingly not directed towards me; but, as there is no one else about, I must assume that I am her audience. She doesn't seem to expect a response so I ignore her and continue my search.

The mushrooms, I discover, seem to thrive in deep shade under a dense, low canopy, the ground wet and thick with leaf mould and clear of long grass. Ludmila rejects most of the mushrooms I offer for her inspection with a little flick of her hand. She draws my attention to one with an orange coloured dome. *"Mugamor,"* she says.

"When you see *Mugamor,*" Sasha tells me, holding it out for me to see, "there are always other mushrooms," and he looks intently under the collapsed branches of a birch tree for more.

It seems that those with very thin stems are immediately rejected whereas the fat-stemmed ones, of a certain type, coveted. I watch as Sasha cuts and lifts a mushroom from the loam then slices through the stem and inspects it; if the flesh is firm and clear, the head is sliced open and similarly inspected. Most often the flesh is wormy and old, the flesh already breaking down. These are tossed away with the word, *"Starry,"* which I have not heard before - and then, suddenly, I remember the word from *A Clockwork Orange,* referring to an old person.

"Old -" I say to Ludmila and she nods and smiles.

Off to one side I hear a cry of delight and I come upon Sasha kneeling before a small, fat mushroom with a rust-coloured head. *"Beligriep!"* he tells me - the best one! He separates it from the leaf mould as one would a delicate insect.

Slowly we fill our buckets; the mosquitoes begin to wake and take an interest. On the way home, we stop off at their *dacha,* a plot of ground 20 X 25 metres in size with a small, one-roomed house, containing a kitchenette, table and two chairs and a bed. Sasha and his mother dig out potatoes and carrots and pick green tomatoes, peppers and cucumbers for the house. Opposite their *dacha* is another small field planted with potatoes.

"Not legal," Sasha tells me. He and other *dacha* owners next to his have extended their land by clearing trees and underbrush, fencing it and planting crops. No one seems to mind - when you consider the size of Russia and its vast tracts of unused land, a few stolen square metres used for growing potatoes is not going to bankrupt the country.

*****

My life has become a hiatus, a week-long intake of breath while I stand outside myself and wait for the exhale. I look about me at a country that has become strangely familiar, like someone in that half-wakeful state between the dream world and the sudden inrush of reality and I ask myself: *What am I doing here?* I tell myself that I am in the middle of Russia, that the people outside my window speak a different language to me; yet, despite this, it has all become familiar now, like a home that is not a home: the gaily-coloured children's playground; the old men sitting on benches outside the apartments watching the world pass by; the worn car tyres painted blue and yellow that demarcate the flower beds; the pot-holed road; music leaking out of the corner *magazin...*

It is somehow surreal. I am half-caught in that moment that Eliot writes about: "Between the idea and the reality, between the motion and the act, falls the shadow"; I am insect caught in resin; I am the still point in my own turning world. I am a stranger here, home but not home; a non-person, waiting.

And, strangely, the key to this state of self-imposed limbo is an old, dirty bike trapped in the dark interior of a truck. Perhaps even at this moment in the distribution centre just three kilometres from where I sit, a fork-lift is adjusting its steel prongs under the pallet that holds my bike, lifting and drawing it into the heat and the light again; soon a telephone call to Sasha saying, "The motorcycle is ready," and he will make his excuses from work, get into his car, drive to the apartment where I sit, now, writing, waiting, reading, and I will hear the muffled bump of the metal outer apartment door and the shuffle as he removes his shoes and then his face will appear around the door and he will say, "Lau-rence, my friend -" in his Russian accent, "come, your bike is here."

I have waited thirty-five days for that. *Will have* - because it has not come yet. It was supposed to have been here six days ago. But then it was still 2,500ks away. Then it would be here yesterday, they assured me. I waited, as I am waiting now, in a bubble of expectation, of nothingness, until the phone rang and Sasha's disappointed voice said, "The bike not come today. Maybe tomorrow..."

And with the word "maybe" hanging heavy in my ears, I take the *auftobus* into town. The lady behind me is rude and shouts at me because my sandaled foot rests briefly on the edge of the seat; the conductress shouts at me to get off the bus when we reach the depot (I've taken the wrong bus) and when I try my usual apologetic Russian that I have used to good effect so often in the past - *I'm sorry, I don't understand... I'm from England and I speak little Russian* - she shouts at me even louder as if the volume of her voice will compensate for my lack of comprehension.

The boat trip along the River Om is nothing more than a distraction, a filler of time. The *auftobus* trip back to the apartment is more successful. I prepare supper for my good hosts as an attempt to say thank you for their patience and their generosity. They are good people but I feel I am now close to outstaying my welcome.

After seven they arrive home. Sasha smiles apologetically and says, "Lau-rence, your bike - they load it now in Novosibirsk on a truck. Here tomorrow."

And so, I wait, reading book after book, devouring words that have been denied me for two long months, revelling in them, the joy of them. Words...

And they wonderfully help to fill the void between the tick and the tock of time that drags her feet in a way so perverse that it almost seems personal.

Another cup of coffee? Another day.

There, I can hear a fumbling at the door!

It is Sasha. "Your motorcycle has not come," he tells me, looking sad, knowing what it means to me. "This is Russia," he explains. "If they tell you twenty years you have to believe them - but you don't believe them," he adds, shaking his head.

Chapter Forty One

Why can't it just be easy?

And then one day the call comes. Sasha and I drive to the depot. On a raised platform, a plastic-wrapped crate that seems to have been hashed up from bits of scrap wood washed up on a beach; inside, I can see the blurred outline of my bike.

With the help of a few men with crowbars, we release her. All seems OK. She looks as if she's just been dredged out of a canal, but that's the way she's always looked. I open the petrol taps, pull out the choke and press the starter. On the second try she takes, much to my relief, but then dies and won't start again. The men push, I drop the clutch and she fires up again.

A quick ride to the apartment and I check her over and begin pack, ready for an early start in the morning...

*****

A heavy mist hides the city of Omsk as I set off early through damp and sparsely populated streets, my goggles misting over as if it were raining. Then the traffic lights and intersections thin and, with that, the mist disappears revealing a big sky. The bike is eager and responsive and I am going home! *Heppy-heppy!*

This, I realise with a sudden tightening in my chest, is what I have been looking forward to, imagining, for the past five weeks. Anticipation has become reality and it is good.

A flat land passes on either side of me, bright with newly-harvested wheat stalks catching the yellow, early-morning light; with the flatness of the land, lakes both large and small appear; reeds in the water tug this way and that like the wind-ruffled hair of an animal, and rooks squabble and wheel in the wind; two yellow-billed kites twist and play above me and where the dark soil has been ploughed the air is damp and smells of cellars long kept closed; from newly-cut wheat fields the air is warm and fresh like Sunday afternoons and cut grass wet with sprinklers.

Around midday I turn off a road heavy with trucks and follow a small lumpy road, almost empty of vehicles and the bike is going well and the sun is bright over the wide, open land. Then the clouds begin to gather and blacken and, ahead, a gauze of rain obscures the horizon and I stop to don my wet-weather gear and then the heavens darken and rain falls in a deluge but still I am happy, feeling the elemental essence of the world against my skin - rain and sun and wind - and loving it and then my engine shudders and dies - not a hesitant, tentative death, but an instantaneous ceasing and I quickly turn the fuel taps onto reserve knowing that it's not that with a hundred kilometres at least still in there and I pull off the road onto the muddy verge with the trucks blundering by and the rain in my face and I am unhappy again.

After a little sulk she fires up again and I ride on in the rain until I find a roadside motel with no water and a very rude woman in the restaurant.

*****

The early sun lying soft on the land is warm with promise. The air is cold. All morning I ride across land flat as a table; other than fields of wheat, the only thing of note is the trees and the occasional small village. Trucks swarm at me coming from the west but my side of the road is relatively uncluttered.

A long truck overtakes me and cuts back too early, the thundering wheels, shoulder high, creep closer until they push me into the dirt. Still on the soft verge, I accelerate past and address him sternly with my middle finger before waving him past. I believe that he understood that I was angry.

In the early afternoon I notice a change: after days, weeks of flat land, ahead of me a range of low hills appears on the horizon, soft wrinkles on a smooth piece of paper - the foothills of the Ural Mountains that run from the Arctic Circle south to the Aral Sea, a distance of some 1500 miles.

I had expected something more dramatic, to be honest, something akin to the Pamirs of Central Asia, a towering barrier stretching across Russia through which roads would weave their way over high passes; these would, in my mind, be all snow and rocks and grand views. After all, the Ural Mountains - one of the oldest mountain ranges on earth - are the outcome of the same cosmic forces that have produced the Himalayas, Andes and the Pamirs. But it is not to be. The coming together of the Kazakhstania tectonic plate and the ancient Laurussia continent have produced a gentle, rolling landscape some 200km wide and little more than 800m high. The hills (can one call them *mountains?*) are tree-covered and beautiful and I pass through them in a few hours, leaving Asian Russia behind me and entering European Russia, with Moscow due west some 2000ks away and, just 600ks beyond that, the border with Latvia.

By late afternoon I have descended into the plains again, the north-south wrinkle across the smooth map of Russia behind me. I ride on into the setting sun, the very air turning yellow again and the bike purring under me. After over 12 hours on the road, I am tired but happy.

*****

It is midday. I eat *borsh* in a small truck-stop cafe on the side of an almost deserted road. At the table next to me four men eat their meals and, together, open and finish a bottle of brandy. When they get up to walk to their car, I notice that one carries another bottle of brandy - I assume in case they get thirsty on the road.

My hands shake as I spoon up my *borsh,* more from nervous tension than exhaustion, although that is part of it. It's my first voluntary stop since I set off this morning.

The day started well with the bike purring contentedly along a good road through pretty, rolling countryside of woods and wheat fields and bright yellow splashes of mature sunflowers. I was making good progress with the new, larger front sprocket I'd fitted the evening before, the old one looking remarkably like a Ninja throwing star with its stubby, sharp-pointed teeth worn to the nub over the past two months of travel. Then I did that which all experienced motorcyclists know *never* to do, the ultimate no-no and something that ought to be taught to little children at their father's knee: I said to myself, in a glow of hubris, that my little bike was going really well, sweet as a nut, in fact.

Well, the curse had been spoken, nemesis released from his dark cave. Within ten minutes, near the top of a long, slow hill, the engine hesitated once, lost power and died.

I pulled over, climbed off with that sinking feeling one gets when facing the unknown, and did what I always do in situations like this: retire to the bushes to have a pee in the hope that, when I get back, the bike will have got over its petulance and be ready to continue on as usual.

It didn't. There's nothing worse, I find, than the lonely, helpless feeling of standing next to a dead bike surrounded by silence and one's personal fears.

Begin trouble-shooting (once again): Oil - OK. Engine temp - hot but within limits (using the sophisticated gauge of a hand on the clutch cover). Fuel - plenty. I was about to test for spark when I thought I'd give her another squirt and she fired and died. Again: fire up and die. But in the end she kept going and, with a handful of revs and clutch-riding, the engine stuttering and hesitating, we made it over the brow of the hill.

I now ride on with a knot in my stomach that I know so well from past experience, unpleasant because it's a fearful thing waiting for the engine to die again, perhaps not re-start, listening to detect the slightest change in engine note, a suspicious noise, feeling the hiccoughs and hesitations in my bones. And what makes it worse is that we have begun to pass through vast tracts of empty countryside interspersed with the occasional small village, chickens and goats claiming the long grass between the houses and the road, children playing, an old woman walking bent to the village well, small potato fields behind each house. It's an almost empty landscape and there are few cars on the road. I pass through an oil field so large it takes me an hour to cross, hundreds of small nodding donkeys paying homage to the god of oil, bowing and swaying and sucking up the stuff.

Chelyabinsk and Ufa and Oktyabrskiy pass by relatively unnoticed, Ekaterinburg some hundred or so kilometres to the north. I wanted to visit Ekaterinburg for the simple reason that it was there that, on 1 May 1960, pilot Francis Powers was shot down by a Russian ground-to-air missile while flying his U2 aircraft on a spying mission. The Lockheed U2 had been designed to fly so high that it was impervious to attack by Russian MIG fighters and any known defensive system, but the Russians had developed the S-75 Dvina missile which was able to reach heights of over

66,000ft at a speed of over Mach 3. This was at a particularly sensitive stage in the Cold War and just fifteen days before a major east-west summit. The Americans didn't know that Powers had ejected, been captured and confessed all so made up a cover story (let's be blunt - they lied) and said that the U2 was a weather research aircraft and that the pilot had passed out because of problems with his oxygen system and, as a result, had strayed into Soviet air space. At the summit, the American delegation continued to voice this lie until, with a rabbit-out-the-hat flourish, Khrushchev produced an embarrassed and chastened Powers - much to the embarrassment of the Americans and Eisenhower. *Oops!*

But I bypass Ekaterinburg and press on, suddenly finding myself on a small, deserted road. (I have a feeling my GPS was having an off day.) An ominous sign informs me that in 36ks the road will end. I decide to ignore it. No other cars join me and I fear for the worst. At 18ks I am again reminded that the road will end - and so it does. A new road is being constructed but a service track runs alongside so I take it, riding first across a section of deep aggregate followed by soft sand into which I manage to drop the bike. But after a few kilometres I make my way through a deep ditch onto the newly-constructed road and ride for about twenty kilometres to the next village where my GPS rather smugly says, "Told you so."

I have to admit that I had been rather fearful riding through this section because the engine is still unhappy and I dreaded the thought of breaking down where there were no people to offer assistance. For me, breaking down is not an adventure - it's the Sword of Damocles that hangs over me whenever I ride through remote regions alone. With a partner to share the burden, it's not so bad; if nothing works, your buddy can always tow you out or go for help (unless, of course he's like my Finnish friend who wouldn't). Alone, it's far more worrying.

We pass the large city of Kazan far away on the left, the city built on the banks of the Volga and Kazanka Rivers; were they join, the water surface is over 35km wide. Then on past Novocheboksarsk and Vcheboksary, just two kilometres apart on the banks of the Volga, as the sun begins to sink in front of me and the air begins to cool. A bed for the night; a shower and a cold beer for my 650ks today. Moscow is a tantalising 700ks away.

Keep going, little bike; nearly there. Two more days, God willing, to the Latvian border.

*****

I continue heading west: Nizhny Novgorod... Dzerzhinsk... Vladimir... The dual carriageway is clogged with trucks both coming and going, the land flat and uninteresting. I am travelling along one of the many spoke roads that make their way towards the concentric circles of *five* ring roads around Moscow, the furthest out being a mere 530ks long; the hub of the wheel, Moscow itself, a city of over twelve million people, drawing all roads for over a thousand kilometres towards itself.

The afternoon offers some respite with a cloudburst that reduces visibility to twenty metres and floods the road. I ride on, enjoying the soaking and the cool, wet feeling of the rain, the air still warm and smelling of tar.

Later, under a threatening sky, I joust with a million trucks that clog the road into Moscow. These diesel-breathing behemoths outnumber cars by at least 4:1 and, as most of them travel faster than I do, I am constantly aware of a massive truck, its engine bellowing, the driver ten foot above me, almost nudging my back wheel as he holds it in check just long enough to force his way through a gap.

Partial grid-lock snags traffic and reduces it to a crawl a good 80ks from the centre but, fortunately, being on a motorbike, I am able to duck and dive through small gaps, use the hard shoulder and even the dirt beyond the road itself and, in so doing, I continue to make progress.

And then it starts to rain again. Heavy traffic, grid-locked roads, an urban sprawl and rain - I find myself bewailing my fate and crying out to whoever is listening, "Why can't it just be easy - just for once? Just for me?"

No one answers.

But I eventually make it to Mr Moto Company who, after a two-hour wait, fit a new rear tyre and chain to my bike. The manager approaches me, concerned about my front brake pads, which have been soaked in fork oil for weeks, but I assure him I still have brakes - I just need to factor in a longer stopping distance. He remains concerned but accepts my assurances. I open my wallet to pay for the work done but, just like the manager in Yakutsk, he shakes his head and says, "A gift from Russia. I am a biker too."

How does one respond to generosity and kindness such as this when a mere thank you is quite simply not enough?

Then on, through the rain, to Sasha and Dasha's apartment for a welcome meal and a sleep on the blow-up mattress at the foot of their bed.

*****

The next day, the sky is clear, the early-morning air cold on my last day in Russia as I make my way through the suburbs on roads already clogged with traffic. I ride hard along a delightfully pretty, narrow road heading due west towards the Latvian border. Forest darkens both sides of the road for most of the 600ks and, at times, I have the whole world to myself; traffic is light and human habitation noted more by its absence - such a contrast to the thousand kilometres to the east of Moscow, as if Russia's whole being yearns towards the Urals rather than mainland Europe.

I arrive at the border just after two and am ushered through the Russian side with alacrity and a smile. It could not have been more pleasant.

Relieved, I present myself at the Latvian border expecting to be nonchalantly waved through. My realisation that it might not be quite so easy begins when a uniformed man asks me for my Green Card.

"I don't have one," I admit.

He looks shocked. "Insurance documents?"

"I don't have insurance," I tell him, a little sheepish now. "I'm going to buy it there -" and I point vaguely to where I hope there will be some tatty kiosks with women inside selling short-term insurance as elsewhere in Central Asia.

"Not in Europe," the man says. "Wait here." He goes away and leaves me for a long time.

Another man approaches me and asks, "You have MOT papers?"

No, I tell him, I have no MOT for the bike - "The bike was in Kyrgyzstan for two years," I explain, somewhat lamely and beginning to get worried.

He, too, goes away - for a long time.

Eventually I am summoned to a large office where an impatient looking man in uniform looks serious. He nods to me, without smiling, and says, "We cannot allow you into Latvia without insurance. You must go back to Russia, buy insurance and then come back."

It's a long story: I plead, he looks stony-faced; I plead some more. Eventually, he concedes, a little ungraciously, "You can come in, but you must push the bike."

I assume he means to the gate of the border compound and not right across Latvia - so I do and I'm free!

And then there are apples - tree-laden, branch-snapping, abundance of apples dropping their excess so that the long grass under their shade is yellow and lumpy with the windfall. It is the apples that remind me that I am in Europe and as I ride along almost deserted roads through overhanging woods dark and shady, I find myself shaking my head in disbelief that I have actually made it, that the bike purring along under me has not destroyed itself, that the officer at the border has let me through. And the churches have steeples instead of golden onion domes and there are cows and the smell of cows, that warm, comfortable smell of dung and urine and warm skin pressed to your cheek while you feel the udders responsive in your hands. *That* smell.

The land, too, is different - the softly lumpy, undulating landscape left behind by continental glaciation, as if the ice stopped when it reached the border with Russia. And aquamarine lakes and small towns without a single brutalist *khrushchyuvka* apartment block or log-built house in sight.

It is Europe - *my* Europe - and, strangely, it feels smoother, gentler, more *refined*. I don't say that in a critical way at all, just trying to capture the difference I feel when passing through a part of Europe after spending three months in Russia. Even the trees are different - in Russia, trees seem to taper upwards, broad at the base and pointy at the top, branches sloping downwards to shed snow; here, the trees taper downwards, their trunks bald, the branches radiating outwards near the top as if they have their hands raised to catch light from the sun. If I were to mix my metaphors a little: In Europe it seems the rough edges have been sanded down a little more diligently; the hem of Russia's garment is still a little frayed.

And I cross both Latvia and Lithuania in *hours*, not days, not Russian time zones.

With the setting sun in my eyes, I stop at the ancient town of Kaunas and am directed to a hostel behind a pretty chocolate shop. And, later, after a rather pleasant beer, I walk down narrow, cobbled streets in the Old Town, drawn by live music on a balmy street corner. I sit at a cafe and eat Buon Giorno pasta with truffle cream while a saxophone plays jazz and young people sip their drinks at tables lining the pavement in the continental way and I know that this sort of evening ought to be for lovers only and it reaffirms in my mind, yet again, that I am old and far from that.

The prices are European; English is fluent and I know that I am a time-shift away from Russia. I look about me and I see the faces of people who can voice their dislike for their leaders or the church or royalty and know that they are safe from arrest; that freedom of speech and movement and all the other things that we cherish so dearly is a given. Yet, just across the border in Russia, it is a crime to ridicule another's Christian beliefs and one ought to consider very carefully before expressing dissent towards anyone in the ruling party - a denied freedom yearned for so deeply by many Russians I met.

And then it's through Poland with its cool avenues of white-painted tree trunks, the heat so terrible that through the cities my piston begins to pinch in the bore but I just manage to keep moving sufficiently to cool it and then a cloudburst kills my engine again for an hour but it starts again when the rain has passed and I press on, into Germany with tumultuous clouds in a dramatic sky so vast and dark and turbulent that it could be a rehearsal for Armageddon and I stop for the night in a delightful village where everyone speaks to me as if I am a neighbour and, without thinking, I answer in Russian.

And then, at last, the next day late I make my way across the channel and the rain and the wind lash me and it is because of this I *know* I am finally in England and within minutes of setting my wheels on my own soil a motorway cop pulls me over and demands, "What's with the plate?" (I having taped a hand-written, cardboard Kyrg number plate over my illegal UK one during the crossing) and I tell him, wanting to plead, *I've come so far, please, please don't stop me now!* and even before I've completed my well-rehearsed explanation he says, "That's fine, buddy," and he pats me on the shoulder and tells me that if I get stopped again between here and Manchester to say that Kent officer XXX, force number XXX, has already pulled me over and said that's OK for me to continue and then through the rain I find a B&B in Folkestone and there's fish and chips for supper and toast and marmalade and butter for my breakfast and when packing up my bike next morning for the final run to Manchester the B&B help arrives to work, seventy-something and trim as a sparrow, with wasp waist and bright red lipstick and rouge and I say, "Sorry, I'll move the bike," and she says, "That's OK, my lovvie, I can manage," and her wrinkled face cracks into a smile.

And it is then that I finally know I'm home.

POSTSCRIPT

For those of you who have followed the journeys that my son Gareth and I have shared over the years and that I have written about in a number of books, you will be aware of how we were forced to abandon our bikes high up in the Pamir Mountains of Tajikistan, Gareth's DR350 with a seized engine and mine, later, when the track we were following disappeared into a river. We walked out but returned two days later and recovered my bike, leaving Gareth's (a total loss, we assumed) to the elements.

(The whole adventure is covered in my book "A Pass too Far".)

This is the story of how Gareth's bike returned. I wrote it as a magazine article and thought, as a postscript, it might be of interest.

The Raising of Lazarus

Lazarus was stinking when he emerged from the tomb. His sister, Martha, remonstrated with Jesus - "Come on, he's been dead for four days - there will be a smell."

This is the story of a plucky little DR350 that my son, Gareth, re-christened "Lazarus". Like the rotting, cloth-wrapped body of Martha's brother, this bike was resurrected from the rocky grave of Matt's Pass in Tajikistan in a manner that rather smacks of the miraculous.

There were two DRs; Gareth and I purchased them for £1500 each from a dealer and rode them home. We planned to use them for a few trips into Central Asia, opting for lightness and durability to cope with the Bartang Pass and other things that riding in the Pamir Mountains tends to throw at one. Very little preparation was needed: new wheel bearings, pannier racks designed and welded, new chains and sprockets, long-range tanks. Sorted.

In 2015 we rode them from the UK to Osh in Kyrgyzstan via Turkey, Georgia, Russia and Kazakhstan where, on a particularly bad piece of dirt, I T-boned Gareth and broke a couple of his ribs - but he's got lots so we carried on, making it over the Kegeti Pass just days before a snowstorm closed it for the rest of the year. In Osh, we left the bikes under a corrugated-iron lean-to in the walled yard of MuzToo, a company that runs tours around Central Asia and has handy workshop facilities for riders in the Pamirs with mechanical problems (and, judging by the number of wrecked bikes in their yard, that would be most of them).

The following year, Gareth and I flew back to Osh and spent a month in Kyrgyzstan and Tajikistan, riding the Bartang Pass and reaching the snout of the Fedchenko Glacier after getting a bit lost amongst the boulders of a dry riverbed.

After that, things started to go downhill. You see, Gareth is not normal. He tends to want to go to places most ordinary people steer clear of - and, because I'm travelling with him, I'm involved. Which doesn't do my body or my mind much good but afterwards gives us lots to talk about. He had read about a small pass named after someone called Matt, 36ks long, that makes its bolder-strewn way across a remote mountain range in Tajikistan before joining the Langar-Kargush road. Naturally, he wanted to attempt it.

So we did.

After drowning his bike in a river at the foot of Matt's Pass, we pressed on over an increasingly narrow and rocky track until, somewhere deep into the mountains, the engine of Gareth's DR seized. Knowing that it would be impossible to get it out and with Gareth becoming increasingly ill, we pressed on with my bike until, to our dismay, the track disappeared into the river against a high cliff - there was no exit to the main road.

To cut a long story short, we abandoned my bike too, walked out and, after sleeping the night in an empty hut that we stumbled across, set off the next day to walk the 32ks to Langar; eventually we were picked up by a 4X4.

At our local home stay, Gareth explained to the Tajik owner where his bike was and told him he could have it if he could get it out. Where we were concerned, the DR had come to the end of its days.

Two days later, carrying spare fuel, we made our way back to my bike on foot, backtracked over Matt's pass, and rode two-up + luggage the 600ks back to Osh. Once again, we left my bike under the partial shelter of the corrugated-iron-roofed lean-to and flew back home.

Two little DR350s: mine left to gather dust for two years until I flew back this year, replaced the wheel bearings and battery and rode it, with no other preparation, 20,000ks across Russia and back home; Gareth's, when we last saw it, forlornly leaning on its side-stand amongst the rocks and stunted high Alpine vegetation of Matt's Pass, partially stripped of a few bits and surrounded by a scattering of our gear that we abandoned after lightening our load to make it out on the one bike.

*****

The next we heard about Gareth's DR was when a Kyrgh local working for MuzToo reported that the home stay owner and a bunch of his mates had made their way into the mountains and manhandled the bike out. How they did it we are not sure but, really, if you've got sufficient time, a large group of friends and determination - all three readily available in the remote mountains of Tajikistan - you can carry a bike, especially one as light as the DR, pretty much anywhere.

Gareth was philosophical: if they had the balls to get it out, good luck to them. For him, the bike was gone, written off as one of the outcomes one has to be prepared for when travelling through the world's remote places.

It was a few months later that the next piece of news filtered out of the mountains. Inexplicably - and we've never been able to find out why - the local police turned up at the home stay, confronted the owner and confiscated the bike. It seems that all his hard work had gone for nothing. Once again, it was lost and, as the bike wasn't registered in his name, there was nothing the man could do about it. Chalk it down to experience, as Gareth had.

And for the next year and a half, Gareth's DR, we assume, remained in some police shed in the Langar region of Tajikistan. The men who had confiscated it weren't riding it - the engine was seized; so, like my bike, it sat for nearly two years, gathering dust.

Some time in 2017, Gareth heard that the guys at MuzToo were leading a group of bikers into the mountains near Langar. Gareth phoned them, more in hope than expectation: Can you contact the police there and ask them if I can have my bike back? Please...

They did and, for some reason, the police agreed. The bike made its way back to Osh on the back of a 4X4 and was parked under the corrugated iron next to mine. I like to think they greeted each other: *Howzit, mate! Where you bin', man? Long time...*

Now at MuzToo they have a Russian mechanic who, in a Heath Robinson-ish, *'n Boer maak 'n plan* kind of way, can repair anything. (How long it lasts after he's repaired it is another story.) Gareth asked him to pull the engine apart and find out why it had seized. It turned out, as predicted, that the bolts holding the timing chain gear to the camshaft had worked loose. As a consequence, the valves were bent but, other than that, all seemed OK. Now, in order for Lazarus to be fully resurrected, all it needed was a repaired engine and someone to fly out to Kyrgyzstan to ride it back home.

When, in June this year, I flew out to collect my DR for my trans-Russia journey, I took with me new valves and left them with the Russian mechanic who, leaving off a few nuts and bolts here and there in the process, cutting stray bolts to fit and generally botching things back together, Lazarus was running again, peeking his nose out of the cave, smelling a little high and dangling soiled bandages.

And so, while I was half way across Russia, Gareth flew back to Osh. His ride back can best be told in his own words that I copied from a few social media posts he made along the way.

It was, as you will see, somewhat touch and go for both him and the bike.

Sept 8

Well, I didn't think I'd make it this far when I saw my bike for the first time in over two years. It's pretty battered. Made it across Uzbekistan and into Kazakhstan. The bike sounds like a bucket of bolts but it's still going. Now I'm waiting for the ferry in Aktau. 4000km to go.

Sept 9

Fitted new rear wheel bearings and clutch plates while I wait for the ferry. There's no schedule so you wait for one to turn up, then it leaves when it's full. There's a hotel here but I'm the only one in it. £10 a night and the security guard looks startled every time I walk through the front door. He didn't mind me working on the bike outside the main entrance, though.

Sept 10

Had some electrical problems a few days ago whilst still in Uzbekistan. I stop on the side of the road entering the town of Kungrad to investigate. Turns out a wire has shaken loose from a soldered joint on the back of the ignition barrel. The owner of a cafe comes out to see what I'm up to and indicates for me to wait as he gets on his bicycle and rides off. About ten minutes later he reappears and points at his bicycle for me to use and motions that I must ride on about 1km with the ignition barrel. I pedal off leaving my bike in bits on the side of the road. Up ahead, an old guy waves me down. I think he's hailing one of the taxis which are everywhere, and try to ride around him, but he steps into my path and points to a workshop just off the road. Inside the workshop he looks at the ignition barrel and then breaks out this soldering iron that looks like it was taken from Michael Faraday's lab shortly after he discovered electromagnetic induction. He pokes the bare wires of the soldering iron into a socket and turns it on. After a time it gets hot enough to melt the solder that is already on the joint and eventually manages to re-join about 16 of the 24-strand wire onto the back of the ignition barrel. (He didn't have any solder wire so the joint is a bit rough. In future I'll add a short length to my tool kit. Flux is your friend.) He won't take any money from me for his work, just waves me off. I pedal back to my bike, put it back together and it fires up! I thank the cafe owner and ride off to see the stranded ships in the desert at the Aral Sea memorial at Moynak. One repair made with zero common language amongst any of us.

Sept 12

I had a few issues getting to the port when I arrived here a few days ago, which are probably worth recounting. I make it to Aktau at about 6pm. The ferries leave from the new port at Kuryk, another hour down the coast. By the time I get to Kuryk it is dark and I head to what looks like the port on the map after being followed briefly by a group of screaming children. It's just a pedestrian pier and someone points off into the far distance where I can see the glow of lights.

Looking again at the map, there is a track going in that direction so I follow it for about 15km when the track suddenly becomes new tarmac with no road markings on it. I can see a razor wire fence and the yellow floodlights illuminating an industrial complex that looks like it's preparing aggregate for the new road. A couple of hundred meters further on, a mound of stone blocking the road, with a No Entry sign propped up against it, looms out of the darkness, so I turn back to the industrial complex. Security guards appear and tell me to just keep going past the barrier, and going back to it, I see there is a dirt track leading off to the left into the darkness past the pile of stones.

It's pitch black now, and looking at my GPS, there are no roads or ports mentioned. My paper map doesn't even show the track I was on earlier. I can see the port lights and razor wire fence surrounding it, but I can't find a way in. There are dirt tracks criss-crossing the area, and I blunder around for about half an hour in the blackness until I stumble across a gap in the fence after coming over a small rise. I can see a ferry tied up, with railway wagons being rolled into its hold. It's the Professor Gul, one of the Caspian Sea ferries that takes passengers. This is good news. Maybe I won't have to wait days and will leave tonight.

I cross the railway tracks and ride towards the workers loading the ferry and they wave me closer and ask for my ticket. I have no ticket, and they look confused. A soldier comes over and also asks for my ticket and then wants to know how I got in here. I point to the gap in the fence and he looks aghast. He gets quite agitated and says something to the effect of: "This is a border control zone, get out!" He's got an assault rifle slung over his shoulder so I disappear through the gap in the fence sharpish. I can't risk too much scrutiny because my fingerprints are on record after stumbling into a restricted area on a previous trip.

After another 10 minutes of following dirt tracks, trying to stay close to the fence so I can find the actual entrance, brand new, unmarked tarmac abruptly appears again. It quickly leads to the main entrance where the barriers are lifted, and I'm waved past after security have phoned ahead. Later, I find out I had missed the un-marked turn off to the new port on the main road from Aktau about 20km from Kuruk. I'm too late, the ferry is full and it leaves without me. The Merkury 1 arrives three days later and I leave on that instead. (The Merkury 2 sank a few years ago.)

Sept 16

The last few days have been fairly un-eventful. After docking in Alat in Azerbaijan, it took about three hours to get off the ferry and through customs. You pay for freight on arrival in Azerbaijan rather than upon departure from Kazakhstan. I had wondered why my fare seemed so cheap when buying my ticket - I had only paid for myself and not the bike. During the crossing I had snuck down into the hold to swap my Kyrg registration plate for my UK one. I had a brief moment during the customs check, hoping that no-one would notice the registration change between leaving Kazakhstan and arriving in Azerbaijan. The next day I crossed into Georgia after being given grapes and pastries by a Turkish couple waiting in the queue at the border with me. I skirted around Tbilisi and then took a southerly route through the Borjomi-Kharagauli National Park before crossing into Turkey. I made it across the D915 pass to Bayburt as the light was fading and found a cheap hotel for the night.

This morning, rain on a tin roof outside my window wakes me up at 5:30 and it's still 1200km to Istanbul so I decide to get going. I set off in the rain and about 20 minutes after leaving I'm on a dual carriageway doing about 80kph on a sweeping down hill right hand bend. Something has been spilt on the road and the next thing I know, the back wheel has lost traction and I'm sliding along on my back. When I come to my senses, I look up and see the barrier of the centre reservation fast approaching. My bike bounces off the barrier back into the outside lane, and I disappear under the barrier between the uprights. I jump up and try to pick my bike up to get it out of the road but my left arm hurts and doesn't work and my boots are slipping around on the road surface so I can't lift it.

I look around and my gear is strewn across both lanes - tent, dry sack, both fuel containers; there's a fan of gravel spread across the outside lane where my bike slid into the dirt by the barrier. I pick everything up and put it in a pile by the inside barrier, then shrug off my jacket to see what's wrong with my arm because it's quite sore. There are no abrasion marks on my trousers or jacket where I slid, not sure what has been spilt on the road but it is very slick. My left shoulder feels a decidedly odd shape and its range of motion is severely limited so I grab my left arm with my right hand to see how far I can make it move. I feel a pop and suddenly the range of motion is greatly improved so I manage to pick my bike up and get it out of the road. I notice my number plate is snapped in half and I find the rest of it in the ditch in the central reservation along with my tyre levers and spindle nut spanner. My bungee chords are snapped so I tie knots in them so I can strap everything back on my bike. Two trucks and a car have passed by this stage but no one stops.

I ride on but my left shoulder, elbow and wrist are very sore and I can't squeeze the clutch properly. I think I banged them on the barrier when I slid under it. After about 15 minutes' riding with my left arm resting on my tank bag, I stop at a roadside cafe and come across two French cyclists getting ready to head off for the day in the direction I have come from. I ask them for some ibuprofen and sit drinking tea and feeling sorry for myself.

Later in the day, I get flagged down by police doing spot checks. They want to see everything, passport, visa, driver's licence, insurance, bike registration. The only thing they're not interested in is my snapped-off number plate. The other half of it is in my backpack.

Late afternoon I stop at a roadside stand where a guy is selling fruit and tea. He doesn't speak any English but shows me an old photograph of him and three friends with road bikes. He points to one friend and draws his finger across his throat indicating that he died in an accident. When I leave he won't take any money from me for the tea.

I stop at a motel on the side of the road as it's getting dark and my elbow, wrist and hand are very swollen. I ask the receptionist about a pharmacy but he does not understand. After showing him my wrist, he calls the owner who gets on his phone and about 15 minutes later a friend of his turns up in a car with a box of ibuprofen! He won't take any money for it either. He speaks a little English and I mention to him how good the roads are apart from the slippery bits. He says he is ever grateful to Erdogan.

Sept 19

Through Serbia, Bosnia, Croatia and Slovenia. It's been nearly three weeks of almost relentless riding to make the distance in time and I'm feeling pretty run down. I stopped at Nis in Serbia to take a look at the Bubanj Memorial, huge fist-shaped sculptures erupting out of the ground, symbolising the resistance of the people despite the execution of thousands of men, women and children at that site. The following day I get in to Mostar in Bosnia at about 7pm. The roads twisting through the mountains are slow going. I had planned to do a section of the Trans Euro Trail towards the end of that day but it would have added another two hours' riding and I wasn't feeling well. I probably would have ended up getting a puncture and having to fix it in the dark. Had a look around the old town and the bridge then went to bed.

The clattering from the top end of the bike is awful so in the morning I check the tappets as a token gesture. Exhaust clearance is a bit wide but it still clatters.

The next stop was another WWII monument in Croatia, Monument to the Revolution of the people of Moslavina. I was hoping to get there before the sunset but it was a 620 km ride and my late start meant that it was dark by the time I got there. Was going to stay at a local hostel which turned out not to exist. The last thing I wanted to do was put up my tiny tent in the dark; I had no food or water and I wanted a shower. I found a hotel on my phone about 20km down the motorway. Something makes me turn and look over my shoulder and I notice my tail light is out. So I'm riding down an un-lit motorway with no tail light, a number plate reflector that's actually in my backpack, and a 4-candle-power headlight while being overtaken by trucks. The adjuster on my rear brake stop light switch is just a plastic thumbscrew that I move all the way over so my brake light is always on. At least I can be seen now. Hotel cost 60 euros but I don't care. Bought a new tail light bulb at a service station the next day.

Sept 22

Made it home with the bike now called Lazarus, back from the dead. 8988 km in 15 riding days...

(By the way, if anyone's interested, I've got a lovely example of a 1995 Suzuki DR350 for sale. Recently had a new clutch, timing chain and exhaust valves. Well maintained, never abused.)

Other books by Lawrence Bransby

Travelogues

There are no Fat People in Morocco
Venture into Russia - Three Motorcycle Journeys
The Wakhan Corridor - A Motorcycle Journey into Central Asia
By Motorcycle through Vietnam - Reflections on a Gracious People
A Pass too Far - Travels in Central Asia
The Plymouth-Dakar Old Bangers Rally
A Walk to Lourenco Marques - Reminiscences of a 12-year-old
By Bicycle to Beira - Reminiscences of a 14-year-old

Adult Novels

A Matter of Conscience
Life-Blood - Earth-Blood
Second Sailor, Other Son

Young Adult Novels

Down Street
Homeward Bound
A Geek in Shining Armour
A Mountaintop Experience
Of Roosters, Dogs and Cardboard Boxes
The Boy who Counted to a Million
Outside the Walls
Remember the Whales

Printed in Great Britain
by Amazon